DON'T TAKE ME HOME

On Tour With The Red Wall at Euro 2016

DON'T TAKE ME HOME

On Tour With The Red Wall at Euro 2016

Bryn Law

ST DAViD'S PRESS

Cardiff

Published in Wales by St. David's Press, an imprint of

Ashley Drake Publishing Ltd
PO Box 733
Cardiff
CF14 7ZY

www.st-davids-press.wales

First Impression – 2016

ISBN
978-1-902719-51-1

Typeset by Replika Press Pvt Ltd, India
Printed by Akcent Media, Czech Republic

Contents

Acknowledgements

First and foremost, I've got to say a massive thank you to my wife, Rachel and my daughters, Megan and Millie, both for tolerating the endless hours spent planning and just generally daydreaming about the summer trip to France and then my prolonged absence through the trip itself and for forgiving me when I missed stuff I should have been at. I'm a very lucky chap.

Thanks also to my travelling companions, Steve, Andy and Fergus but Steve in particular for shouldering the burden of driving the camper van up, down and across France.

Thanks again to Ashley at St. David's Press for all the encouragement and support in putting this second book together so soon after the first. Thanks also to the incredible Lucy Mason and her team at the FAW, who did such an amazing job of sorting out so many tickets in such a short space of time. I have had great help from the players and FAW staff subsequently as well, as they've been happy to share their memories of an incredible summer. They're such a great bunch, I'm so glad they seemed to have enjoyed it every bit as much as we did.

Finally, thanks to all those amazing Wales fans I met along the way, some of whose pictures I've used in the book. The games were great but the bits in between were even better. To see tens of thousands of happy, noisy, friendly Welsh people doing such a brilliant job of supporting the team and enhancing the good name and reputation of our country was such an uplifting experience. The UEFA award was the least you deserved, you did Wales proud!

Preface

If you ever meet Bryn, his love of Wales and Welsh football in particular will be evident immediately. Not because he makes an effort to let it be known, it just comes across naturally and subconsciously.

This book is a journal and a celebration of his reward for those years of disappointment, suffering and heartbreak.

It gives a voice to many of his travelling companions and fellow sufferers of those barren years.

It tells of the indomitable spirit of the long suffering football fan, the bond between supporters and the unbridled joy of seeing your team not just winning but surpassing all expectations.

Zombie Nation Awakes was the story of the journey to France. *Don't Take Me Home* is a record of the culmination of that epic journey.

Nobody could be better placed or better informed to document and tell the wonderful story.

Barry Horne

Foreword

I've had some great experiences as a player, for club and country, but I'll be a lucky man indeed if anything I ever experience in the future matches the summer of 2016. It was just the most unbelievable, enjoyable few weeks of my life!

I've always loved playing for my country, always felt tremendous pride when I run out in that red shirt, but it hasn't always been easy. There have been tough times, awful times, in fact. Playing games in front of small crowds, losing matches and not qualifying. All that wasn't the best of times but nothing at all could compare with the dreadful tragedy we experienced in 2011. We were all so close to Gary Speed, had such love and respect for him, and as a group, we had to help each other through that terrible time.

I'm sure that bond has helped us since, through the tough times when Chris Coleman took over, through Serbia away and all the other setbacks that followed. The job Chris did then, and is still doing now, also deserves to be hugely recognised and appreciated by every Welsh fan, just as it is by the players.

That group strength certainly came to the fore in the Euro qualifiers as we came through so many challenges together and it then helped ensure the summer was the most incredible thing, it carried us all the way to the semi-finals!

In the build-up, then in the camp, we just grew closer and closer as a group. Living the dream with one of my closest ever mates Aaron Ramsey, and the rest of the squad. I've never known team spirit like it, we truly were that 'band of brothers', but the special bond wasn't just with each other, it was with everyone who came out to support us in France, the tens of thousands of 'bricks' who formed that amazing 'red wall'. We were as one, staff, players, fans, all united. There were so many of my friends and family out there and they were all telling me what a fantastic time they were having. We could sense that every time we walked up the tunnel and looked towards the hordes of happy, noisy Welsh suporters. We proved to the world we have the best anthem as well. I've never heard it sung like that before and having spoken to some of the other players about it, they said the same as myself, about having to just try and hold it together during each rendition of *Hen Wlad Fy Nhadau*.

The celebrations after games were just beyond anything I've ever experienced before. Seeing grown men in the stands crying with joy after the games still give me goosebumps now. Even in Lens, against England and that defeat, the fans were with us, they kept their chins up!

When my playing days are over, I'll go back to being a fan again, and I really, really hope I'll get the chance to experience something similar, with a beer in my hand and a bucket hat on my head!

I've got to know Bryn well as he's been covering the national team since I made my debut. I know how much it means to him to see Wales succeed because, even though he usually has a job to do, he's just a fan as well. He's been dreaming all his life about the chance to travel around another country all summer, supporting the team. This is the story of the summer of 2016 when that dream finally came true, when he got the chance to switch back from Wales' reporter to Wales supporter. I'm pretty sure we managed to give Bryn a few good memories, as we'll see in his story of the greatest summer of all of our lives, enjoy!

Chris Gunter

Introduction

At 9.40pm on Saturday 10th October 2015, I was standing by the side of the pitch at a rain-soaked football stadium in the Bosnian city of Zenica, both arms punching the air with a microphone clenched tightly in one hand. In my headphones I'd just heard the news that Israel had lost a home game against Cyprus, meaning that my team, Wales, despite a 2-0 defeat here in the Balkans, had finally qualified for a summer tournament for the first time since 1958.

As I waved my arms in triumph, the travelling supporters who'd been shouting to me for score updates just moments before, realised that their team's time had finally come. For many, it was too much to take in and I could see some, whom I regard as friends, in tears. It was an incredibly emotional moment, after decades of desperately hoping, the dream had finally come true.

I enjoyed my moment of elation but then I had to compose myself as there was important work to be done. In my role as the touchline reporter for Sky Sports, I had interviews to do for our live coverage of the game. The wild scenes of celebration on and off the pitch were the backdrop to those interviews. It was one of the most enjoyable nights of my 25-year career as a football reporter but, I've been a Wales supporter even longer so it was truly special to be present at the moment when qualification was finally confirmed. After the show was over and the interviews all done, I celebrated with my Sky colleagues back in the hotel in Sarajevo. We'd covered all the games in the qualification campaign and many more besides, so a strong bond had developed between us, particularly over the 13 months of the Euro 2016 qualifiers. It was the most rewarding experience of my professional career.

The broadcast agreements are different for the actual finals though. Having shown all the qualifiers, Sky Sports had no rights to show any of the games at the tournament in France and access to the squad and manager would also be restricted. For well over a decade, I've been covering Wales for both Sky Sports and the Sky Sports News channel, which meant I'd had the chance to build up great relationships with the coaching staff, the players, the admin team and lots of people working at all levels at the Football Association of Wales – the FAW. All those contacts couldn't really help me cover the team at the Euros as UEFA have strict rules about who is and isn't allowed in: it's their event, they decide.

So, if I was going to work in France, it wasn't going to be the same experience as I'd enjoyed in Bosnia, on the pitch with the players and the manager conducting live interviews at full-time. I'd be kept at a distance with a different broadcaster benefitting from the sort of access I'd usually enjoyed.

All that was a consideration in the decision I made in the immediate aftermath of that game in Bosnia but it wasn't the major reason I submitted a leave application for the first two weeks of June, a day or so later. That was merely the professional justification.

The main reason I requested leave was far more straightforward, it was emotional. I'd been hoping to see Wales play in a World Cup finals or European Championships ever since I saw my first Wales game, against the USSR in 1981, aged 11. I'd seen my country miss out so many times, often falling at the final hurdle. I'd begun to wonder whether it was actually going to happen in my lifetime. Whilst I've been lucky enough to get paid to watch football, I have always – first and foremost – remained a fan, willing to pay to watch football. Whenever work allows I still go and watch Wrexham – my club – and, before I got the job of reporting on the internationals, I'd travelled across Europe supporting the national side. I loved the experience and I wanted to know what it would be like to spend a couple of weeks travelling around a country following the team. This was my chance. A couple of days after the leave application was submitted I got an email to say it had been approved.

Finally, my dream was coming true and the planning could begin...

Bryn Law

1

France
Euro 2016 – Group B

'So much hard work had gone on behind the scenes in the months prior to us arriving in France. I had been part of a team that had attended numerous inspection trips to Dinard and all the venues that we were to play at in the group stages to make sure that everything was as it should be for when the team arrived. We needed to make it our home both at the hotel and at our training base camp and I can honestly say I think we succeeded.'

'I don't think it hit home though of how big an occasion and event it was until I arrived at Bordeaux for our opening game. Coming out of the tunnel and just seeing that wall of red from our supporters was such a surreal and amazing moment and one that I'll remember for a very long time. Thousands and thousands of them singing and having a good time. It's sent shivers down me and I know for a fact that it got to the boys too. It lifted them. It made them feel proud and even more passionate about the shirt and they then gave us a performance for every Welsh person to be proud of. We had won our opening game. Wow! What a feeling.'
Dai Griffiths (Kitman, FAW)

The Plan

On Saturday, 12 December 2015, two months after confirming their place at the finals, Wales finally learnt who and where they'd be playing in France. I watched the draw after getting home from covering a game at Hull City, a dull 1-0 win for the home team. My mind had been on that night's event in Paris so it's probably a good job there wasn't much to report.

With the draw live on TV, I was all set up and poised, laptop at the ready, as the teams came out. I'd already done a lot of research, having studied the rail links between all the venues and I'd pondered the idea of getting a central base, Paris perhaps, then heading out from there for each fixture. The TGV, the SNCF's fast train, made this a viable possibility. By getting in ahead of the draw, accommodation prices at least would be lower.

The format of the competition was certainly going to present its own challenges. UEFA had made the tournament bigger than ever before, with 24 teams and 10 venues. UEFA had also decided to scrap the traditional concept of basing a group geographically, where fans could also base themselves for the first two weeks. Not this time. The group games could be staged anywhere, at any of the host venues. This was going to be the big logistical challenge. France is a big country, the biggest in Western Europe, so three group games looked like a whole lot of travelling and a whole lot of organising. Hence the laptop, plus my iPad with a new app I'd just added, booking.com. It provides an instant cross check on an extensive range of accommodation on any given date at any given location, usually offering free cancellation on any bookings made.

Of course, I wasn't the only one ready to spring into action when the long pre-draw preamble was finally over. Across Europe, hundreds of thousands of people were all waiting to do exactly the same as me. Hotel rooms, air fares, and train tickets were all about to shoot up in price as fans of all the participating countries began the race to book transport and accommodation as quickly as possible. I can't remember how we did all this stuff before the advent of the Internet, was there someone we used to ring?

As well as my bank of computers, I had a tournament chart on which to try and plot match dates and venues. This draw was going to be incredibly complicated. People study for years to be able to figure this sort of stuff out and I needed all the help I could lay my hands on. I also knew what the competition was up to elsewhere as many pals of mine who'd organised far more trips than I have, without the assistance of a travel department like we have at Sky, were all working as a team to secure the best rates. I was a one man operation.

The first stage involved allocating the top ranked sides to a group. In travel terms, this gave their fans a significant head start. As soon as the top seed was allocated to a group, their fans knew which three venues they'd be playing at and when and could make a start. They just didn't know who they'd be playing until later in the draw but that didn't matter. If you were planning on going to all three games, you just get booking!

France already knew their schedule. As hosts they'd been pre-booked into Group A, so the organisers could ensure they played in the opening game in Paris. Next up was Group B, and England were the team whose name popped out for that one. I'd already identified Group B as being one to avoid as I'd calculated the travelling distances between each venue for each group – yes, really I had – and Group B was the worst. It would involve long trips from south to north and back again. England were looking at Marseille, then Lens, then Sainte-Étienne. I knew their fans would already be booking flights for these venues, before even the next ball came out of the bowl. I bet by the time the next team in Group B were drawn, the travel-savvy England fan would already be sorted, feet up, smug smile, confirmation emails pinging melodically as they arrived in the inbox.

For us, the wait went on, but not for long as bottom seeds like Wales were to be drawn out next. Albania came out first, alongside France in Group A. Then to Group B, and guess who? My heart sank as I saw the red dragon symbol appear. We'd be in the same group as the *Saison*! That meant our first confirmed fixture was England v Wales – our second game – in Lens on 16 June. That much we now knew. It was the one game I definitely didn't want.

I wanted the focus of our Euro 2016 to be on playing in a tournament but now, for many – particularly in the media – the focus would fall on one game. England qualify for football tournaments regularly, so their journalists really need to find an angle to make it all a bit more interesting. England sailed through with an easy but uninspiring qualifying campaign and now their press pack had something to get their teeth into; a Battle of Britain! I looked at the venue with a sense of foreboding. It was the closest tournament venue to the channel ports, that meant England fans would be likely to travel in huge numbers. On top of that, my research had already thrown up Lens as one of the smaller stadia and as the smallest host city, with a population of just 35,000. Even before I checked, I knew there wouldn't be a lot by the way of hotels on offer and it's certainly not a tourist area so campsites also wouldn't be an option. In fact, I was already checking a map of the area as Slovakia popped up as the next team in Group B, which meant we'd begin our tournament on 11 June in Bordeaux. That was better. I know the area well from numerous recent holidays to the Vendée region. If nothing else, I knew there was a coastline within striking distance so hotels and camping would both be an option. Then Russia joined our happy band and the final fixture could be confirmed as being in Toulouse on 20 June.

Okay, I had all the information, now it was a race for the line! Within half an hour, I had somewhere booked for the day of each game. I'd gone for Lille for the England game – it's half an hour away by train – and had two options in Bordeaux – either Arcachon, a nice coastal town I've been to before – or a place in the city centre itself. For Toulouse, I'd also got a place in the city on the night of the game. The late kick-off time was important here, our only 9pm game, so transport out of the city almost certainly wouldn't be an option after the final whistle. I weighed up all this stuff as I flicked between apps, websites and social media. I was never very good at maths but I'm as scientific and detailed as Stephen Hawking when it comes to calculating and formulating trips to football matches. I was only missing the big blackboard with lots of squiggles and arrows.

That was just the match days sorted, but the biggest test promised to be getting out there and then sorting out what happened on the days in between, especially given the huge distances involved. Between now and the day of departure, it would prove to be pretty much all consuming, I mean my family were talking to me and I might be nodding but really I was working out where I might stay *en route* from Bordeaux to Lens. The itinerary ebbed and flowed, adapted and grew, until finally, with departure day in sight, it was ready. Or so I thought...

I was in regular contact with other seasoned away travellers throughout this long and complicated process, hoping to get a handle on what they were doing. One of the potential options thrown up by this was a room in an old abbey near Bordeaux. My pals Gwilym and Rhys were organising this and another friend, Gary, would be joining them. There were loads of rooms, twenty or more, so there was potentially space for me but I wasn't sure I wanted to stay in the same place for the duration. I liked the idea of this being a road trip and that pushed me in the direction of camping. I had experience in this field, having organised the family holidays to France for the last decade or so. I knew about ferry crossings, journey times and French budget hotel chains. I'd also had plenty of experience in sorting out trips to far flung corners of Europe to watch Wales in the past but that had always been on a 'find a flight, find a hotel, watch match, go home' basis.

The one thing I lacked was a group of mates to go with. I'm based in Leeds and usually, in recent years, I've been travelling out to games as a Sky employee, with flights and accommodation organised by our travel department. I do take a part in that process, discussing options that might best suit our plans for filming and covering training sessions, but the brass tacks stuff is handled by someone at HQ. Here, I was flying solo in every sense.

Talking of flying, Bordeaux as a base became an early option for the Abbey crew because they quickly established that you could fly – with the French budget airline called Hop! – from Bordeaux to Lille and back in a day, a drive that would normally take seven or eight hours. Because they were onto this option so swiftly after the draw, using all the experience gained from not missing an away game for about 30 years, they got return flights for £60. By the time they'd mentioned this option to me, still just hours after the schedule had been finalised, the flights had shot up in price to an unjustifiable level.

Budget was also a consideration. I'd set aside the royalties from my book, *Zombie Nation Awakes* to finance this trip. Although sales were great; JK Rowling was still sleeping easy, I still hadn't hit number one in the Amazon bestsellers list or sold the movie rights so 5 star hotels and helicopter transits were out of the question.

Instead, I started investigating the camping option. This was what I knew best from all those previous holidays. I'd been staying on French campsites since I was a lad. Months before we'd even actually qualified, I had actually indulged in a little optimism, unusually for me, by looking on eBay to investigate how much a second, third or fourth-hand camper van or caravan might set me back. I'd had a look at tents as well, although I'm a big fan of having a floor under my feet and a mattress for a bed. Oh, and a toilet in situ that doesn't involve traipsing across a field in the middle of the night.

The problem with the eBay camper van option was that anything that looked as if it might actually get to France in one piece was pretty expensive. After the qualifiers were over, the prices – even for clapped out old things – were already clearly rising. This was also the case with camper van hire. It's a service lots of companies now offer but the prices for a fortnight, particularly for a single traveller, were already looking scary.

I kept musing on it, right up to the point of knowing the match schedule and beyond. Then I had an idea. Instead of hiring one in the UK, why not look at getting one in France? So, I put the phrase camper van and the French word for rent – *Louer* – into Google. It threw up a few more possibilities, including a website called *JeLoueMonCampingCar.com* [IRentMyCampervan.com]. This looked right up my *rue*! Using my 'O' level French and a dictionary – well, mostly the dictionary – I ascertained that you could rent camper vans from private owners, collecting them from locations of your choice – subject to availability – and the prices were considerably lower than those being charged by companies specialising in a rental service.

This set me thinking. Most vans seemed to be available for one or two weeks so I focussed on getting myself to Toulouse and back, from Bordeaux. I already had accommodation for the first and last game and it was possible to travel between the cities fairly easily, it was the long haul north that needed covering, so, I investigated further.

There were a few options, although some companies said they wouldn't be renting camper vans to football fans during the Euros. I was going to be on my own and I hadn't driven a van since I worked during the summer for a fruit and veg wholesaler after graduating from Uni. so I didn't fancy some massive Winnebago-sized thing. I eventually found a pretty new vehicle, available in Bordeaux, that didn't look ridiculously large and it offered unlimited mileage or should that be kilometrage? The price was okay, so I submitted a request to be passed on to the owner via the host website, like Airbnb. It came back in the affirmative. Now, things were taking shape!

I requested a Sunday to Sunday hire period, 12th to 19th June. That meant me driving down to Bordeaux, collecting it the day after the first game, making my way up to Lens or Lille where I had a budget hotel booked, then driving back down to Bordeaux to arrive the day before the final game to drop it off. Then I could collect my car and either drive or get the train to Toulouse. After that, who knows? If Wales were out, I'd be on my way home. If not, I'd be working on another plan! With that in mind, I booked a one way overnight ferry from Portsmouth to Le Havre, for Wednesday 8th June. I just needed to find somewhere to stay Thursday to Saturday. I had a room on hold in Arcachon, an hour away by train.

Then, everything changed. I have a number of pals in Leeds who follow Wales and when we'd meet up, they'd ask me about my plans? All of them have been abroad to watch Wales before, a couple of them on trips I've helped organise. I play football with these two chaps on a Wednesday night, a practice that started when we all used to work at the BBC together, many moons ago. Andy, or Evo as he's more commonly known, had already declared an interest in trying to get out for one of the games at least, then Steve, or Shoney, asked how I was getting on with the planning. When I outlined the itinerary as it stood, he said he was keen to come along, if I could get tickets.

Tickets were already on my 'to do' list. Fans who had travelled as FAW members to away games had accrued points that should have put them at the front of the queue when tickets went on sale on the UEFA web portal but I had no reward points despite attending pretty much every game for years – being a member of the media crew doesn't count – so I'd find myself right at the back of that line. Still, I was fairly confident that I'd get some help from the FAW, particularly as I do quite a lot of work on their coaching courses, and if not, then I had lots of contacts in the game.

So, the solo happy traveller scenario was now looking like becoming a two-man trip. The camper van was, it said on the website, a four-berth. It was difficult to tell from the few pictures of the interior, but that sounded fine for two of us. The ferry cabin was also a four-berth and even the hotel the night of the first game was a triple. But with the costs now being split, that allowed me to think a little more ambitiously and soon Plan A was ditched, or adapted, to become Plan A2. This involved scrapping Arcachon and looking for somewhere for three nights in Bordeaux instead. At one point in this process, I had three different places to stay in Bordeaux, all on the same night! I was booking then cancelling with gay abandon on my booking.com app. It was all too easy; I was the scourge of hotel receptionists across the city. Except that I suddenly discovered that not all their hotels work on a no fee-cancellation basis, including the very first one I'd booked. This discovery was made just as I happened upon a decent looking apartment in the centre of town that was available for the three nights and offered parking, at a reasonable price. So, I put my hotel up for sale on Twitter and quickly found a buyer, the Assembly Member (AM) for Wrexham, Leslie Griffiths. She's a big football fan and was planning her own trip out. So, Bordeaux was sorted, at last. Overnight ferry, long drive down, apartment, game, camper van. Boom! Next stop Lens.

Again, there was a budget hotel in Lille booked but I didn't need it now I had the camper van so it was cancelled. Instead I now needed a place to park. I studied maps to see where you could catch trains into the city. Paris was an option but probably not great for driving a van or finding campsites with easy access to the TGV station. I looked further north and Amiens presented itself as an option. I checked on campsites and there was one near the town centre as cheap as *frites*. I booked it for two nights, before and after the game. It was an afternoon kick-off, so there would be ample opportunity to get back to Amiens.

That left Toulouse as the last big gap in the itinerary. I had a single hotel room booked there after the game so Shoney was either going to have to find himself somewhere or Plan A3 was in the offing? Then Plan A in all its guises got scrapped.

The Super Furry Animals are my favourite ever band. They're Welsh and they're big football fans so rumours had long been circulating that they might combine a trip over to watch Wales with a gig somewhere in France. I'd checked this out with Gruff, the lead singer. We'd got to know each other through a mutual pal, so I was looking for any heads-up on a gig so I could shape the itinerary accordingly. Bordeaux was mentioned, two nights before the game, a venue was even mentioned but when I checked, it wasn't true.

Weeks went by with no news and then came the announcement of a headline appearance at the Rio Loco festival in Toulouse on Saturday 18 June, two days before the game. This was the day before the van was due to be returned to Bordeaux. I didn't see the point in going

8

to Toulouse, then back to Bordeaux, only to return to Toulouse so I asked if I could extend the camper van booking by 3 days? *'Mais, bien sûr!'* was the response so now we were going straight from Amiens to Toulouse.

There's only one campsite anywhere close to the city so I was all set to book it when, coincidentally, I went to see the Super Furry Animals gig in Leeds. Gruff sorted out tickets for me and some pals, including Tim Williams, the Bala lad who's responsible for the thousands of bucket hats that have become part of the uniform for Wales fans to wear at matches. Tim, like me, loves his music as well as his football so he was keen to get his newly launched Euro 2016 bucket hats into the hands, or rather onto the heads of the Super Furry Animals. I suggested he come over for the gig and bring some hats with him; it was all a bit short notice. I was still trying to organise it as Tim was catching the train over from Chester, but it all came together nicely with Tim handing the hats over to the guys on the tour bus at the end of the gig and with the obligatory pictures taken. We all sat and chatted over a couple of beers and our respective Euro plans were discussed. When I mentioned the camper van and staying in Toulouse, the tour manager got interested. "Does it have a shower?" he asked. It did. "We haven't got one on the tour bus, do you fancy parking up alongside us at the gig so the lads can have a shower?" This was a spectacularly crazy development. The prospect of being official shower provider to the Super Furry Animals was quite an exciting one. "I'll be in touch", he promised as we said our goodbyes.

I was a bit giddy at the prospect of sharing a shower with my musical heroes but I immediately clicked onto the complications as well. The lads had no plans for the next two nights other than to stay on the tour bus, so would my services be needed throughout? Would there be a water supply to tap into? If they only needed water for one night, where would we then go? I let the issue lie for a week or so, occasionally checking the campsite website to see that there was still somewhere available if at all fell through.

SFA played more gigs, the tournament was getting pretty close and I heard nothing more so I replaced giddiness with hard-headed practicality and went ahead and booked the campsite anyway, all three nights. If the call came from the Furries. If they needed to clean themselves. I'd make the necessary adjustments but I felt more at ease for knowing that whatever happened, Toulouse was booked.

Almost immediately after Toulouse was sorted Evo got back in touch. He could definitely make it out for that fixture and could I get him a ticket? I'd made contact with the FAW in the form of the wonderful Lucy, the person who oversees the ticketing operation. She's a fantastic person, loves football and music, and genuinely tries to help whenever she can. She suggested trying the portal which was about to open but understood my problem in not having the points to would push me up the ladder.

A few days later she came back with good news, I was going to be going on the FAW list and a form arrived shortly afterwards. It gave me the chance to book up to two tickets for each round, with the option to request more if they became available. So now, I could get group tickets for me and Steve and ask about the extra one for Andy. Another pal, Alun, Gruff's record label boss, was also in the market for tickets, so I asked on his behalf as well. They were all at category one or two level, so the most expensive, but I could now tick a box that would guarantee me a ticket all the way to the final! I duly filled in the form, requesting cat two throughout although I asked for only one ticket for the first knockout stage and quarter-final as I didn't know if either Steve or Andy wanted anything other than tickets for the group matches. I also didn't ask for any at all beyond that last eight match. Even if by a miracle, we got there, which I was pretty sure we wouldn't, the prices shot up. In fact tickets for the final were going to cost either €675 or €895! Unjustifiable.

The form was submitted and a couple of weeks later I got confirmation that I'd got all my group tickets bar the one extra Russia ticket for Alun, but by then he was on the case anyway so that wasn't too much of a blow. For the other two lads, this was great news. *'We like to sing, we like to dance, The North Leeds Dragons are going to France'*!

The Pre-Tour Tour

The date set for departure to France is just over a week away but it's late afternoon on Tuesday May 31st and I'm at Leeds Bradford airport, heading out to Dublin on the official pre-tour tour. It's by way of a little treat for my wife, Rachel, as she's never been to Dublin before. It's also by way of a little attempt to say 'let's go and spend some quality time together before I clear off for a couple of weeks having fun'. It's also by way of a present for her 'special' birthday, which she will be celebrating in the next few weeks, possibly on the day of the round of 16 knockout game?

We've left our daughters with their grandparents so it's just the two of us going away for the first time since they were very, very young. I've been to Dublin many times before, it's the perfect city for doing very little except drinking and shopping, which is fine by the both of us.

We arrive on the airport shuttle bus, right outside our hotel, drop the bags off and head into town to enjoy our evening in the city centre. I've researched, via the internet, the five best pubs to visit, as recommended by a Dublin barman. I know from previous experience that the Irish capital has some fine looking buildings, the Guinness factory tour and the famous GPO building on O'Connell Street but there's not much on offer that beats finding a decent bar and enjoying a pint or two of the 'black stuff', so that's pretty much the itinerary for the next couple of days.

The first pub we enter – which is not on the list – is just off O'Connell Bridge. It's got a decent enough menu so Rachel orders mussels, I order fish and with two pints of Guinness we settle down at a table which, as luck would have it, is in clear line of vision of the big screen that seems to be showing a game between the Republic of Ireland and Belarus, this is an unexpected bonus! For me, at least.

By the time we've eaten and seen Ireland play very poorly and lose 1-0, it's getting on a bit but the first pub on my list, Bowes, is very close so I suggest we end the evening there. It's a great choice, a fantastic bar featuring a very narrow 'snug' to the right of the entrance and adjacent to the main bar. Apparently the 'snug' was originally designed to be used by the womenfolk – as an act of enlightenment! As he pulls more pints, our barman describes how the pub was the first in the city centre to admit women but they were confined to sitting on the bench in the 'snug'! He's an interesting local historian. He's also a very knowledgeable football fan and, it quickly becomes clear, he watches Sky Sports. Not only that, he's off to support Ireland at the Euros in a camper van in a few days. For the next hour we discuss games between the Republic and Wales, our team's prospects in

France and the best place to park a mobile home in Bordeaux. Rachel retires to the 'snug'.

From the capital of the Republic to the capital of England – I should have tour shirts done. I unpack my bag from Dublin last night and repack for London this morning. On arrival in the Big Smoke I head first to meet up with my pal, Adrian Chiles, then the two of us head for the London Welsh Centre on the Gray's Inn Road. The people there have organised a pre-Euro event with myself and Chris Wathan, the chief football writer for WalesOnline – the company behind the Western Mail and Wales On Sunday newspapers. Chris has also written a book about Wales' progress to qualification called *Together Stronger* so we're both there as authors. We aren't the only people who've written books since the qualification was confirmed, in fact there have never been so many books about Welsh football. The English may chuckle away, safe in the knowledge that they always qualify, but our country has revelled in the fact that we've finally qualified and it seems everyone wants to write a book or sing a song about it.

There have also been enough Euro tunes released to fill a double album. Things have got so mad that I've even appeared on one, *Dyddiau Coch* by Tigana. They asked me to record a bit of commentary for 'the middle eight' as we call it in the rock business and I couldn't refuse a band named after one of the coolest footballers of all time. I'm hoping we may be a good bet for this year's Christmas number 1. Mind you, the competition is fierce for that top slot. The Manic Street Preachers have recorded the official FAW track, also called *Together Stronger* and my favourites, the Super Furry Animals have released their first new track for many years, *Bing Bong* in celebration of our qualification. I love it and the video's great. I've purchased tickets for the Toulouse gig now, costing a whopping €8, so I'm hoping they'll perform it there.

It's my performance that's under scrutiny first however as a decent crowd turns up and I take my place on a panel with Chris and a very special guest: Cliff Jones. Cliff played for Wales in the World Cup in 1958, our only previous appearance in a summer tournament. Wales confounded the odds to get through to the quarter-finals, losing 1-0 to Brazil, the eventual winners. The goal was scored by a young lad called Pelé, who went on to do okay.

Cliff's one of the last of the boys of '58 still with us and it's an absolute privilege to be sharing a stage with him. He's impeccably turned out, looking almost as fit as he did when he was pushing up from full-back for Spurs in the 1960s and has a great range of stories to tell about that campaign 58 years ago. The crowd roar their appreciation. I'm a little more downbeat. Chris predicts a potential semi-final slot for Wales and outlines the reasons why he thinks this is possible. I laugh, and castigate him for being ridiculously over-optimistic: ah, the folly of youth. I have a different outlook. I tell the audience I will be happy if we all have a good time, regardless of what happens in the matches.

In my defence, I have, at the back of my mind, the country we're heading to and the state it's currently in. In November last year, Paris was hit by a series of terrorist attacks. The second time in recent years. This was even more horrific than the *Charlie Hebdo* massacre and it all coincided with a match between France and Germany at the Stade de France in the St. Denis district of the city. In fact, suicide bombers attempted to gain entry to the stadium but were thwarted and detonated their explosives outside the ground. In the city centre, gunmen attacked a concert hall during a performance by an American rock band, slaughtering dozens of people in the audience.

Other locations were also hit and in total 130 people were killed with hundreds more injured. I first noticed something was happening in Paris via my phone as I sat on the sofa at home watching the Wales v Netherlands friendly. It wasn't being shown on Sky, our contract only covers qualifiers, and I had a game to cover in the North of England the following day so I hadn't travelled down for it. Social media carried the first suggestion of loud explosions being heard during the match in Paris. Footage from the coverage was quickly available and then the reports of attacks started coming in.

The worst news came from the music venue, the Bataclan. I love football and I love music. Tonight, both had been targeted by terrorists claiming to operate in the name of religion. They had not sought a battle with police – armed and trained – an opposition on equal terms, instead they had simply gone out to kill people enjoying themselves. I knew this was going to have a profound impact on the concept of staging a large scale public entertainment event. I started to doubt whether France could stage the European Championships.

Would France even want to stage the tournament now? There are things in life much more important than watching football. Would it be right to invite hundreds of thousands of football fans to come and enjoy themselves in the summer when the scars, physical and mental, clearly would not have healed? It sounds terribly selfish but why should I worry about going to see a tournament when people had been slaughtered? I felt a bit ashamed, despondent and angry but it did feel like an attack on our entire way of life, often frivolous perhaps, but essentially civilised and liberal and accepting of others.

Over the coming days, the topic of the Euros was discussed at high levels. I had an inkling it might be moved, England seemed a good option, but France – quite rightly – clearly didn't want to be seen to 'give in' to the terrorists, mainly home grown and seemingly still at large. A State of National Emergency was declared but the message was clear – the show must go on. I understood this but it felt like UEFA and the French government were taking a massive gamble with people's lives, with the fans potentially in the frontline of what France's President Hollande had described as a war.

I had real worries about this in the build-up to the tournament. When I mentioned them to others who were planning to go they said, 'Yes, but that's what they want isn't it? That's why we have to go.' I know of one friend of a friend who said he was going to go specifically for that reason: to show 'we' wouldn't be cowed into changing the way 'we' lived. Again, I understood, but it was hardly the carefree anticipation of a summer festival of football I'd always longed for. I tend to brood on this sort of stuff.

Then, in March, it happened again. This time it was Brussels. Three suicide bombers detonated explosives in the departures hall at the airport and at a metro station in the city. Thirty two people were killed and hundreds injured. Subsequent investigations and arrests showed clear links between this group and the attacks in Paris. The horror of this was that these attacks once again showed how just about any location where people gather in large numbers could now be seen as a legitimate target to people intent only on killing as many people as possible, indiscriminately, regardless of race and religion.

Documents seized by the police indicated the group involved in Brussels had been planning to target the Euros but, with the authorities apparently closing in on them, they'd gone ahead with the attacks in Belgium instead. It was hard not to think about the location for the forthcoming game against England in this context; Lens being just 100 miles from Brussels. This was a fixture the authorities were already identifying as being one of the most problematic from a security perspective and that was as much to do with the potential for hooliganism, which was a issue but totally insignificant in the context of this greater threat.

On 24 May, it had been announced that Lens would be subject to an alcohol ban on the day of the game. In fact, it would start the night before and finish the morning after. Supporters without tickets were also warned to stay away from the town's fan zone. By now it felt like I was preparing to go off to war. The alcohol ban was said to be as much about people having their wits about them – in order to stay alert to the potential for a terrorist attack – as it was to keep them from getting so drunk they'd want to throw plastic chairs at each other. All that hooligan stuff seemed even more ridiculous and 'old school' given the State of Emergency in France: 'new school' was far more frightening.

European Union states share internal open borders. It's the laudable ideal of peace and cooperation between nations who'd previously ripped each other apart in wars for hundreds of years but, with the mass movement of people in and out how could France realistically prevent another attack, no matter how many extra police were on duty or security officers hired?

So, clearly, I'd thought about this stuff a lot. I don't know if anyone else in the crowded, atmospheric room at London Welsh has thought as much about it but I certainly don't get any questions about Islamic State tonight, only about team spirit and how well we might do in the tournament? Clearly, people are really looking forward to the coming weeks, many in the room are planning on going and that's exactly how it should be, it means that 'we' win.

2

Bordeaux
Wales v Slovakia

'We were determined to ensure that we met everyone's expectations off the field as well as on, it was our first time at this level and we think we nailed it and we want to do it again. Toulouse and Lille were fantastic evenings but to me the best atmosphere was at Bordeaux, so many Welsh fans enjoying the occasion, what a stadium, what an anthem and a great win. The departure from the hotel with thousands of our fans was amazing and we never looked back.'
Mark Evans (Head of International Affairs, FAW)

Wednesday, June 8th

Given the amount of planning that's gone into this trip, perhaps even the proximity of the date, D-day seems a pretty apt way to describe my day of departure. The car's packed pretty full on the drive but, as I'm ready to climb in amongst my stuff – essentially a big bag full of Spirit of '58 T-shirts and hats – there's no delegation on the front doorstep waiting to tearfully wave me off. The dog looks on quizzically from the window of the front room but that's it, I'm alone. Rachel's at work and the children are at school. Hugs and kisses were swapped earlier, we said our goodbyes without knowing when we'd be reunited as a family.

For weeks, no, make that months, Rachel has been asking, "When will you be back?" and for weeks, no months, I've been answering, "I don't know, it depends." Rachel has always struggled with the concept of my football travel and it's apparent fluidity. She still asks me pretty much every Saturday as I set off to cover a game, "What time do you think you'll be home?" I've been covering football ever since we first met, 23 years ago, and she's still asking me! Obviously, I display consternation whenever she asks. "Same time as the last 20 years!" I reply but really I like it, it keeps our relationship fresh.

Of course, there's a lot more riding on my answer than the prospect of my tea not being ready in this instance. There is that 'significant' birthday to consider this time, just over two weeks hence, right in the middle of the knockout phase. I know the possibilities: first place, Paris on the 25th; second place, Nice on the 27th; third place, Lille on the 26th. So, if Wales go out at the group stage, I'm sad but she's happy – well, she is English and not at all interested in football. If Wales qualify, first or second might work for me. Third does not. Something of a club v country conflict looms! Despite or because of this, there is only a one-way ferry booked, Portsmouth to Le Havre, tonight. At least it was Portsmouth to Le Havre until I got a text message late on Monday to say that, due to strike action, the ferry had been cancelled so could I ring to sort out alternative arrangements. As if France wasn't facing enough turmoil, now industrial unrest – the French Government is wanting to introduce new labour laws and some of the unions have reacted with fury – is threatening to cause chaos at Euro 2016.

During last week's half-term break, many UK travellers experienced fuel shortages and delays and cancellations to ferries and flights. More strikes are planned for the duration of the tournament, clearly aimed at embarrassing a left wing government into diluting or abandoning its proposals. Already, before even leaving my drive, I've felt the effects. The call to Brittany Ferries was duly made. The strikes closing the port were fairly localised and there was some availability from Plymouth to Roscoff instead. It meant a longer drive down through England but it's the most straightforward solution. I've kept Steve, my fellow traveller, up to date with developments. He's all for cancelling that ferry and going from Dover instead but that means lots more rearranging for me and, frankly, I've had enough! After months of wrestling with the itinerary for this adventure, there's no fight left in me. So, Plymouth it is.

Inevitably I'm also missing other important domestic events and, also inevitably, it's the longsuffering Megan who feels the most impact.

She was born on the day Wales beat Belarus in a qualifier. I watched the highlights on a little TV just above her mother's head shortly before she arrived, courtesy of an emergency caesarean. Great header from Giggs to win it. Unfortunately, that first weekend in September is still a part of the international calendar so I've been away for lots of her birthdays, especially since I started working on the Wales games for Sky.

During the last qualification campaign, I was in Cyprus on her 16th birthday, the wonderful advance called Facetime was the nearest I got to being at home with her to celebrate. I don't miss a birthday this time, not Megan's anyway, but she's started her GCSE's so I've been around to help with some of the revision. You know, the, 'Tell me all you know about the effects of global warming on the people of Peru?' and that sort of thing but I won't be much help to her over the coming few weeks. My consolation is that she's very bright, hardworking and used to getting on with things without me being around. Mille is younger and seems fairly relaxed about my being away. No birthday, no exams and no competition for the TV remote.

I've had a bit of time alone to reflect on the enormity of my upcoming adventure since they left for school. I also had time for a bit of a health panic about a swollen gum that led to a race to the GP who said I needed to speak to a dentist. Good advice but not much help as the dentist isn't available. Still, by the time I've flapped a bit, I can't feel the supposed swelling anymore anyway so I can go back to panicking about going away instead. It's actually PTT I'm suffering from, Pre-Tournament Tension.

As I reverse the car off the drive, the satnav is set for Plymouth but the first stop will be a little closer to home, Headingley, 20 minutes away on the other side of North Leeds. I'm picking Shoney up. I must admit, I'm nervous about this as I originally envisaged travelling alone to France. I wasn't daunted by that prospect, I travel up and down the country alone during the football season, as I've done throughout my 18 years at Sky. I don't mind my own company, I can even happily eat alone in a hotel restaurant. When Shoney said he was keen to come, I couldn't say no on those grounds, I'd seem like a 'right miserable git', and nobody wants that. Still, although I've known Steve almost as long as I've lived in Leeds – which is most of my adult life – and we've travelled away to watch Wales before, it's been in a group, not just me and him for two weeks in a car or camper van. We're mates but we're not bosom buddies, forever in touch and sharing experiences, although we might be after a couple of weeks on the road in a small camper van. Alternatively, we might hate the sight of each other.

Like me, Steve was born in England, in Cheshire, but his family all come from north Wales and as a lad, his father would take him to watch Wrexham and Wales, my two teams. Growing up in Crewe meant his club allegiances switched as his pals started to go and watch the local team but he's held onto his support for the national side. Our previous Wales trips together haven't been entirely successful. We drove down to Cardiff for the crucial qualifier against Romania in 1993 – seeing our team lose 2-1 and miss out on USA '94 – and then we were in a six-strong travelling party from Leeds to support the side in Milan in another big game against Italy in 2003. There were 10,000 away fans there that night, in a so-called cathedral of football. Our treatment was less than reverential though and everyone in our group was hit by spit from the Italian fans on the tier above us; others had worse experiences as all sorts of horrible stuff rained down. On top of that, we conceded four goals in 16 minutes during the second half and after the match they closed all the bars in Milan. Yet, we still go.

Steve used to work with me at the BBC in Leeds, as an editor, but he left just before I did and he's been editing and making films ever since as a freelancer. That means his time is largely his own to organise and with no projects on the slate for June, he's footloose and fancy free. He's waiting for me as I arrive, bags at the ready. He's also brought an old kettle as the camper van doesn't have one on board, nor does it offer outdoor seating so we've both been in our respective garages to find old camping chairs. On top of that, I've bought a portable barbecue as the camper van is also lacking an oven, so 'barbies' might be a regular event in France. To add to the impression that we're recreating the opening credits to *The Beverley Hillbillies* (kids, ask your mum and dad, in fact, ask your granny and granddad), Steve has also included a small wooden table as part of his inventory. Add to that a bag of provisions, some beer and a couple of boxes of *Zombie Nation Awakes* and we're filling the back seat as well as the boot. I've also created a special display for the front of the car, consisting of a small flag of Brittany and an FAW pennant; I'm hoping this may get us preferential treatment on the ferry tonight.

Steve's daughter, Ellen, is home from college so she comes out to take a picture and wave us off. With that, we depart; next stop Devon – 328 miles away – a gentle warm up compared to what lies ahead across the channel. Having driven in France pretty much every summer for the last decade or more, I know the bit on this side of *La Manche* is likely to be a whole lot more stressful than over there. Our roads are packed while French roads tend to be comparatively empty. As it turns out, we do encounter holdups around Bristol, as usual, but by and large we do okay. We find conversation easy, there's lots to discuss at the moment, not least the forthcoming referendum on staying in or leaving the EU. Steve's already voted to Remain, I intend to do the same, by proxy, as the voting is on 23rd and if Wales are still involved, I might still be in France. It's a good job we're both singing from the same hymn sheet on this issue, or tensions may have started to rise the closer we got to the big day.

Six hours later, having put the world to rights, we're quayside and ready to embark. If there's been some good news to come out of the late strike-enforced change of crossing, it's that we've been upgraded to an outside cabin. As the crossing to Roscoff is longer, we also get more time in bed before we dock tomorrow morning. That means we can afford to drop our bags off, examine the porthole that denotes 'outside cabin' – it's dark so we can't see anything anyway – then head to the bar for the first pint of the Euro 2016 experience. I have a suspicion that it may not be the last. We find a table and sit down. Almost immediately two guys come over, a father and son. "Have you got any spare tickets for the England game?" they ask after introducing themselves as being from Cardiff – both him and his lads are referees apparently. His son looks about 17. Why do teens want to be refs now? Is it the Clattenberg effect? We haven't any spares but there are more Welsh fans settling themselves down in the bar area now so they head off to ask someone else.

There's another guy who wanders past a couple of times, clutching bottles of champagne, before coming over to introduce himself. Having covered Wales and football in general on the TV for a long time, quite a few of the travelling fans may recognise me, I guess. He's from Wrexham, which explains why he's drinking champagne! He says him and his mates have worked hard for months to put money aside to pay for this trip, doing lots of overtime and working extra days, so they're determined to make the most of it. By the look of a couple of the lads in his party, they're already well into that process but the atmosphere onboard is universally chilled-out and happy. Nobody's being boorish or loud and small groups chat, with conversations now turning to what lies ahead. This experience, the one we've all waited a lifetime for, starts with Slovakia in three days time except, with the time change it's now 1am so, actually, we're only two days away from the opening game. All of a sudden that realisation makes the ordering of another pint seem a tad reckless. We're not young men anymore and that time switch means an hour less in bed, so we retire to our cabin, clamber up to our bunks and I drift off to the gentle hum of the ship's engines and Shoney's snoring.

Thursday, June 9th

I awake, too few hours later, to the somewhat disconcerting sound of Breton harp music. One hour ahead of arrival, the tannoy system in the cabin is piping the music through the speakers to ensure we're all up in time to disembark. I roll off my bunk and into the shower, both to freshen up and because I've never had a shower on a ship before. I glance out of the porthole *en route* to the shower. A thick mist means I can't even see the sea, never mind the coast of Brittany.

Steve and I move gingerly around the small cabin space, each searching for tops, trousers, towels and the like whilst trying to avoid bodily contact. We're going to be living almost cheek by jowl for the next couple of weeks but we're still at the 'getting to know you' stage of our courtship. Once we're up and ready we head for the restaurant, or should that be the ship's galley? A cooked breakfast and a pot of tea provides our last taste of home before we immerse ourselves in a Gallic lifestyle and *croissant et pain au chocolat* for the next fortnight or more. Actually, it won't. I've packed Weetabix.

We dock on time, the passport control is swiftly negotiated and we head into the murky morning; next stop Bordeaux. We've got 670 kilometres to do today – 416 miles – so there's another long day's driving on the cards. It doesn't start well. Surprisingly, for France, we hit road works. In all the years of driving over here, I've rarely seen cones or high-vis jackets but we see lots of both in the first hour, until we clear Brittany and then the French roads revert to type. I set the cruise control to 80mph and have a little snooze whilst Steve steers the car. I'm joking! Actually, after a couple of hours, a roadside coffee and a fuel refill – despite scare stories in the media, no problems on the fuel front it should be noted – we swap seats and Steve takes over.

As Bordeaux gets closer, we pass long lines of van full of *Gendarmerie*, presumably heading to the same place we're going. I'm guessing it's 'all leave cancelled' for these guys for the next month. We leave them behind and I begin to consult my phone for any messages from the people in charge of the apartment we've booked. I have a number for somebody called Gilles. I'd suggested we'd be there about 3pm and we aren't going to be far off, so I confirm an arrival time. We leave the main road, cross the river and head into the city itself. I've had nightmare drives around Bordeaux in the past. The *Périphérique* – the ring road – used to be a loathsome stretch of motorway and, as a family going on holiday, we've spent hours stuck on it – so near yet so far from our intended destination on the Vendée coast. The only time I've previously been to Bordeaux was by accident, on an early morning return to the ferry port. I took a wrong turning and we were soon driving across cobbles in front of a big old building. It was so early, revellers from the previous night were still making their way home. I took that as a good sign.

We proceed without delay even though there are big road works taking place in the vicinity of our apartment, but a one-way system takes us right past the end of the road we're on, Rue Malleret, and we're there, number 58. Gilles, a middle-aged Frenchman, steps forward off the pavement and waves us in when he spots the GB registration plate.

After handshakes, he leads us in for a quick tour. The apartment's on the third floor of what must be an old stone building, as we climb up a narrow, windy staircase to get there. Inside, it's been nicely and, I'd guess, recently refurbished, with exposed roof beams and a mezzanine floor with a double bed over the living area. Below is the bathroom, a sofa and TV and a kitchen with breakfast bar. Gilles asks about the sleeping arrangements. It's a slightly awkward conversation in his meagre English and my meagre French but I attempt to convey the message that we will definitely be requiring sheets for the sofa bed, something I'd already made clear in an email prior to arrival. My suggestion that we are '*amis pas amours*' seems to work, although he doesn't laugh. He's either not got a sense of humour or he's not got a sense of what I was trying to say. This requirement for extra bed linen causes a moment of panic on his part and he has to phone the office. Just as I begin to envisage an awkward top and tail situation, he disappears somewhere and returns with sheets and another pillow. Job done, he departs and we go down to the car to carry our bags up the narrow, windy staircase. It's been a long couple of days but we can envisage some settlement for the next couple at least. We both decide to start proceedings with a whimper and go to bed for an hour, a siesta if you will: middle-aged madmen!

A kip works wonders for the spirits and the next priority is to get some food and drink in the fridge, to add to the provisions I've brought from home. There's a Carrefour Express just round the corner and we load up a bag full of baguettes, beers, ham, cheese and crisps. By way of a nod to our surroundings I source a nice, cheap, bottle of *rosé* as well. *C'est la vie mon frère*!

We eat and drink and then set about making our mark on the neighbourhood. This doesn't involve marauding the streets and chanting. No, we're much more twee than that. Instead, it involves hanging the Welsh dragon bunting my wife bought me as a pre-trip gift across the front of the building, window to window. It looks rather nice. Rue Malleret now knows it's home to a small party of Welsh fans as the masses begin to arrive in the city. This being a Saturday fixture and given the enormous significance of the match, tens of thousands of Wales supporters are expected, we are amongst the advance party.

We set off to find them and also to meet a pal of mine who's on duty for UEFA in the city this week. Trevor has a dual role, he works for the Premier League as a 'Match Manager' on a lot of the games I cover for Sky and he oversees various aspects of the media coverage of UEFA games as well. He's based in Bordeaux for the duration of the group stages. A few minutes from base we come across a small bar, a couple of flags hanging up and a small group of Wales fans sitting at an outside table. Only one of them is wearing an identifiably Welsh top but I hear them speaking Welsh and can immediately make an educated guess about where they're from by their accents. I'm guessing north west Wales and, as it turns out, I'm right. We sit down with them and they're keen to talk about Wrexham. I'm President of the Supporters Trust that owns the club and whilst that doesn't mean I have any power or input into what goes on, it does mean I have a some insight. It's been a difficult year for us, particularly recently as we've had to agree to take possession of a stadium we previously rented and we're about to lose our training ground. Financially, things are pretty tough and the challenge of getting the ground up to scratch whilst keeping the squad competitive is going to be a big one, the biggest we've faced since we took control four years ago. There's no point denying the reality of the situation but I'd rather not focus on it today, the eve of Wales' long awaited debut at the European Championship finals. Still, it's to our club's credit that these bright young guys from as far away as Caernarfon and Pwllheli want to discuss it. Following Wrexham means a three to four hour round trip for them, just for home games. No other non-league club in the English pyramid system can claim that sort of loyal support.

Whilst we chat, I text Trevor to let him know where we are, he sets off to find us and another round's ordered – the bar has a nice atmosphere and the owner's friendly even when we admonish him for the lack of a Welsh flag – so I promise to rectify that for him. I'm interested to see to what extent France has embraced this tournament, I've seen a few footballs in shop windows but nothing that screams out 'major event!' I wonder if the French are ready for this? The country's relationship with football has always seemed an odd one. When I first came here on holiday in the very early 80s, I wanted to take a football shirt home as a souvenir and I spent most of our fortnight dragging my parents around sports shops looking for one. There was nothing, anywhere. Eventually, right at the end, I spotted one in a shop in Béziers. It was the amazing Saint-Étienne shirt with the SuperTele sponsors logo and horizontal pinstripes. It was worth the wait, all the leg work and most of my spending money. The point is, at that time France really didn't seem interested in football. I returned a year later, just after their brilliant team featuring Tigana, Platini, Giresse, Tresor and the rest, did really well at the World Cup in Spain and things had begun to change. I got a lovely French national team shirt that summer, plus a big poster of the team that stayed up on my bedroom wall for many years to come. That was maybe a turning point here? When I returned to the same southern corner of France 25 years later, we stayed at a predominantly French resort that had two shops on the main street just selling football gear, mainly Marseille and Lyon, and everyone seemed to be wearing a football shirt. Some things hadn't changed, as I was still after a souvenir and brought a Rennes shirt back with me.

Now, after years of having a competitive top league with a good spread of winners, PSG with their Qatari investment are utterly dominant and have just won the title for the fourth successive year, finishing 31 points ahead of the second placed team! Bordeaux won the league themselves not so long ago, but this year they finished mid-table, 46 points behind the Champions. That can't be good for the game; an uncompetitive league must surely lead to a drop off in interest?

At least the national side has seemingly turned the corner after the ructions that accompanied their recent tournament campaigns. Many people have the host nation down as their favourites to win Euro 2016 and the country could surely do with the boost after all that it's suffered over the last few years. France open the tournament tomorrow night and I'm sure we'll get a better idea then as to the level of excitement and interest.

Trevor arrives and, after introductions, I ask him, "What's the mood here?" He says there's a lot of nervousness and the terrorist threat is the main cause. The German intelligence services have just warned of a credible threat to the tournament that their investigations have uncovered. Everyone seems to know that no matter how much security you put in place, if a maniac wants to launch a random attack, they can't be easily stopped. There are going to be tens of thousands of people wandering around city centres carrying rucksacks. To me, it looks like an exercise in crossing your fingers and hoping for the best, although I'm sure the French authorities would say there's a bit more planning to it than that. Trevor warns us to set off for the stadium in good time on Saturday as there are going to be numerous security checks to negotiate on the way in. He says he's been asked to show his pass at every occasion he's come into and out of the ground. It could all take an hour, he suggests. We lighten the mood by having a bit of a chuckle about Newcastle, Trevor's team, talk about Wales' and England's prospects and then wish him farewell as he heads off to join UEFA colleagues for a meal: which is a timely reminder that we haven't had a meal a since that cooked breakfast many hours ago, so we should head into town as the evening's flown by and it's getting late.

The beauty of the location of our apartment is that it really is only a five-minute walk from the centre. So, a couple of hundred yards on from the bar, we get our first sight of Bordeaux and what a sight it is! We walk along a wide boulevard towards *Centre Ville*: there's a large 3D Euro 2016 sign in the middle of it, restaurants down both sides and then, at the end of it we find the *Grand Théâtre* and the *Place de la Comédie*, all creating a very impressive first impression. There are lots of places to eat and crowds of people are sitting at tables outside. There are lots of Welsh shirts and bucket hats in evidence but there are lots of locals enjoying a Thursday evening out as well, and both groups appear to be mixing happily. There's the sound of singing from a side street somewhere, the atmosphere is great and there's not a police van in sight.

It's the sort of place where I'd be happy enough just to wander the streets, soaking up the sights and sounds. It's quite late now but it's a warm evening and there are crowds of people doing exactly the same. Still, we are on a mission and there are the first signs of chairs being stacked outside some of the bars. We happen upon a Chinese restaurant, empty but apparently still open. We dive in and order quickly before the chef decides it's time to go. The service is attentive and the food's good. Somewhat bizarrely, there's a large picture of a naked woman as a centrepiece of the wall decoration and, as we pay the bill, Steve asks the waitress if it's her in the picture? She blushes, laughs and runs off to tell the rest of the staff – now gathered by the bar – what's just been said. There are more laughs from her colleagues and nobody comes at us with a meat cleaver so it seems she probably wasn't the model or offended by the suggestion she was.

After finally filling our stomachs, we seek one more drink to round off our long day. Off one of the main streets we find a quiet square where a large group of smartly dressed, middle-aged French people are gathered around tables, thin jumpers draped over shoulders, drinking wine and talking loudly and animatedly; all shrugs and hands. Nearby, there's a good looking young couple; he's resting against the seat of his motor scooter and she's leaning into his body. They canoodle before she climbs aboard behind him and they roar off into the night, *amours* not *amis*. I feel like an extra in a Robert Bresson movie. *Fantastique!* This is France...

Friday, June 10th

....But this is France too. We wake up the news that there's been trouble involving England fans in the Old Port in Marseille. Social media is awash with footage of plastic chairs being thrown, lines of police outside bars, aggressive chanting and thugs chasing thugs; all the scenes that have become so familiar from England games abroad down the years.

There's an extra element reported in this instance, with some of the chants apparently being 'anti-EU' in nature. This might just be a wind-up, a good laugh at the expense of the media who duly report it, or it might be evidence that the presence of a far-right element amongst the English support remains. If you had to make sweeping generalisations, you'd probably suggest the majority of England fans would vote Leave. Maybe it's the tiny minority that seems 'anti-everyone' but their presence puts many people off. I have lots of mates who are English, who are big football fans and yet they won't lend their support to the national team; it's the politics they don't like. It's a game they're going to, not a rally. The national anthem probably doesn't help in terms of inclusivity either. Can you really be a republican and an England fan?

Meanwhile, back in Bordeaux, the biggest risk of aggro arises from the fact that Steve wants some of my Weetabix for breakfast. I've calculated how many I'll need for the fortnight so if Steve's starting his day with a couple as well, we're not going to have enough and I have a suspicion that you can't get Weetabix in France. Unless this situation is resolved there could be some chair-throwing at 58 Rue Malleret. For all my fancy talk of being a Francophile, I've brought my own cereal, cans of bitter and a box of Yorkshire Tea. In fact, if you dig down in t'scran bag, I think tha'll even find a tin of baked beans!

The other bit of bad news centres on the weather and the fact that it's raining. I have some knowledge of the climate in this part of the world and I have to report that hot, dry weeks are not something I've experienced too often, even this far south.

I have a mission to undertake this morning which will involve a walk into town, whatever the weather. My wife loves her *brocante*, or 'French junk' for want of a better translation. She likes old French things; signs, boxes, bottles, that sort of stuff. She's not alone in this. There's a pretty big market for it in the UK and people travel over on buying missions. In the same way that I always look and hope there's going to be a local club playing a pre-season fixture whenever we go on holiday to France, Rachel hopes she's going to come across a *Vide-grenier* – 'empty attic' – the French equivalent of a car boot sale, only the stuff tends to be a tad more *chic*. I've done my research and Bordeaux has a district where there are lots of *brocante* shops. She's tasked me with bringing her a gift back so if I can get that box ticked this morning, I can relax for the rest of my time in Bordeaux. Steve's a bit of a antiques buff as it happens. He's done buying trips to Europe in the past, filling up a van with old furniture then bringing it back to sell, so he's more than happy to accompany me. We'll use it as an excuse to have a look at a bit more of the city centre as well, before we adjourn to a pub for a few eve-of-match beers.

We can walk along the river to reach the *Basilique Saint-Michel*, our intended destination. *En route* we call in at our 'local' and I drop a Welsh flag off with them: I've packed one huge one and one small one so they get the small one. We then head on towards the fan zone which is due to open for the first time in a couple of hours – there are lots of police on site already – then we arrive at the side of *La Garonne*, the broad river that runs through Bordeaux. Opposite the river, as we turn to look back towards the city centre, we get our first glimpse of the magnificent river frontage and the grandeur of the *Place De la Bourse*. In front of it there is a huge square and in front of that, an incredible water feature, the *Miroir d'eau*. It's called that because it is, according to the guidebook, the world's largest reflecting pool. It isn't just that though. As we stand and admire it, jets of steam appear to rise up from it, from all across its vast area, creating an eerie foggy effect. People who are standing in its midst almost disappear from view. A TV crew is filming a group of football fans standing in the middle of the pool, just the sort of thing me and Alex, my Wales cameraman when I'm on Sky duty, would be out doing if we were working together on this game. The water feature is new whilst the *Place de la Bourse* was built in the mid-eighteenth century but the two constructions complement each other brilliantly and the effect created is pretty stunning. Bordeaux is starting to make a big impression.

We have an easy landmark to head for in terms of our onward destination, the tower at the *Basilique Saint-Michel* and our route takes us down some exotic backstreets. There are kebab shops, shisha bars and cheap clothes shops. A police patrol walks down one street towards us. Between us and them a car is parked, hazard lights flashing, in front of one of those places that seem to sell phone airtime, for cheaper calls abroad. Clearly, there's an issue with the car being parked in the street because the tallest of the three officers stops in front of it and appears to report it into his walkie-talkie. A white-haired chap emerges from the phone shop, of North African appearance I guess you might say, seemingly indicating that it's his car. This isn't enough for the giant cop as he continues his conversation via the walkie-talkie and speaking, or rather shouting at the older man in-between. I don't understand the words but I get the drift. This road is closed to cars but this guy's driven up it anyway and then left it. It's clear what the 'issue' is as tensions rise quickly. The two are now shouting and gesticulating at each other, the commotion now attracting other people who start to appear from shop doors to have a look. One or two guys move out of the doorways, edging towards the scene whilst the two other cops start moving their hands in the direction of their heavily laden belts. Very quickly, I feel uncomfortable. Steve's behind me, keen to watch what happens, but I've got a bad vibe and I let him know I'm off. We've been strolling through a seemingly relaxed, urbane city centre, but the mood's switched suddenly and perceptibly. This is a country in a State of Emergency, on high alert. It's a relief to emerge into the light and a square at the foot of the tower.

The square's also busy, it's become a kind of *Vide-grenier* with lots of people standing behind stalls. I don't get the sense they're dealers though, the faces and the clothes suggest they might be immigrants trying to raise some cash by selling any old stuff. I'm no expert but Steve is and he confirms my guess that it's less junk, more rubbish, a bit like Wetherby car boot sale.

The actual *Brocante* shop lies across the other side of the square. In contrast, it's got some great stuff and we browse happily for a while before I make a couple of purchases, including the French sign demanded by my other half. That's mission accomplished, let's get drunk!

We head for a *café* on the edge of the square but it's still a bit early for beer so *café au lait* is the drink of choice; a little more calm before the storm. Except that the storm comes in pretty soon afterwards as the skies darken and torrential rain sweeps across the city and the square. We're under the cover of an awning but soon it's leaking badly. People caught in the deluge scuttle over to try and find shelter until it passes. An elderly couple tuck in by us and Steve gets talking to the old chap, so I talk to his wife. Steve's conversation revolves around the referendum, they're from the Republic of Ireland and he's worried about the impact on their economy if the UK votes Leave. I talk to his wife and the conversation's a bit lighter in our corner, she's a big sports fan and says she'd love to go and see the Wales game. She talks about the impact Jack Charlton, and the national team he built, had on the country. She reminisces about the run to the quarter-finals in 1990, when David O'Leary's penalty in the shoot-out took them to the last eight. It's an event the guy behind the bar in Bowes back in Dublin had also talked about, as being life changing – how Ireland had become a different sort of place after 1990. They've both talked about Jack Charlton in tones that suggest he's still idolised by the Irish people. I wonder if Chris Coleman can inspire something similar. I've never doubted the impact this tournament might have on the Welsh nation and its place in the world. This conversation with a very sweet, elderly Dubliner emphasises the magnitude of what we're about to embark upon here. Economically, the Republic's been right up and down since that O'Leary penalty but even on that quick visit last week, Rachel and I took a boat down the Liffey towards the sea and the building work and major redevelopments have resumed on both sides of the river.

The rain eases off sufficiently for our Irish friends to resume their exploration of Bordeaux, but for me and Steve it's delayed our return to base. I have an appointment in a couple of hours as I've arranged to sell copies of *Zombie Nation Awakes* in a pub called the Charles Dickens and I've advertised the fact that I'll be there at four o'clock. We've got to go back to the apartment to pick up a couple of boxes and then cart them back to the pub, which is just on the edge of the *Place de la Bourse*. The sun's back out again and we walk back through the city centre, now thronged with people. It's the same mix as last night, lots of locals and lots of Wales shirts with the occasional Slovakian top or hat but then there's an unexpected addition to the street scene. Walking towards us there's a patrol of soldiers, four or five fresh-faced young guys wearing berets but carrying automatic rifles. They look from side to side, not catching anyone's eye. High alert.

I'm looking from side to side as well but I'm on high alert for any good shops. I spy the *Girondins de Bordeaux* club shop beyond them and, just like I would when I was twelve years old, I need to go and have a look. It doesn't disappoint, there's a lovely T-shirt featuring the traditional 'v-stripe' that's always appeared on the *Girondins* shirt but instead of being in the club's dark blue and white, it's in red, white and green. It says 'Wales' and 'from Bordeaux' on the front. Needless to say, it gets bought.

As we emerge into another square, a bar on our right is packed with Welsh supporters. There's a bit of street theatre going on alongside, those people in costume on a metal frame that makes it look like they're levitating, except that they've picked exactly the wrong spot today because the real theatre is going on right behind them. The French stop to look and listen as *Les Gallois* sing, dance and generally have a good time. The strains of *Don't Take Me Home*, rise up from somewhere within the crowd. It's the song I first heard in Brussels during the qualification campaign. I joined in with a mad, massed chorus after the game that night, in an alley crowded with delirious Wales fans. It went on and on and we've been singing it ever since.

We cross to the other side of the road and there's a shout, "Hey Bryn!" and a familiar face emerges from under an umbrella at a table in front of the Intercontinental Hotel. It's my pal Johnny Owen. He's a Merthyr lad who's done very well for himself, got into acting, appeared in films and more recently, started making them himself. Incredibly, through the film industry, he knows Steve as well, small world eh?! We follow Johnny back to his table, he's with another guy I know pretty well, Andy Legg, a former Wales international who also honourably served both Cardiff and Swansea. Johnny introduces us to his partner, the actress Vicky McClure. They're enjoying a bottle of *vin rouge* and watching the daftness on the other side of the square. Vicky's not Welsh, she's from Nottingham, but she says she's really enjoying the atmosphere. It's non-threatening, the singing isn't against anyone, it's for Wales or for the players who wear the red shirt.

Chatting with Andy reminds me I need to give Barry Horne a shout. He's here as a guest of the FAW and flew out on the same plane as Andy this morning, so he's back at the hotel having a rest. I double check with Andy; 'Any travel problems? Everything on time as it was meant to be?' Andy assures me that, yes, Barry has had a smooth trouble-free journey out here. After all the travel nightmares through the course of the qualifiers, this hints at the new world order we now find ourselves in.

With time moving on, we reluctantly need to excuse ourselves from this happy gathering and work our way back through the crowds to the flat. I get word to Barry that we'll be heading for the Charles Dickens later and he promises to come along and join us. On our way back home, we pop into the little supermarket for more baguettes but also for some food we can cook for tea; we're eating in tonight.

As we pass our 'local', I note with satisfaction that my flag, *Y Ddraig Goch*, is now fluttering alongside those from other countries from the front of the bar: job done. Our turnaround time is now pretty tight if I'm going to make it to the pub for four o'clock, so we basically bolt down another cheese and ham baguette, fill a big bag with books, take another box of books and head back the way we've just come. It seems a longer walk when you're lugging 30 books each, that's for sure. It's a relief when the crowds gathering in the *Place de la Bourse* indicate we've almost reached our destination. The crowd is at its reddest and deepest in front of the pub. It's packed! As we weave through the supporters gathered outside, I spot Eleri Siôn of Radio Wales in the corner by the door. Eleri's married to a big mate of mine, David Hughes. Dave's on the FAW coaching staff and he's out in France as he'll be scouting games. Eleri's been broadcasting from the pub and she's just come off-air so we can have a chat before I find another corner to set-up shop whilst Steve battles his way through to the bar.

This pub is owned by the Charles Wells brewery, one of a lengthy list of establishments the Bedford-based company now has in France; thirteen in all. The prospect of having a decent pint of real ale is quite enticing because, if France has a major failing, it's the quality and breadth of choice of its beer. Everywhere you go, it's the same four or five brands. Lots of wine of course, but that only really comes in half a dozen different flavours doesn't it?

As Steve's queuing for a couple of 'Bombardiers', I arrange books on the window ledge, arrange a couple of bar stools, hang up the *Zombie Nation Awakes* flag I've had made specially by way of a backdrop, then wait for the crowds to descend. Whilst I wait I talk to the lads gathered around the adjacent tables, the excitement is palpable. All ages are represented and it's the older fans who are surely the most excited. We've spent a lifetime waiting to be right here, right now. There have been so many close calls, near misses, and hard luck stories. One of the lads, my age, asks me if I can "Really believe it?" When I answer "No, it doesn't seem real yet", he tells me I've got to start believing, it's real. "We've made it!"

The pints arrive, the first drink of the day and it's nearly 4.30pm, how's that for abstinence? Shortly afterwards, Barry arrives. He's walked from the FAW hotel, further up the river. He's been waylaid all the way by people wanting pictures, and was then mobbed outside the pub. No wonder. He's a popular figure with the fans, 59 caps and a former Wales captain, even though he didn't make his first international appearance until he was 25 years old. He was a late starter – after completing a degree in Chemistry – before his professional career began at Wrexham. He's maintained his link with the national team through his role as Sky Sports' co-commentator on the Wales games, throughout the period since Sky won the broadcast contract in 2004. We've become really good mates in that time and I'm always pleased to see him, never more so than today, here, ahead of this momentous event. There's an embrace, introductions, then I scuttle off to put a pint in his hand as quickly as possible.

The next couple of hours pass incredibly agreeably despite the fact that there's very little trade on the book front. In fairness, there's lot of interest, people come over for a chat but potential customers have other priorities today and I think quite a few fear that if they buy a copy they'll only end up leaving it somewhere before the night's out, so they pay or order and ask for the books to be posted to them which is only fair. I fully understand this fear. I'm constantly checking my pockets to make sure I've still got my phone, wallet and camera, and I'm sure I'm not the only one. Actually, the books are impacting upon my plans for the evening as well. We can't really lump boxes and bags around with us for the rest of the night, so we decide to head back home again and make sure we're back in time for kick-off in the France v Romania game, the tournament's opening match. It's a 9pm start, so we've got a bit of time yet.

I cook pasta and we have it with the sausages, chopped up, mixed in with red pesto and some mushrooms, hunks of bread and washed down with a glass of wine. Quick and easy so we can head out for the main event.

As we pass 'our' bar for the fifth time today, the owner is outside talking to customers. He spots us and waves us over. Beers are swiftly produced, on the house, this is our reward for adding a Welsh flag to his frontage. It would be nice to linger longer but we have to meet Barry before the France game starts so we head back towards the river, passing the fan zone, which is now filling up with people and ringed by a police cordon. They're dressed in the full 'Terminator' costume and Steve senses a good photo-op so he bravely advances on them, waving his camera. He smiles, they scowl, "*Pas de photos!*" one barks at him. Steve continues to smile but backs away, sensing that these lads are probably not in the best of moods. A long month stretches ahead for a police force that's already under enormous pressure.

We turn left at the river and look for somewhere in the direction of Barry's hotel. Having found a restaurant with tables outside and a big TV erected in front of the terrace, I make contact with him. It seems straightforward as I try to describe our location to him on the phone but he starts asking about landmarks I should be able to see, but can't.

"Can you see a big ship?"

"No mate".

"Can you see two big chimneys?"

"No, I can't."

And so it goes on, until it seems we might actually be in two different cities. He walks as he talks and I have an inkling that he's getting closer to us all the time, he has to be, we're down river. We grab a table, order drinks and a few minutes and another tense phone call later, our intrepid traveller arrives, out-scowling any riot cop. I know the best cure for a grumpy Barry and get the waiter's attention. Now, finally, we can sit back and enjoy.

Except, there's not much to enjoy in the first half. France have all the attacking talent but Romania are well organised and defend as well as they had done during the qualifiers. They almost score from the game's first corner, then France hit the post before the break. During the second half, with France missing decent chances, I suggest they won't score tonight. Barry replies, "I bet they do", so I wager €5 they won't. Then Giroud rises to beat the keeper with a header and suddenly the French are up from their chairs and celebrating.

I'm €5 down so I make another bold prediction. There's no way back for Romania. Barry takes the bet, another €5 and minutes later Romania get a penalty: 1-1, I lose. I try again. That's it now, no more goals I insist. Barry's worked out I'm a clown and takes the bet. In the 89th minute, Payet shoots from just outside the box and it flies into the top corner. My only defence for this disastrous performance is to point out that this is why Barry gets paid to give his opinion, it's an unfair advantage to actually know what you're talking about!

Actually, from this point onwards, and it may have been a factor, things get a bit blurry, super blurry. I know that at one point Guto, from the Super Furry Animals, walks past with his partner and comes over for a chat but I'm not sure about the details. Barry heads off, probably. That means it's time to head home and that presents its own challenges. I get a bit confused about where we are and start insisting to Steve that we need to get back across the river but as he points out, we haven't actually crossed it yet.

As we stumble homewards with Steve leading the way, we are – being weak – tempted into another bar. That's almost as much as I can recall except for flashes of trying to speak French with some students from Paris, then singing *Le Marseillaise* and waving a French flag about with them and others, then inevitably, there being a chorus of *Don't Take Me Home*, in the street outside the bar. Actually, what we really do need now is someone who will take us home, we shouldn't still be here, drinking all the beer.

Our meandering homeward journey continues and, incredibly, I bump into some Welsh lads who introduce themselves as being Tigana, my bandmates! I think I then attempt to lead them in a rendition of our hit record *Dyddiau Coch* but that may be just a dream. At some time in the wee small hours, we arrive back at 'Spirit of '58 Rue Malleret' and discover there's now a Slovakian flag flying from the window of the apartment below. Luckily, it's too far up for either of us to attempt to do anything other than navigate the spiral staircase and collapse on our beds.

Saturday, 11th June – Euro 2016 Match Day 1

After a late finish, the inevitable late start. As I lie on my bed, head thumping, I realise that I've probably not prepared very well. I've overloaded in my final training session before the big game. It's some time before I can drag myself up and force down a cup of tea and the obligatory Weetabix, banana and honey. Unfortunately, as healthy as it sounds, nothing stays in my system for too long. It's an early kick-off today, 6pm, so the clock's already ticking and I need to get up and out, not least because I've been invited to an FAW Trust event in the city in the build-up to the game.

Getting to this is my sole focus at this stage. Steve's in better nick. He's been out for a coffee at a little *café* across the road by the time I manage to get my act together, to some extent. The weather's not the best again – overcast with a hint of rain in the air – so I choose my outfit accordingly. I'm going to wear the Spirit of '58 T-shirt that's been designed especially for this match, with a logo on the front depicting the stadium, the date and the two teams. This will match nicely with my SO58 bucket hat in red, yellow and green. There will be literally thousands of these hats on show in the city and the ground. Tim, the creator of these items, will see the full fruits of his labours over the next few hours. The bucket hats have sold in huge numbers and, such has been the demand, they've been changing hands on eBay for big sums. Cheap attempts at something similar have appeared as well, imitation apparently being the sincerest form of flattery.

As well as Tim's gear and considering the weather, I err on the side of caution and go for jeans and my new black Adidas ZX500 trainers. I've also got a small bag for my *Zombie Nation Awakes* flag, and camera. Because of the security checks, it's been recommended that everyone travel light, so phone and wallet – with ticket – are the only other items I leave the apartment with.

As we head towards the FAW event venue, we pass the Euro 2016 letters again and they're a great sight to set us up for the day. There are fans clambering all over them, Welsh and Slovakians taking pictures of each other and posing – all smiles – with each other's flags. In Marseille, it seems, there have been more clashes overnight between England supporters, locals and the police. Tear gas has been fired, arrests made and it looks like a bar might even have been set on fire. Here in Bordeaux, we've seen nothing but peace, love and happiness. This is absolutely what I'd hoped to experience at Euro 2016, this is my festival of football and it's all so uplifting. The positivity goes some way to shifting my hangover.

From there onwards, the city centre is absolutely packed with Wales fans and it's a sea of red everywhere you look. We walk down to the *Place de la Bourse*, the venue for the FAW reception but we're early so we go for a wander instead. All the pubs and bars are packed with people eating, singing, drinking and, in a small square – the *Place du Parlement* – young Wales fans are playing football around a fountain, whilst the adults look on from their tables. Barry's sent me a text, he's somewhere close by but we fail to locate him before the appointed time for the event, so we'll have to come back to find him later.

Back in the *Place de la Bourse*, we weave through the crowds of singing supporters outside the pubs and then we enter the door of the impressive venue. The very high stone ceilings mean our feet echo as we walk along the corridor to the imposing, sweeping staircase. At the top of it is the low sound of polite chatter from inside a room. Heads turn as we walk in. We're not exactly dressed for a posh drinks reception but I wasn't about to pack a blazer. For me one of the beauties of just watching, not working at, a game, is not having to wear smart clothes. Still, I'm in tune with some of the sensibilities of the occasion as I take off my bucket hat and put it in my bag.

Steve and I head in the direction of the drinks. There's a selection of reds and whites, produced by a local vineyard owned by someone from Wales. Despite the fine pedigree, last night has taken its toll and we both ask for a still water. More importantly, for me and my still empty stomach at least, there's food. An excellent selection of *canapés* is on offer and we descend on them greedily.

There are quite a few familiar faces in the room including Neil Ward, the man in charge of the FAW Trust, the organisers of the event. Neil's been in touch over the last few days to see if I might be able to help out by hosting one or more of the next couple of gatherings, in Lens and then Toulouse. The Trust are the people who organise the grassroots coaching and coach education programmes that take place in Wales. They're keen to use the Euros as an opportunity to let people know about all the good work they're doing. I can testify to this myself, as I help out by holding media training sessions for the UEFA A and Pro-Licence courses they run. I was at the National Coaches Conference a few weeks ago and it was a fantastic event with an impressive guest list. Star names like Thierry Henry, Marcel Desailly and Patrick Viera have all been through the system in Wales and, due to this connection, they've all been enlisted to share their experiences of playing in international tournaments with the organisers at the FAW. This experience and advice must have been invaluable to the Welsh coaching staff as they prepare for a first crack at tournament football.

Jonathan Ford, the FAW's Chief Executive is also present and he comes over for a chat. A lot of money's been spent on getting everything just right for the first stage of the tournament. It's been pretty much 'no expense spared' as Wales have made the Breton seaside town of Dinard their base for the duration. They've worked closely with the hotel where they're staying, to ensure they have everything they need on site including the chartering of a plane at Dinard airport, which is just a few minutes from the hotel, to fly to all the games. I've been told that all the money earned for qualifying has been spent on the training camp and the FAW will only start to make money if the team progresses from the group stage. Given that three of the four teams are likely to go through, it seems a gamble worth taking.

The opportunities offered by involvement in the tournament are immense. This will be the legacy element that always gets talked about in relation to events such as these. Sarah Powell, the head of Sport Wales, speaks about this as the presentation begins. As she explains it, the legacy in this case will be to get more young people involved in and enthusiastic about sport. For me, the legacy will also be in creating heroes of the fine bunch of young men who make up the squad. They're genuine role models. Also, selfishly, to see young people in south Wales routinely choose football over rugby. We need first call on the sporting talent in the south!

Jack Charlton's legacy was to create a love for football in the Republic of Ireland that matched the nation's passionate ties to the

Gaelic sports or rugby. As a result of the success at the European Championships in '88 and particularly at Italia '90, the Republic suddenly became a soccer-mad nation and remains so to this day.

After Sarah, the Trust's ambassador, Ian Rush is called up to talk football. I've known Ian a long time, he's a top, top man and one of my biggest heroes. He speaks bullishly about Wales' prospects, particularly in this first game. It's an enjoyable interlude but the windows are open onto the street and through them, throughout the event, I've been able to hear the strains of Wales songs drifting in from the crowds gathering outside and I'm itching to be amongst it. I see the calm, collected, business-like side of football all season long but I'm here for a very different experience. I want to go back to what it was like when I travelled with my mates, in the back of a van from Ruabon to Nuremberg, to watch my first Wales away game. Obviously, I don't want to the experience of sleeping on top of and then under – it started raining – a picnic bench in a motorway service station tonight; I've got a nice bed in a nice apartment. I also don't want to get chased through the city centre afterwards by East German neo-Nazis with mullets and tight, ice-wash jeans but apart from that, I want it all!

Barry's been ringing me repeatedly whilst we've been listening to the various speakers, so when we get out I call him to finally track him down. He's to be found a short distance away, dining on steak and *frites*, and chatting with the former Wales team doctor from the days when he was playing. There's a group of Welsh lads who've all flown over from Australia for the game as well. It's an incredible gathering of the clans. It feels like everyone I know from Wales, or who supports Wales, is in town. As if to reinforce that point, when I step inside the bar to get the day's first beer – we did finally manage to force down a very pleasant Chablis at the Trust Event – I bump into a couple of Wrexham chaps who are amongst the loyalist of the loyal, Capper and Dave. I've been bumping into them at games most of my life. They're happily watching the Albania v Switzerland match on the TV. The Swiss are winning 1-0 and Albania have had a man sent off.

The way the tournament is set-up, one win could be enough to see you through to the next stage so winning the first game is everyone's priority, to take pressure off the next two matches. On that basis, I'd predict the Swiss are likely to concentrate on defending that lead rather than going for more, but I wouldn't bet on it.

I get a round in, but I'm already checking my watch. Trevor's warnings about the time required to get into the stadium are ringing in my head. Of all the Wales games I've ever been to, I don't want to be late for the start of this one. The last game Steve and I travelled to together was in Monchengladbach in 2008. We stayed a little too long in a very fine bar, jumped on a bus, got stuck in horrendous traffic, ended up running the last couple of miles and still missed the first ten minutes of the game. We lost. That can't happen today.

Barry's outside, chatting with a couple of former rugby union players, the ex-Wales captain Ryan Jones and Derwyn Jones who, at about six foot seven by five foot across, is an absolute giant. It's great that these rugby boys are out here to support the football lads though, it's a unifying event.

Together, stronger, we decide it's time to head off. There's a general movement in the direction of the nearest tram stop for the line that goes to the stadium. We use our giant rugby pal like a plough, following in his path as he cuts a channel through the crowds. There are tens of thousands of Wales fans congregated by the riverside and the tram stop. The city's tram drivers have been on strike today but I'm guessing the local authorities must have either offered a king's ransom to strike breakers or forced drivers at gunpoint to drive the trams to the stadium. It's a fair way out and everyone who's going to the game seems to be around us at the moment.

The adrenaline starts pumping. This is truly amazing, what a feeling! I sense that little surge of emotion at the back of the throat and tell myself 'Soak it up, keep it in, there's a long way to go yet.' With our giant leader we forge a route onto a pretty packed tram. As it pulls off, the singing starts. Then the tram stops a little further down the line and more people pile on. It's solid now, we're all jammed up against each other, arms above our heads to grip the straps. If we weren't so excited, it would be pretty unpleasant.

Just over my right shoulder, a Welsh guy is talking to some blokes from Toulouse. They're teaching each other songs. The Toulouse blokes reveal their dislike of Bordeaux and teach him a song about how much they hate *Les Girondins*. In the meantime, the tram keeps stopping at every station which is pretty ridiculous because everybody on this one is going to the last stop – the stadium – so nobody's getting off, which means nobody's getting on. The ground is new so maybe they're still fine-tuning the transport systems.

The tram trundles on, the temperature in the coaches rising as the sun shines through the clouds. After what seems like an age, we arrive at the stadium stop and everyone pours off, almost gulping in the fresh air. The scenes around the stadium are remarkable. There's the odd flash of blue but otherwise it's awash with red. Thousands of bucket hats bob up and down on this red sea. Together, we surge towards the ground, the waves breaking on the first security cordon, where tickets are checked, then we roll on towards the next check. This is where the frisking and the bag checks takes place so there's a greater density of people waiting patiently for the queue to move forward.

When my turn comes, the security guy asks me to empty my man-bag then he wants to see my flag. They are primed to check to see if flags have the necessary fireproofing but also to see if there's any political message on it, or unsanctioned advertising – the so-called bandit marketing. In a sense, given that my flag carries the name of my book, he's missed a trick when he gives it the nod and I fold it back up and head on towards the stadium.

Finally we can see it. In keeping with what we've encountered architecturally in Bordeaux so far, it's a striking construction. It was designed by the same people who did the Allianz Arena in Munich. The theme here is trees, specifically the trees of the forests of the region so the exterior is a series of thin stanchions, in lines from ground level to the roof. It creates a fine and highly unusual effect. As we walk towards it, there are assaults on the senses from all angles. Ahead of us a band are playing samba-like music and there are Wales fans dancing around them. One big-bearded guy in a Wales shirt is busting some of the moves we all became with familiar with from the qualification celebrations on the pitch in Bosnia then Cardiff. "Look!" his mate shouts at me, "He's a fat Joe Ledley!"

One more check, a barcode reader at the turnstile and then comes the final step – a small step for man, a giant leap for Welsh football fans – as we cross the threshold from outside the tournament, to inside the tournament. In front of us there's a bank of steps. I get halfway up then stop and turn to Steve to say, "Take a picture!" It feels right to mark this moment, I'm seconds away from seeing the pitch, taking my seat and watching Wales play at the European Championships. He takes the picture. It's already so exhilarating and those next few steps are even better. We climb up, towards the light, and then we're in. I've always loved that first view of the pitch and the stands in a new ground. I've been lucky enough to visit some amazing stadia around Europe and beyond but this, this is something else. With about 20 minutes to go before kick-off, the ground's already pretty much full and everywhere I look I see red, I see Welsh dragons. We have fans on all sides, in all sections, bar one block of blue behind the goal to our left. It's incredible, we've taken over the city and now we've taken over the stadium!

We find our seats. These are 'category two', not the best on offer but still not cheap at €105. In fact, for anything other than Wales, there's no way I'd ever pay that much for a ticket for a game of football. Luckily, as I'm a Wrexham fan, ticket prices have never been a dilemma before. Still, we're well positioned, quite close to the pitch – in the corner – and because the tickets have come via the FAW, quite a lot of people I know seem to be sitting around us. There are lots of little reunions going on, up and down the stand. I have my own when Gruff from the Super Furries arrives and takes up a seat right in front of me. He's wearing the SO58 hat Tim hand-delivered at the Leeds gig. We embrace. The Manic Street Preachers may have done the official song but it's the Furries who are here in force. Guto turns up, then Cian, another who's wearing his bucket hat. *Bing Bong*!

There's a lot of 'man on man' hugging going on, none more so than when I get a tap on the shoulder and turn round to see Alex, my cameraman and Sky-brother! There's a prolonged embrace but no kissing, we're not French. He's finished his filming for Sky Sports News – with a reporter called Geraint Hughes – for the day, and those UEFA restrictions mean there's nothing more they can do now the game's about to get underway. It's the first time I've seen him in ages because of the long gap since we last had a Wales game to cover. He's from Wolverhampton but he's become a proper fan over the years we've been working on the internationals. More than that, unlike some who does his job, he actually loves football as well so he'll have been desperate to make sure he was inside the ground, for this game of all games. All the work we've done together over the years, all the days and weeks away from home, it's all been about this, Wales in a major championship. We've done long trips to bad places for rotten results but this makes it all worthwhile.

Being a professional and 'sort of' on duty, he's got team news. I've already heard a rumour that Danny Ward might be starting in goal in place of Wayne Hennessey and this is correct, Alex confirms. The other news is that David Edwards gets a start as well, with Joe Ledley and Hal Robson-Kanu, who've both had injuries, on the bench.

Twitter tells me Wayne has been suffering with a back spasm so it's a big, big day for Danny and already his selection means good news for Wrexham. We sold him to Liverpool before he'd even played a first team game and one of the add-on payments in the deal relates to his first competitive cap. Today's the day, so Wrexham get £50k! Whatever happens this afternoon, that'll put a smile on Barry's face. He's our Director of Football and balancing the books is an ongoing battle so every extra bit helps.

Before the teams appear, there's a choreographed display on the pitch involving children holding two massive team shirts, a UEFA logo and big letters spelling out BORDEAUX. It's the kind of thing that might appear cheesy to the neutral but to the Wales supporters it's further evidence of just where we've landed. The children get a massive ovation as they file off the pitch in front of the fans. Then the big screens cut to a camera in the tunnel, we see Ashley Williams looking fierce and seconds later the two teams file out to a huge roar. Behind me, the guy I was talking to in the Charles Dickens yesterday leans forward and says, "Now do you believe it?" "I still can't!" I reply.

Then the moment that so many of us have singled out as being the moment when it really is time to believe, the anthems. The Slovakian one is first, we all stand and to a man, woman and child, listen respectfully and applaud at the end but there was little singing to be heard. It wasn't that sort of anthem. *Hen Wlad Fy Nhadau*? Now this is an anthem and the whole world's about to find out. The fans' rendition starts a little behind the PA, so it's incredibly loud but the whole thing really takes off when we catch up. '*Gwlad! Gwlad*!' is that meeting point and it's glorious. I've never been sure about the anthem going up at the end, on '*i'r hen iaith barhau*' – it never used to – but it works so well here to create a massively emotive climax. Needles to say, by the time it's over, I have tears rolling down my cheeks. Now, now it's real!

It's an all-seater stadium of course but they've wasted their time putting in seats for this one. Nobody sits once the game's kicked-off. Everyone stays on their feet, all around the ground as far as I can tell. Perhaps, it's different in the proper posh seats on the far side, but here it might as well be a terrace.

I'm not sure what my hopes are for this game. Ian Rush was bullish about our prospects earlier but he did make the point of saying a draw would be a good result; getting your first point on the board and all that, and I'd be inclined to agree. I don't know much about the opposition but they had an excellent record in qualifying – with their win in Spain being the stand out result – and in Hamšík they have their own Gareth Bale equivalent. There aren't too many familiar faces apart from him and the big, bald head of Martin Škrtel. He's a no-nonsense centre-half the same as me, albeit taller, faster and actually quite good but I'm not sure either he or I would be able to do much to stop a rampaging Gareth, bar the obvious jumping on his back as he runs past.

Mind you, all the play is at our end early on and with just a couple of minutes gone, Hamšík picks up a ball midway inside the Wales half. He sets off on one of those runs that lasts so long you get ample opportunity to think, 'Why doesn't someone tackle him?' but they don't and his diagonal progress takes three defenders out of the game, leaving him with a clear sight of goal, dead centre on the edge of the penalty area. Danny Ward advances but Hamšík puts the shot past him and it's clearly flying in for the first goal. Time stands still, luckily Ben Davies doesn't. With my hands already on their way to my head, Ben throws himself full length and manages to hook his foot round the ball and clears it away. My hands carry on up and I celebrate a clearance like a goal, what amazing defending! It feels like a big moment, a Slovakia goal so soon might have deflated all this positive energy. The players seem to realise it's a let-off and a warning.

This is tournament football, there's no time to work your way into a game. Things begin to tighten up and Wales show the first signs of being able to take the game to the opposition. Nobody does this better than Jonny Williams. He loves to run with the ball. I'm not always sure where he's heading but then, often, neither are defenders and

44

I've seen him get chopped down so many times, both for club and country. The Bosnians kicked him out of the game, and out of action for weeks, in the qualifier in Cardiff. The same happened to him in a game in Macedonia. I saw him playing for MK Dons a few weeks ago and he must have been fouled at least half a dozen times in the first half: proper fouls as well, late tackles sweeping his legs away from under him. Given the number of times he's been injured in such incidents, I wince every time I see it.

He sets off on another run, turning out of one challenge and inviting another. It's late, he tumbles to the ground and the ref blows for a free kick. The anticipation levels around me rise, it's a fair way out but this is Bale! His first ever goal for Wales was free kick against Slovakia. I remember it well, the one bright moment on a bleak day when a sparse crowd at the Millennium Stadium saw Wales lose 5-1. Our goalie, Paul Jones had a dragon and '50' shaved into his hair as he reached an appearance landmark, then spent the afternoon picking the ball out of the net.

Times have changed, we didn't know much about Bale or what he could do in those distant days but now, as he steps back from the ball, we know the trademark signs, we know the routine. A couple of long strides back, one step across, eye on the ball throughout. The *Viva Gareth Bale* song echoes from the fans behind the goal. "He's going to score, I've got my camera ready for it!" Steve shouts and he is indeed poised, ready. I feel the need to dampen expectation, to help take the pressure off Gareth, "No chance!" I suggest, "He's too far out." Gareth runs in, strikes the ball and, just like Andorra and that beautiful, crucial goal in the qualifiers, it lifts up, just high enough to clear the wall before it dips dramatically – swinging a little to the left, swinging enough – to ensure that when the Slovakian keeper catches sight of it and dives, he's moved too far the wrong way and the ball's beyond his outstretched arms and hits the back of the net! And then, and then? Pandemonium! We're leaping over seats, leaping over each other, hugging and screaming, screaming and hugging. The 'Welsh end' of this fantastic stadium is now a writhing sea of celebration. We've scored a goal! We're 1-0 up in our first ever game in the European Championship finals! Us, Wales.

The players and coaching staff are involved in another mass embrace in front of the dugout, just like in Cyprus. Good enough. It feels like we can all go home now. Ten minutes gone in the first game in Group B and we are now officially top of the group, or as the fans describe it, '*We are top of the league, we are top of the league*'. Chorus after chorus, song after song, the atmosphere's charged now.

But this is where the nerves start to kick in. At 0-0 there's no need to be nervous, at 1-0 up I have hope, but hope dashed is the recurring theme of so many stories involving our national team. It's so early. This team's a bit different from teams in the past though. I mean, we're here for a start. They have great confidence in their ability, they don't have the inferiority complex that seems to have dogged so many of our performances in the past. They score a goal and get better, as if that was the cue that confirmed what they've been told in the dressing room, that they're every bit good enough to play at this level. It's no fluke and they set out to prove it. It's Wales who take control, keep the ball better, win it back better and we look good.

We look even better after a dominant 20 minutes. Jonny Williams gamely chases an overhit through ball into the penalty area. It's to the right of the goal and Škrtel tries to hold him off and let it run for a goal kick but Jonny has other ideas. He wriggles away and just as he's actually going to get to the ball, he's sent crashing to the ground again. We're a long way away but it looks like it might be a foul and there's the extra official watching the whole thing from no more than a couple of yards away. The ref gives nothing but a goal kick. Then a remarkable thing happens. Surprisingly, they run the TV replay of the incident on the big screens around the stadium. Everybody sees Škrtel throw an elbow at Jonny's head and knock him to the ground. There's a collective gasp from the Welsh end, replaced swiftly by anger. It's a red card offence and a penalty. It's amazing that we get neither, what the hell's the extra official doing? It's literally right in front of him!? As ever, Jonny ruefully picks himself up, shakes it off and gets on with the game. He's an absolute hero. He gets smashed about constantly, but he gets on with it.

The let-off seems to encourage the Slovakians to think maybe there's something in it for them after all. With Hamšík and Weiss getting back on the ball, the momentum begins to shift. As half-time approaches, we're hanging on a little. Nothing too dramatic but I'm holding my breath when Slovakia start playing in our box. Somehow, we manage to get a toe-in just at the key moment, but one false move and maybe we will be seeing the ref award a penalty. Ben Davies has already made his massive contribution and James Chester's doing his bit now, reading the game so well he can step in front of the attacker to nip the ball away. A shot sails over Danny's head but also over the bar. A free kick flies over and another ball into the box almost picks out Škrtel who's unmarked and onside. He's getting booed every time he touches the ball now, but I can't imagine that's something that's going to phase him unduly. He doesn't have his hair shaved to the skull to make friends. He'd certainly have enjoyed getting the equaliser there though.

We make it to half-time with the lead intact and, as the whistle goes, there's a chance to draw breath. A moment for reflection on what we've just seen. It's only at half-time that I realise just how intense the whole experience has been already. Watching this game is almost as physical as playing in it. We're singing, standing, jumping, shouting and the full focus is on the game in front of us. Steve nips off to try and calm the nerves with a crafty cigarette somewhere in the bowels of this no smoking stadium. I chat with the Furries. I could go home now, then never turn on another TV, radio or phone and we'll always have won 1-0.

Alex appears at my shoulder. "No problem here. These are rubbish", he opines about our opponents. He's done something similar previously, notably at half-time in Israel when I banished him back to his camera position as I feared his optimism. He was right, they were. We won 3-0. It worked then so I do the same again and send him and his ridiculously upbeat outlook packing.

The teams emerge all too soon, 'Come on then, let's get it over with', I murmur to no one but the heavens and the early evening breeze. I'm sure Slovakia can play better, they beat Germany away, in the week before the tournament began for God's sake. Sure enough, after a quiet five minutes, they start to play. Mak is the biggest threat, more so than Hamšík. He has a run, shoots over and Slovakia take a grip in midfield. A second goal is needed here to settle the nerves and a breakaway almost brings it. The build-up begins right down in front of us. Chris Gunter takes a quick throw to Joe Allen, almost on the by-line, who controls then flicks a cross into the box almost in the same movement, with Gareth Bale waiting at the far post. It's a standing

47

start but he gets up and above the defender and heads the ball down towards the bottom corner. This time though, the keeper does better than he did with the free kick and he gets across to push it away.

I'm doing that thing again by now, the thing I did all though the qualifying games, where I feel like I have to ration myself to glances towards the clock in the corner of the big screen behind the goal. I shouldn't do it, it's like torture because it doesn't seem to make any discernible progress. Time passes slowly. Still, to get to an hour would be significant. Just before we reach that point, the board goes up and the Slovakia coach makes a double change. Duda and Nemec come on and I wonder if Chris Coleman is planning to freshen it up as well. There's a key period in the game coming up. Ten more minutes and we're nearly there but one or two in our midfield are starting to look tired. The way we play demands high energy levels and it's a big ask to put it in for 90 minutes.

As if to reinforce the point, Mak picks up the ball inside our half, on the right. As he races towards the box and away from Aaron Ramsey, who's struggling to keep up, I'm thinking this could be dangerous, we've let him go here. Then he moves beyond another covering defender and he's up to the edge of the area. He cuts the ball back into the path of a teammate who's clear in the box and jabs the ball past Danny Ward and in, 1-1.

I swear, as do others around me but all the noise is up the other end. We look up to the big screen to see the replay. It's Duda, the guy who's just come on. It's his first touch! Talk about an impact substitution.

It's a blow but, as Ian Rush said, a draw is still a good result. Except now Slovakia sense there's more in it for them. Finally, their supporters raise their voices and, for the first time today, they're noisier than the Welsh. It's 'backs to the wall' stuff for us now and Danny Ward's our saviour – just – as he blocks a shot with his legs and a defender rushes in to hack the ball away with blue shirts bearing down on the rebound. We haven't had to defend desperately up until this point but it's now us, in our legs and minds, looking tired. I'm glancing across to our bench now. There's activity, lots of it. Incredibly, it looks like Joe Ledley's coming on. The man who broke his leg just six weeks ago. Can he really be fit? It seems like a miracle! Never mind, it'll be worth the risk just for the chance to sing my favourite song, *'Ain't nobody, Like Joe Ledley, Makes me happy, Makes me feel this way'*, which we all do as he comes on. Dave Edwards leaves the pitch to warm applause, he hasn't let anyone down.

It looks like there's another change to come and I see the number 10 flash up on the board. Really? Ramsey?! He did look laboured in that build-up to the goal I guess. He sets off towards the touchline in response but then there are gestures sending him away again. The change doesn't happen. Is it a rethink or did the official just misread the card that needs to be filled in and submitted before a substitution can be made? A minute or so later the board goes back up with the number 20 on it, which supports the latter theory. Jonny Williams goes off to huge applause from the fans and there's an even bigger roar as Hal Robson-Kanu steps onto the playing surface. The Barry Horns, the excellent supporters band, are sitting just a few rows behind. They serenade him with the Salt 'n' Pepa track *Push It* that's now become his theme tune. The fans respond with '*Hal! Robson! Hal Robson-Kanu! – Hal! Robson! Hal Robson Kanu!*' We're all chanting it, arms aloft. It's like we're imploring Hal to help us out. It must be incredible to hear fans chanting your name like this, or is it just too much pressure? He's not even touched the ball yet!

Joe Ledley's already made one big interception in the couple of minutes he's been on, Hal comes out wide and suddenly we have shape again. There's an outlet. Hal's powerful and he crunches into a couple of challenges just to let the Slovakian defenders know they're going to have something new to cope with for the last 20 minutes or so. Seeing Hal and Joe come on lifts me. They've been a massive part of our success. It's great to be able to bring such quality into the game at this late stage. Almost immediately, Hal emphasises that by battling down the right-hand side, swings a cross over and there's a flash of peroxide blonde as Aaron Ramsey, eight yards out and dead in line with where I'm sitting, leaps in ahead of the defender. Chance! Over! OOOOHHHH!

That's better. The fans respond, taking the noise to another level and from my right I can hear a chorus of the anthem developing, now is the time, now the players need us. The sound ripples across the section behind the goal and grows and sweeps across every pocket of Welsh fans in the stadium. Everyone, everywhere is standing with arms spread wide, singing their hearts out. '*Gwlad! Gwlad!*' booms out. We still believe. I still believe.

Just as in the Belgium game at Cardiff the previous year, the players seem to be lifted. A free kick into the Slovakia box comes to nothing but the pressure's back on them. We're snapping into tackles again and James Chester makes another great interception on the halfway line. He rolls the ball to Joe Ledley, who looks up and slides a pass down the side of Aaron Ramsey – one he can run on to – heading for the penalty box. He makes a first touch, then stumbles and I think the chance has gone, but Hal Robson-Kanu is close by and he swings at it. The ball should be going to the right of the keeper but it isn't, it's going to his left. He's wrong-footed, unable to get across in time, and the ball just rolls beyond him into the back of the net. The next minute's insane. Just madness. No words. Off the scale.

When the madness subsides just a little, it's replaced by pure ecstasy. We're still hugging, jumping, screaming but now we're all chanting it again and again, *Hal! Robson! Hal Robson Kanu!* – *Hal! Robson! Hal Robson Kanu!* over and over, forever and ever, Amen.

I don't know why it hasn't happened before but, at this point, I actually think we'll win. I don't think Slovakia can score again. It just wouldn't be right. I don't think they can compete with this: what we are, what we're feeling and the wall of noise that we've created. *Men of Harlech* booms out for the umpteenth time today but this is full-on, bigger than any chorus before because every single person supporting Wales is singing it, everywhere you look. Even as it rings around the ground, across Bordeaux and over Europe, a cross from the left lands on the head of Nemec, just left of centre in the area. He wins the header in front of Ashley Williams and directs it beyond Danny Ward's dive. It strikes the post and flies back into play. We just keep singing.

Still, we have the chances to make it a certainty. Ramsey and Bale break as Slovakia throw bodies forward. Bale shoots but it's too straight and the keeper blocks. The board goes up and it shows four added minutes. Now it's the new anthem ringing out, '*Don't take me home, please don't take me home, I just don't want to go to work*'. Again, it's universally adopted. You couldn't be in the midst of these marvellous, happy people and not join in. Unless you're from Bratislava.

As the clock ticks down, Ben Davies does something else brilliant, just as he did right at the start of the evening. With Slovakia on the attack, he charges out of defence and makes a bone crunching tackle.

Then, as the ball rolls away to another opponent, he makes another one and wins the ball again. That's it – in a nutshell – that is what this team is. It gets better as Škrtel flies into a challenge on Davies. It's late, and Neil Taylor, little Neil Taylor, runs over to push Škrtel and then square up to him. Škrtel's booked and walks away smiling but he knows what we know. God, I love this team.

The ref blows the whistle and that's it. We've done it! Wales have won it! There's so much more hugging to be done now. Shoney first. Now we're getting more intimate! Then Gagey bounds over and we virtually leap into each other's arms, like long lost lovers. Basically, we just laugh a lot and make happy noises. Then he has to head off to sort out work-type stuff and I'm free to do what I've always wanted to do. I dance with various members of Super Furry Animals, I sing at the top of my voice for ages, I applaud the players who come over and stand in front of us and I don't have to do any post-match interviews!

After a huddle and another wave to the fans, the players head to the other side of the ground and the dressing rooms and we reluctantly start to drift away. Outside the stadium, we see the Slovakians exiting from their end and the Wales fans stop to clap them on their way. It's not patronising, it's just an acknowledgement that they've done their bit to make this a great football day. They then stop and return the gesture. With the ground now behind us, Steve points at a sapling. They've landscaped the area around the stadium with trees. At the foot of the sapling, there's a big Slovakian guy, slumped against it. He's wearing a very big felt top hat in red, white and blue. Steve remarks that he looks like a knight who's just been knocked off his horse and goes across and pats the fallen giant on the shoulder. The dejected Slovak looks up and raises a weak smile.

We head to the tram stop, along with 20,000 others. I had a thought on the way here that these little trams might not be quite enough to deal with a huge surge of potential passengers post-match. The long, long queues suggest my concerns may have been well-founded. Steve has a plan. "We'll walk to the next stop and get on a tram going back towards the stadium", he suggests, "Then we'll already be on it instead of having to queue." I'm convinced there must be a flaw in this somewhere but I can't work out what it is, so I follow him. As we're walking, alongside a line of stern looking riot police, a young lad runs past us. He's big unit. He's looking to his right – not in front – as he runs. That's unfortunate as there's a metal signpost in the middle of the pavement and he hits it at pace – bouncing and spinning away – leaving the post vibrating like a tuning fork. For the first time, we see the cops laughing.

Now, back to the plan. We get to the next stop and, sure enough, a tram approaches soon afterwards heading in the direction of the stadium. We're not the only ones who've come up with this cunning scheme as a group of north west Walians have also had the same idea. They jokingly suggest they're going to 'out' me in the tabloids for jumping the queue. If it comes off, I'll take all the bad headlines. We get on then pull off, celebrating the fact that we're actually going to have a seat for the return trip. Moments later, we're back at the ground and we're ready for the tram to turn round and head back into town. It stops. The doors open. A bloke in a high-viz jacket gets on. "*C'est termine!*" he says, "Off! Off!" Another guys gets on, he speaks English, "Sorry guys. It terminates here. You can't stay on." We argue our case, pointing out that it's surely just going to turn round and come back again but he's having none of it. So, reluctantly we alight. It's not all bad, however, as we then hop across the tracks and join the crowd waiting on the platform. They're regulating the numbers of people being allowed in at any one time, so they're holding thousands of people back, all of whom have just seen us hop off one tram and prepare to hop on another. I pull my SO58 bucket hat down low over my eyes.

As a result, once the tram that we've just got off has, as predicted, turned round to head back into the city, we're able to squeeze into a carriage. It's even more packed than the one to the stadium before the game. After a full day's drinking, singing, dancing and sweating, the aroma is somewhat exotic. The tram lurches as if it's carrying too many people, and, just like the journey out, it proceeds at a snail's pace. It stops at every station, despite the fact you couldn't squeeze a cigarette paper on to any of the carriages. Then, it stops altogether. For ages. For the first time, tempers rise with the temperatures. This is getting a little bit scary. It's really hot, we can't move and we aren't going anywhere. Some Cardiff blokes start to get a bit annoying, which doesn't help. They've been singing tasteless songs about the English, very much at odds with the mood of the day and now they're demanding the doors be opened. But there's no one who can hear them. In the end, they try to use the hammer to smash the emergency bell. When that doesn't work, they use it to force the doors open instead. Then they push their way out and start walking. Seconds later, the tram starts going again and the whole carriage cheers as we pass them.

Eventually, we arrive back and hop off, relieved to breathe fresh, clean air again. Bordeaux has a great stadium and a great transport system in theory but it simply couldn't cope today. As we weigh up our options, I make a suggestion. The England v Russia game's just getting underway, we could head back to the apartment to watch it, picking up a take-away as we go. Then, a quick change and back out for post-victory celebrations. Like the tram plan, it's a goer.

We head home via somewhere called *Speedburger*. The name is a difficult one for me, today of all days, when we've heard Gary's name sung at the match, seen his name on the back of so many shirts and his face on so many flags and banners. It almost seems to be in bad taste but they don't know that on this Bordeaux backstreet of course. Reluctantly, I follow Steve in and we order the biggest burger on the menu. We've only had those *canapés* all day. I guess Gary would understand, needs must.

Then it's back home, telly on and beers out the fridge. The England game's scoreless at half-time. Apparently they've been well on top and we settle down to watch the second half. England again dominate and finally make the breakthrough their play merits in the 73rd minute as Dier scores from a free kick. With the 90 minutes up, I'm almost on my way to dive in the shower when a ball into the box isn't defended properly and a Russian pops up at the far post to head-in an equaliser. At this moment, I'm sure, the fan zone in Bordeaux has just erupted. *'We are top of the league, say, we are top of the league!'*

As we get ready to return to the biggest party Bordeaux has ever seen, reports are coming in of more trouble in Marseille. Throughout the day, England fans have apparently been targeted by small packs of Russian ultra-hooligans. They've launched vicious attacks, inflicted some serious injuries and been seen using mixed martial arts moves armed with knuckledusters and knives. This sounds like hooliganism at a whole new level, way beyond the haymakers – up on your toes, arms outstretched, posturing – and chair and bottle throwing associated with the English in the past. At full-time, it seems, Russians smashed through the ranks of stewards separating them from England fans, many of whom had to leap over high walls to escape. We play Russia in Toulouse in nine days time.

Our own experience remains so utterly at odds with what's happened in Marseille. As we walk towards our local, there's a decent Saturday night crowd outside. We stop and claim a table.

The owner comes over and congratulates us on our win, pointing at the flag. Then things get a bit bizarre. A couple of Australian blokes come over, one of them wearing an Italy shirt. He's a fairly elderly chap but with a great head of long, silvery hair swept back with oil. He's larger than life, wants to talk about the game and how Bale scored from the free kick because the two guys on the end of the wall moved and left a big gap for him to shoot through. Then he starts slagging England off, saying their hooligans have just got what they've been dishing out for years. I suspect he's no lover of the 'Poms'. Then an English bloke staggers up and makes a beeline for Steve. He appears to be a Geordie and he appears to be very drunk. He's not making much sense but Shoney ascertains that he's been on a stag do, he's lost his mates, and now he's lost. Steve's a helpful sort, I have visions of him putting the bloke up for the night. So, I usher Steve away and pass our Geordie pal on to our Aussie friends. I'm sure they'll get on famously!

Barry's been in touch. He's awaiting our arrival at the Charles Dickens. The square in front of the pub's absolutely rammed with Wales fans. As we emerge from the crowds and enter the bar, we spot Barry and the hugging starts all over again. Barry seems overwhelmed by the whole experience. He must have felt so much love from the fans this evening. They'll have massively appreciated the fact that he's out with them having a beer, chatting and having pictures taken. It's all part of 'Together Stronger', everybody mixes, everyone gets on. After the hugging, we get down to the analysis. "What did you think?" I ask? His assessment surprises me a bit, he reckons a few of the lads didn't look fit enough and thought Ramsey was ready to come off when the board went up with his number on it. He says the Davies clearance was every bit as important as the Bale goal. He had Joe Allen down as his 'man of the match' and then he introduces us to Joe's dad. He, in turn, introduces us to Joe's brother. It's a remarkable story they tell. Mr Allen was a rugby man but Joe's older brother Harry suffered hearing loss as a result of a meningitis attack at the age of three. He had a hearing aid fitted but, because of it, he couldn't play rugby, so he played football instead. As a result, Joe followed suit. Both were good players, but Joe went that little bit further with his career. Now Harry's out in Bordeaux celebrating Joe's success.

After a couple more pints of real ale, the bell rings in the Charles Dickens. I can only imagine this has been a pretty successful couple of days for the Charles Wells brewery. With Ireland and Belgium on their way, the shareholders bonus should be significant this year. The staff have been brilliant, keeping calm and good humoured under the incessant barrage of requests for beer, all apart from the grumpy looking bloke in the kilt who orders everyone out at the strange time of 1.20am.

Joe's dad is all for going on somewhere and wants Barry to join him but we can't find him. I send a text. He calls me back saying he's heading home. That, ladies and gentlemen, is unprecedented. Barry never goes to bed first!

We should be off as well. We have to pick up the camper van and then drive it to Brittany tomorrow, so we need our wits to be kept about us. We say our goodbyes and set off. We haven't left the square however, before I spot another mate, it's TC – Tommie Collins – and his brother Chris. I see Tommie everywhere, we go back a long way with Wales' away trips. He's Porthmadog-born and bred and his brother's living in the North East of England. Tommie supports Chelsea – travels all over to see them – whilst Chris supports Everton, but both support Wales, everywhere. They have a great camper van story about a group of lads from Abergele who've hired one and driven it over. They forgot about the extra height, tried to drive under a low bridge and tore the roof off. They've been staying in it ever since: regardless. It's nice to be sleeping under the stars apparently.

I make a note to keep my eyes peeled for low bridges over the next ten days. Before I can sleep, I have to watch the goals again. I drift off counting Hal Robson-Kanus.

3

Lens
England v Wales

'To be part of history and especially being at a major tournament with Wales was a very special time and something that I and my family will never forget. Everyone played such a big part in the success of the team. Our preparation was meticulous, we worked with a high level of professionalism, we remained humble throughout but most importantly we were together. The fans, the families, the players and the staff – that was the common thread of our success.'
Ian Mitchell (Team Psychologist, FAW)

Sunday, June 12th

It's an 11am departure from the apartment so the alarm's set for 10 o'clock. Not enough sleep really but last night wasn't overly indulgent so I'm in better shape than I was 24 hours ago. Or maybe I'm just getting more practice?

We both shove clothes back into bags, gather up bunting, baguettes, phone chargers and all the other items we've managed to distribute to the four corners of our living space. Steve wanders off for a smoke and I start transferring bags from flat to boot. As I'm doing so, the guy who's coming to check we haven't set the flat on fire or sprayed graffiti across the walls arrives. He's early. This puts extra pressure on as he heads upstairs to do his once-over.

He gives it the nod, so I'll be getting my damage deposit back – good news – and we're ready for the off. We say our goodbyes, it's been an excellent base. Next up, who knows? I type our onward address into the satnav and take the wheel for the next stage of our epic trip. We're heading to an address just to the south of the city centre, really close to the train station. This is where we're expecting to find the camper van, then we transfer the bags and, having pre-ordered and pre-paid for a space for the next ten days, I go and park my car in a car park. This has involved signing up for something called Zenparks and now I have an app on my phone bearing their logo and the details of my booking. The car park is just a couple of hundred metres from the pickup address. That's the level of planning we're talking about here. I needed a car park because the person who owns the van doesn't have anywhere for us to leave my vehicle, which is a bit of a miss.

It's a ten minute drive but the actual address, the house number, doesn't appear on the satnav. I pull the car over somewhere close and get out to look. I'm looking for 55. There's a 53, 54 and 56 but not the one I need. There is a big college building which I wander round and I ring the company rep to say I'm somewhere close. She promises to ring the owner. As I put the phone down, a woman emerges from a small door in a wall of the college. She's looking around expectantly. I figure this is us so I approach and say *"Bonjour. Je suis Bryn."* She responds and contact is made. I haven't seen a camper van parked anywhere during my circuit of the building, so in my 'O' level French, I set about trying to ascertain where it is. Her English is some way below 'O' level standard, so it's a struggle. *"Ou est le camping?"* seems the simplest way to approach this. One thing I quickly work out, it isn't here.

Next, a young bloke arrives. He introduces himself as her partner but there's a big age gap so I think I've mis-translated his explanation. Anyway, we have more important matters to sort out. He speaks a bit more English so we move on a bit. The camper van is about 10 minutes away so he suggests we get in his car to travel there. His car is not very big and we have loads of bags, so we decline that suggestion and tell him we'll follow him instead.

His car emerges from another hole in the wall of the college, it's like Thunderbirds this place, and he sets off at a fair lick. It's a bit like the first French Connection film as we speed through the backstreets. He seems to be intent on shaking me off. We head out of the city centre and finally arrive at a car park. As the electronic gate rolls back, for the first time we see our home for the next 10 days – Gareth The Camper Van – parked under a tree, against a wall. We're already behind schedule and want to crack on with swapping the bags over. Actually, we haven't got a schedule but we're keen to get back on the road.

Our friend jumps in the van whilst the woman stands some distance away, playing with a small dog, and not really taking any part in proceedings. He turns the key in the ignition. It's a new looking vehicle. It said 2013 in the description and I've seen a few photos on the website, but still nothing happens bar a strange grinding noise. He tries again, the engine briefly flickers into life, then dies again. Once more, same thing. Steve and I are leaning against the bonnet of my car, arms folded, watching all this. It's difficult to know what to say, "I think the battery's knackered." Steve suggests. "Well, if it is, I'm not sure what our Plan B is?" I respond.

It's true. There is no Plan B. The whole itinerary for the next 10 days is built around being in a camper van. It's not like hiring from a company when they just go and get you another from the warehouse. We've hired from an individual, who is still standing on the far side of the car park playing with a small dog. Behind the wheel of the camper van, a little worryingly, our man has his head in his hands. This is all beginning to feel a bit surreal.

He tries once more, phone now pressed to his ear. The engine comes to life again and keeps turning over. He manages to edge the van forward. As he draws up to where we're standing, he says he's going to drive around for five minutes to see how it is? By now, another woman has arrived on the scene, maybe this was the woman I'd called. She's younger – his age – and introduces herself. She's a teacher and she teaches some English, he's a friend and he's asked her to help out. This is the first good news we've had in quite a while. The older woman comes across to talk to her but she won't talk directly to me or Steve at all. Her small dog runs around her feet. Steve's worried that the van's unreliable. I can't blame him. When it finally comes back, still apparently working, he seeks assurances via our interpreter. The battery is new, supposedly, the van has just been serviced and everything was okay when he tested it the other day. He did wash it, so maybe some water got in the battery connections. We don't have a lot of choice at this moment but to trust that he's right. So, we prepare to start the handover.

This process, conducted through an intermediary, is not a swift one. He has to describe how everything in the van works, the electrics, water, lighting, toilet etc. It all takes a while. Then we get to sleeping arrangements. He asks, in English, "Do you want one bed or two?" It's that question again. Two middle-aged blokes travelling round France together. Well yes, of course, he tells me, the last two people who had the van were gay. I'm pleased that everyone's so relaxed about this stuff now, but once again, I do my rubbish '*amis non amours*' joke. He doesn't laugh.

What he does do is ask, in English, if I know the game Tetris? I do. He laughs now, and starts building the lower bed. I see why he's asked as he unscrews and lowers tables, shifts seats around and then produces various cushions, in all shapes which fit together in a complicated pattern over the top. I take a picture of it so we'll have a visual record of how it all fits together. We're both beginning to suffer from an information overload by now, so I figure we may need this tonight. Assuming we ever actually get to leave this car park.

The upper level is more straightforward. The bed drops down from the roof and is accessed by climbing a small ladder. One thing that's become immediately apparent, is that the suggestion that this is a four-berth would only be true if Snow White had booked this vehicle for the lads and even then three are going to be disappointed, I'm guessing Grumpy and Sneezy for starters. We have Evo coming out to join us in Toulouse and he's at the opposite end of the fairytale spectrum: he's the guy who lives at the top of beanstalk. I suggest to Steve the chances of us being able to squeeze him in for a couple of nights are slim to non-existent.

That's the grand tour done. Now, there's the paperwork. There are lots of boxes to tick, we have to do a visual check inside and out, and he shows me where the van documents are. I sign something. We have another conflab as there's only one copy of the contract so I'm instructed to take a picture of it and keep it on my phone. We're nearly there but he has one more thing to show us. "Are you going to Spain or Portugal?" He asks. "*Non*" is the fairly straightforward reply. However, that doesn't put him out of his stride. There is a small black box on the panel by the door. It has red and green lights on it. He tells us that there have been cases of people being gassed in their vans by criminals in Spain and Portugal. If they try and pump gas into the van, this alarm will go off. That's reassuring. I do wonder why they only commit this crime in Spain and Portugal but now doesn't seem a good time to ask.

Finally, we start moving bags, barbecues and chairs across from the car to the camper van. There isn't an awful lot of storage so the bathroom at the back of the van gets pressed into service as a large wardrobe as bags are piled-up in the shower cubicle.

Next, my car needs parking. We are in a secure car park now, with numerous empty spaces including the one vacated by the camper van. However, this apparently belongs to the local school and they only have permission to park their vehicle here. They suggest that parking in the street should be okay but I'm not keen and I decide to pay for what I've already booked, so he says he'll lead us back to the car park near the station. Now things get really mad. He jumps in his car, with the old woman – who still hasn't spoken to us – and her dog. I jump in my car and Steve, poor Steve, jumps in the camper van.

I know he's driven a van abroad before, collecting furniture, but still, it's a daunting prospect, driving through back streets in a fairly large left-hand drive vehicle. I'm so glad he's here because I absolutely couldn't have done this on my own. I'd be in tears by now. We set off, looking a bit like something from *The Wacky Races* (kids, ask your parents). Again, he swings his car round tight streets as if he were in a rally, and he finally manages to lose me somewhere near the station. The traffic's heavy here and he gets through a set of lights. I don't make it. Then I'm lost. I'm following my satnav and I have Google maps going on the phone so now I have two female voices shouting at me to go left in 200 yards. Then I see that left is down what amounts to an alley – Steve will never make it – so I have to ignore their advice and get more lost. Then Steve loses me.

Eventually, after several more minutes looping round the station but never quite being where I'm supposed to be, Steve calls on the car phone. Our friend has just spotted him and run over to flag him down. They'll wait for me by my car park. I've pulled over now and reassess. I look at the map. I'm very close. I can do this. A minute or two later, I see the van parked up and two people waving at me. It turns out I've been up this street at least once but didn't see a car park. It is, it turns out, under a hotel. Incredibly, given the shambolic nature of my approach, I open up the app and press the entry icon and the metal door rolls up in front of me, as smooth as silk. I park and exit through the hotel reception, popping up 100 yards further down the road from where I entered. Hands are shaken, goodbyes are said and we finally set off on the next stage of the journey. It's now three o'clock; four hours since we left the apartment and we're still in Bordeaux.

We say *au revoir* to our guide. Fair play, he's worked really hard to help and it's probably been as stressful for him as it has been for us. Madame is conspicuous by her absence. We speculate that she's already regretting her decision to hire out her pride and joy to a couple of daft lads from Leeds. *Que sera sera* and all that.

Now, back to the travel plans. I've suggested heading up to Brittany rather than going straight to Amiens, our base for the next game. We have four days, we're booked onto the campsite in Amiens from the 15th onwards so there's a gap in the schedule. We have a pal in Brittany, a former member of our Wednesday night football gang, and I've been in touch to find out if he's about and ready to accept visitors. I've had positive replies to both enquiries. I don't think we'll get to him today now, it's too far, so I let him know we'll be arriving tomorrow. So, as we finally bid a fond farewell to beautiful Bordeaux, Steve still at the wheel and me on navigational duties, we have no idea where we're going to sleep tonight, our first night in our new home. This is life on the road!

The van moves along well, despite those early problems and, after three hours or so, we pull over to evaluate our situation and to see if we can make a cup of tea. Steve's travel kettle finally gets brought out of the bag but the plugs don't work. After much scratching of heads and fiddling with knobs, we go 'old school' and heat water in a pan on the hob. We're not quite reduced to rubbing sticks together yet.

There's something very satisfying about sitting at the table behind the driver's seat, drinking a cup of tea. If I had a map, I'd now spread it out on the table but there's no map, instead it's an app and it has all the camper van stops along the route. More traditionally, I also have a book with lists of overnight stopping places in every region. I've been reading up on all this stuff before we set off. I'm aware that France has embraced the camper van concept and many small villages, even roadside stops, provide facilities specifically for our use. There are all sorts of different plug-ins and hook-ups to look out for. They work with different tokens, or with money or credit cards or they're free. In my book, there's an exhaustive list of icons to describe what each location offers. There are also photos of the different types of box on offer. It's obvious from studying both my sources that there are a few places we can aim for but there's a municipal campsite with a camper van hook-up facility at a place called Les Essarts, just south of Nantes.

We get back on the road. I would drive, of course, but now, more than ever, I feel my skills are better deployed in the passenger seat. I'm sure Steve agrees. As we come upon the exit from the A83, I'm right on it. We drive to the village, through the village and then the campsite is on the Rue De La Piscine, which seems to be a clear indication there's a swimming pool near there as well. All is as it should be, we travel through a very sleepy looking, nondescript village which seems to have already shut down for the night. Then we pick up 'Camping' signs and turn right into what appears to be a car park. It is a car park, for the swimming pool. On the other side of the car park is a gate and a sign for *Camping Municipal le Patis*, except the gate is shut and the hut that lies beyond is boarded up and the weeds are sprouting around the foot of the gatepost. That's the problem with guidebooks, unlike apps, they're out of date as soon as they're published.

All is not lost though. I've already got overly excited at spotting one of those plug-in boxes, now familiar from my pre-trip studies, so there is still a facility for camper vans here. Surprisingly, given the exotic nature of our location, in a car park on the outside of a dull village, there's no one else here. So, we're able to park right next to the provider of power and water.

We both spring into action, as if we've been doing this all our lives. Steve gets the power cable out of the back, as demonstrated to us back in Bordeaux and plugs it in. I stick a couple of Euros in the slot and we have power. Now the plugs work and we can stick the kettle on, so we do, just for the hell of it! Well, it's all on for one hour at least, then the meter will need feeding again. An hour's worth of charge to the battery should see us through though. We can fill the water tank here as well and get rid of any waste water. We're all systems go!

Now, we have our first chance to unpack the bags. This is going to be quite a challenge. Storage space is at a premium so we squeeze clothes into small holes, and the empty bags go back in the shower unit. My other bag is lodged, still full, in-between the toilet and the side of the van. We're moving around each other fairly well, given the confined space available, but we're both quite hefty, so we keep the side door open, despite a chilly, wet evening. The weather, thus far, has not been kind.

Next, tasks are delegated. I take on the role of chef and Steve is assigned the job of getting the TV working. The van's got a satellite dish on the top and it moves around to find the best signal. As I step out to take a picture of us, the van and our location, it looks exactly like a scene from my old Sky Sports News days. We'd be parked in the middle of an empty car park somewhere, working with a satellite truck, dish up and broadcasting to the world. Now, I'm cooking pasta and sipping from a can of bitter whilst Steve has his feet up, trying to find coverage of Ukraine v Germany. That he succeeds is probably the best moment of today. It's just us, somewhere in the middle of France, a bowl of pasta, some bitter and a game of football, which Germany win 2-0.

Elsewhere, in the real world, all is not so blissful. There's been another mass shooting in the US, Florida this time, with the gay community targeted. We've encountered a relaxed, liberated attitude to homosexuality in France. To me this is further evidence that there are fanatics who can't accept our 'live and let live' outlook. We have to prevail.

In the not so serious news, I catch up on text messages during the game and there's one from Barry Horne. It reads, 'Horne strikes again. Flight delayed!!!' So, he's still in France, he's teaching in Chester tomorrow morning and the flight's due to land – if it ever takes off – in Cardiff. Steve becomes the latest member of my entourage to enjoy a little chuckle at Barry's travel travails.

Another of my pals, who's a teacher, has also had a long trip back, travelling by coach from Bordeaux to Wrexham. He's still at Dover, so he's still got to get to Wrexham and then drive himself to Leeds, so he reckons he'll be heading straight to the school gates tomorrow morning.

As I climb up to my bed, I feel I've made the right choice, even if there's only a six inch clearance between the tip of my nose and the roof. Down below, Steve's completed the Tetris challenge and we settle down for an early night.

Monday, June 13th

I think that probably qualifies as the longest night's sleep I've had since I left home last week, despite the compact nature of the sleeping arrangements. I did spin from one side to the other rather too dramatically in the night, crashing against the ceiling in the process, and I didn't feel the need to try and scale the ladder in search of the bathroom in the dead of night, so the first night 'under canvas' can be considered a relative success.

The weather's no better so we don't throw the sliding door back to reveal a fine summer's day. Still, we take our Weetabix *al fresco* and then contemplate the plan for the day. We're about two hours away from Plouha, which is where Brian lives, so we've got a leisurely drive by current standards and I volunteer to take the wheel.

Steve wanders off for a smoke and to see whether we might be able to use the facilities in the swimming pool. Before he's gets back, I've decided to give the shower a go. I clear all the bags out first – obviously – then slip in and pull the curtain across. It's not a big area and although the water's warm as it hits me, and I get wet, the curtain starts sticking to me like a second skin. Still, I get a bit of a lather on before peeling myself out of it. This now means we need to empty the waste water tank, which is actually an exercise I think we've both been secretly looking forward to. It involves positioning the van over a grid provided specially for this purpose. We were guided through the procedure for this yesterday; the lowering of the waste pipe, pushing a button and standing back to wait for it to empty before remembering to put the pipe up again, or else something very bad happens.

Our run through is somewhat delayed, incredibly, by the arrival of another van that parks up right alongside us, despite the fact we're in a big empty car park. The reason he's here becomes apparent as he goes through the waste water rigmarole and then clears his chemical toilet out as well. We watch attentively and look to pick up a few tips.

When it's our turn, I get behind the wheel for the first time. I give the van a couple of circuits, just to get a bit of practice in, before I reverse carefully over the grid with Steve guiding me in. I stop right over it and feel pretty pleased with myself. Then, pipe down, and the waste water starts flowing out. We both feel a sense of satisfaction at ticking another box in the camper van handbook.

Now, a much bigger test awaits as I strap myself in and we pull away from the car park and head for the open road. I've driven a van before, when I was 21 and working for a fruit and veg wholesalers in Wrexham. It was one of those jobs that helped me pay off the overdraft from college, in the halcyon days when you didn't leave with both a degree and a lifetime's worth of debt. I wasn't very good at van driving to be honest. They asked me to work a Saturday morning shift, which I agreed to do despite the fact I had already just signed up to be the Llangollen rubbish tip attendant at weekends as well.

As I had to be on the road by about 6.30am, I figured I could get my deliveries done, then be in my hut at the tip by the time it opened at 10 o'clock, but my plan started to unravel pretty quickly. Once I'd loaded up I was told to go and put fuel in it, so I did, except I put the wrong fuel in and the van ground to a halt just opposite The Racecourse on the way into Wrexham. Not one nectarine had yet been delivered. The van had to be towed away, unloaded, a new van loaded and then, and only then, could I go and do my round. I had to ring my brother and ask him to go and pretend to be me at the rubbish tip until after I'd belatedly made all my deliveries to scowling shop keepers. I was very unpopular that day.

Maybe experiences like that have coloured me, but the 'driving a van' thing is not particularly enjoyable for me. It's the first time I've driven a left-hand drive vehicle for a start, so changing gear with my right hand is a change I struggle with. Steve talks me through it like a driving instructor with a nervous pupil. "Remember, you've got a lot of weight behind you, so allow extra space between you and the vehicle in front." He suggests, as I roll uncomfortably close to the rear end of a lorry. Eventually, after a hairy moment dealing with the junction onto the A83, I get to grips with it and we're back on the road and heading northwest. I take us round Nantes and then onto Rennes. Beyond there, we stop and I feel happy to resume my preferred role as Navigator.

Brian's sent directions to his house but we plan a supermarket stop first, to stock up on provisions and we pull over in a place called Lanvollen which to me looks very similar to the name of my parent's home town of Llangollen. We're in Brittany now, so there will be many similar sounding place names as the two countries share a Celtic language, indeed the Welsh and Breton national anthem have the same tune as well.

The SuperU throws up a number of exciting purchases beyond mere ham and cheese. I find a copy of a magazine called *So Football* which has a giant Gareth Bale poster in it, so I have to buy that and some Panini Euro 2016 stickers for my album, which is some way from being finished – about 476 stickers short to be precise. The other exciting purchase is something I find in the frozen food aisle where they have bags of frozen meals to pan fry. There's a paella, a sausage and potato dish and a lentil and meat *cassoulet* to name but three. This is particularly exciting because our camper van hasn't got an oven so these meals can be cooked on the hob, they're the answer to all our prayers!

Tonight, of course, we don't have to worry. Brian's waiting for us, as promised, *en route* to his house. We greet him with big hugs. We haven't seen him for quite a while. Brian and his wife, Gi, still keep a house in Leeds but they spend half the year here. Brian used to play football with us, in fact he played professionally a long time ago, but he's into his 70s now so those days are over. However, he still comes along for a post-match drink on a Wednesday evening whenever he can and he's still fighting fit, having just completed a Land's End to John O'Groats bike ride – the second time he's done it. Add to that the fact that he's an acclaimed psychologist, a former lecturer and that he suffered a very rare and potentially fatal form of leukaemia not so long ago and you get an impression of a pretty interesting chap. We won't be short of stuff to talk about.

We follow Brian back to the house and it's lovely. A white cottage with an orchard and well tended gardens around it. The drive is narrow, but Steve does a fine job in getting the van in-between the gateposts and we park in front of the house. Gi comes out to greet us. We've all met before so we can get straight into the kitchen for a cup of tea, some fantastic cake and a catch up.

There are practicalities to sort out as well. Brian has an outdoor socket, so we run the cable out from the van and plug it in. There's a spare bedroom in the house, so I offer Steve the use of that, to save the Tetris challenge tonight, whilst I'll happily sleep in the van.

The rest of the day passes extremely agreeably with beers, Sweden v Ireland, then a fabulous meal with wine and really good conversation. The Brexit issue comes up again, of course. Brian and Gi are both avowed Europeans and the fact that they now have a house in France makes them even more anxious about the consequences should things not go the right way on the 23rd.

Being part of the EU makes it far easier for them to come and go as they please, to start a new life here if they wish. An opportunity that many other UK citizens have taken across Europe. I guess they might be described as immigrants but they've thrown themselves into community life, producing cider with the help of a local farmer and using local builders to help turn a rundown dwelling into a lovely place to live. They're investing in the local economy and Plouha surely benefits from having them here. The village we drove through last night was sadly all too typical of others I've visited in France in recent years with no shops, restaurants or bars, in fact no real signs of life at all in the evenings.

We retire to the lounge in time for the next game and we watch the unfancied Italians beat the very much fancied Belgians, who still seem to have all the players but don't have a team. Off-the -pitch issues come to the fore in the half-time interval, with Wayne Rooney and Roy Hodgson both being shown making an appeal to the England fans not to get involved in any more trouble in Lens.

In the days since the incidents in Marseille, there have been many lurid tales about the Russian hooligans, who were the main perpetrators of the violence immediately before, during and after the game. The level of violence witnessed has clearly rocked the organisers and UEFA has issued a warning that Russia will be kicked out of the competition if there's any repeat but England have received a similar warning, hence the manager and captain making these televised appeals for calm. There's also been a request for ticketless fans not to go to Lens at all, but rather to go and watch the game in the fan zone in Lille. What nobody seems to have noticed is that Russia play in Lille the day before so it has the look of the lion's den about it.

It's hard to make sense of all this angst and unhappiness given all we've seen and experienced in France so far, it almost feels like Wales and England are competing in two separate tournaments and yet we both come together in three days time?

Tuesday, 14th June

After a day on the road, I'm finding I've all but left my old life behind. Not only did I sleep in the camper van, I also start my day by making myself a cup of tea in it, despite the presence of a fully equipped kitchen just a few yards away. I sit on the seat by the door and look out at yet another dull day. It's no real surprise, I've had a few holidays in this part of the world, it's beautiful but it gets the same weather as it's Celtic cousin, Cornwall.

Cheesy appears at the front door, offering a cup of tea and a cooked breakfast. I'm not about to turn down either offer, although I warm up for my trip to the big house by downing a couple of Weetabix; I need my fibre intake. Shoney's clearly enjoyed the opportunity to sleep on something other than a sofa so everyone's in good spirits as we reconvene around the kitchen table. I take my Panini album in with me so I can add yesterday's new stickers. When I lay my book out on the table it causes much hilarity for the Cheesmans. Apparently, their son used to do exactly the same as a lad and they probably weren't expecting to see it from a soon to be 47-year-old. For those of my generation though, this is one of the key aspects we've missed out on as Wales fans.

I was collecting English Football League stickers when I was in primary school in Liverpool, the playground ritual of sifting through swaps – 'got, got, haven't, haven't, got...' – but the international collections have never featured Wales. Over the last few months, I've seen many people even older than myself, gathered round tables that are covered in piles of stickers, clutching lists of those numbers they need and those they've got. Yet again, I'm left somewhat disappointed, five more packets and I've still only got two Welsh players.

Breakfast is very good, Cheesy whips up an *oeuf et jambon* combination which tastes great and sets us up nicely for his suggestion of a little bike ride before we get on the road in the van again. His house is close to the sea and the nearest beach was used as an escape route by allied airmen in the Second World War. Indeed, so many were smuggled through the countryside and onto boats back to Britain, from this point, that a memorial's been erected saluting the bravery of the local *Résistance* forces – the *Maquis* – who risked, and in some cases lost, their lives helping them. Brian has a bike for everyone,

68

so we set off. I'm dressed in a stripy Breton top and I've wearing my beret for the occasion. I'm only missing a string of onions around my handlebars to complete the picture.

It's an easy ride on quiet country lanes and we arrive at the memorial no more than five minutes after leaving his house. It's a rugged bit of coastline with a glorious cove down below. The tracks the *Résistance* members used to lead the airmen are still visible. There was only a short window of opportunity of a couple of months before the route was discovered but in that time they got over 130 back to Britain to rejoin the war effort. When the Germans eventually discovered what was happening, they burnt down the farm being used as a base and shot the owner. We ride to the plaque at this site, arriving to find a tour party already being told the story. As we begin to read it, the skies darken dramatically and heavy spots of rain begin to fall. The tourists dive back into their minibus and pull away and we shelter for a little while under the trees but, with no sign of a let up, Cheesy suggests we follow a cross country route home that's quicker.

It's definitely shorter but we're riding on muddy tracks, through puddles and into driving rain. By the time we get back, we're all in a right mess. I've got mud from the back wheel all across the seat my shorts and my top. I'm looking pretty bedraggled but it was a great laugh and I've enjoyed the chance to get my heart racing again after a week of relative inactivity. My running regime has been on hold since I left Leeds so I strip the filthy clothes off and dive in the Cheesman's shower, feeling good to have shifted even a couple of the pounds I must have recently put on.

Having availed myself of the hot shower, fluffy dry towels, and after one last cup of tea, it's time for us to leave. We don't want to overstay our welcome and it's been a fabulous detour from the route. We wish Brian and Gi fond farewells, I take the wheel and steer carefully out between those two gate posts. *Au revoir* Plouha!

The good news is we're not going far. Rather than getting over to Amiens – about four hours away – I've suggested heading to Dinard, the base for the Wales team for the duration of the group games. It's only a 90-minute drive from the Cheesmans and it's in the right direction in terms of where we're heading tomorrow. I've been trying for several weeks to try and contact the only campsite in the town, without success, so I fear a repeat of two nights ago but we decide to give it a go anyway.

We drive east through Brittany, towards St Malo, and just before the port we see signs for Dinard. The camp site is clearly not in the town centre but the good news is that it is quite clearly open for business. I jump out and go ask the guy in reception if there's a pitch available. He says there is and it 'maybe has a little view of the sea?' He gives me a map and I guide Steve to our allotted position. He was underselling it a bit, we actually have a full view of the sea. It's a great location, so good that we decide to go 'full beans' and get out the awning, the deckchairs and, to complete the picture, I hang the bunting across the struts at the front of the canopy that's now sheltering us from yet another shower. Soon, the kettle's in use again and we sit, sipping tea and looking out across the beach to the ocean. I think I've done pretty well with this stop, even if I do say so myself.

A quick check on Google maps then marks our location as being just about next door to the team hotel. I'm sure the security presence around the FAW base is going to be pretty heavy, so I send Weeksy, one of the medical team, a text to let him know we'll be wandering past shortly if anyone happens to be knocking about. He confirms the tight security, it's passes or no entry apparently. I don't want to cause any hassle or put anybody out, they're busy people, but it would be good to see the backroom boys and girls. In fact, it would be good to see everyone, I've always got on well with the players and if there's one thing I'm missing about being on the other side of the fence for this tournament, it's that distance from something that I've been incredibly close to for over a decade. I've been with everyone in good times and some very, very bad. Still, I made my choice so, as Steve and I approach the hotel entrance a little while later, a crew of half a dozen police officers start gazing over in our direction. It's sufficiently off-putting to cause us to drift away from the approach road and send us round the path that leads to the coastal walk in front of the hotel instead.

I understand the need for it, the security presence. In the squad, Wales have the world's most expensive footballer. It's a sad fact that Gareth would be just the sort of high profile target publicity hungry maniacs would crave. That's probably another reason for the selection of this base. It's right on the coast, almost as west as you can get in

France and whilst it's a long way from even the nearest tournament venue, it's isolation is its strength.

As we walk around the perimeter fence, the sea to our left, and security guards on duty at each level of the tiered exterior of the hotel to our right, it reminds me of a fort. One of the concerns identified during the planning process was the potential for the players getting bored. I know the FAW have gone to great lengths to ensure there's enough stuff provided to keep them entertained – games consoles, table tennis, quiz nights that sort of stuff – but, as me and Steve have found, the evenings are always taken care of anyway as you have a game to sit back and watch. You never know, we might be studying future opposition? One more point should guarantee progress.

I look up towards the terrace and I can see a couple of people in training gear moving around but they're too far away to risk waving and shouting, I don't want to suddenly see one of those red laser dots hovering over my heart, so we keep walking, in the direction of Dinard. The path snakes around the cliffs and we can see the ferries sailing into the port of St Malo just a little further up the coast. It's a bit of hike to the town from the hotel, a couple of kilometres, and as we walk, the rains return. It's a relief to round the last outcrop and sight a beachside *café*, complete with covered terrace. Before we can find a table though, there's a picture to be taken.

We find statue of Alfred Hitchcock that Brian had mentioned. Apparently Hitchcock was very fond of this place and there's a film festival, named after him, here every year. The tourist bit done, we seek shelter and beer. The *café* provides both.

As we sit and watch the world scurry by, I spy someone I know. The media assigned to Wales are all staying here as well, including Alex and Geraint, although they've already been dispatched to Lens, presumably in anticipation of trouble and a three-way tear-up between English, Russians and Welsh fans. The S4C team must still be in town though, as their commentator Nic Parri is striding along the prom, umbrella in hand. I nip out from under cover and intercept him. I've met Nic many times before and he's another fascinating character. He's not full time at this broadcasting lark, in his day job he's a High Court judge! He has become the Welsh language voice of football over the course of many years commentating on radio and television. He's an extremely bright bloke, as you might imagine, and he has a terrific turn of phrase, very poetic, very 'Welsh'. He commentates alongside a former international, Malcolm Allen, who is all passion and crazy outbursts. They make a good team. If Wales get through, Nic will have to negotiate to extend his absence from the judicial system for at least another few days, but we still need that extra point. Sadly, more of the chat is about the potential for disorder. It's a great disappointment to me that our tournament is being overshadowed by this stuff and it's exactly the reason why so many Wales fans didn't want to play England. We've spoken to a number already who are going to the first game and the last game but not the middle match, how sad is that!?

Once Nic has left and we've settled the bill, we go for a walk around town. What is immediately striking is just how much the town has thrown itself behind it's resident football team. There are Welsh dragons on display in pretty much every shop and the flag flies over the hotel in the main square. It's fantastic to see the Breton people getting behind their Celtic cousins to this extent. There are those in this part of the world, as there are in Wales, who seek independence for their nation, particularly those who speak the ancient languages. Welsh and Breton are very similar and share the same origins. They're mad keen on football in Brittany as well and the Celtic nation has a number of top-flight teams. It's only a few years since two Breton sides, Rennes and Guingamp, met in the French cup final, the first time it had ever happened. Before the game, the *Marseillaise* was sung but so was the Breton anthem, *Bro Gozh ma Zadoú* – 'Old Land of My Fathers' – by a singer called Nolwenn Leroy, the footage is on YouTube, and it's amazing.

Dinard is a very pleasant little town. It looks well-heeled; we've seen some amazing houses near our campsite, and there are a host of interesting shops on the main street – independents – not the cheap chain stores, bookies and coffee shops that have colonised just about every surviving high street in towns large and small in the UK. You know things are a bit different when you can purchase a souvenir chocolate bar, with DINARD written across it, that's described as having 80% cocoa content, and is covered in gold dust. It makes a change from a stick of rock.

Steve uses the time available to buy some presents. I've already made inroads into my gift buying of course, but I add a few more items to the collection. After Dinard, I can't see many gaps in the itinerary for wandering around shops; other than supermarkets.

The late afternoon's heading in the direction of early evening and the rain's back so we set off for home, a couple of baguettes poking out the top of Steve's rucksack. We haven't got much further than the front porch of Harry's bar when the rain seems to get heavier and we are forced, once more, to seek shelter. Others have had the same need it appears, as there is a group of Welsh lads gathered around the pool table and, at the bar, I see Mark Pitman, the man who provides the Wales coverage for the UEFA website, now that really is an 'access all areas' role. There's more hooligan talk with him. It's getting depressing. I have a mate, an England fan, who is joining up with pals in France and who might be out in Lens. Already one of their party has decided to go home after what he witnessed in Marseille.

Still, the tournament goes on and we watch some of Austria v Hungary on the big screen. Austria will be World Cup opponents for Wales, so it's good to see them lose 2-0 in Bordeaux. A place and time that already feels a long way away.

The rain refuses to abate so hunger drives us to make the decision to brave it. There's a shorter route back to the campsite which is just as well as we get caught in another deluge and by the time we arrive back at the camper van, we're both soaked, again. I think back to the week of one of the qualifiers when I kept getting drenched, every time I went out, hopefully this is a good omen.

Not only are we very wet but we arrive back to notice something odd about our awning. There's a very big sag in the middle of it and the two supporting poles are beginning to look a little like Bambi's legs as she struggles to her feet for the first time. Needless to say, it's water that's collected and dragged the cover down. We have to very carefully lower the legs so that the water runs off, forming a small river right where we were hoping to sit and have tea.

Tonight, Steve's on cooking duties and we eat whilst watching a fairly dull match between Portugal and Iceland. Mind you, try telling that to Iceland – population of just over 300,000 – who are enjoying their first ever game at any international tournament by claiming their first ever point. Like Wales, they have brought huge, enthusiastic support to celebrate this new experience. Their backing must make up an even greater percentage of the population than ours does: Wales being 10 times bigger.

The pre-sleep check-up on news from back home is full of dire predictions about the likelihood of trouble in Lille, a Russian fans' leader has been deported but he reckons all the top hooligans are already in place anyway, but there are also headlines about the referendum. Polls suggest a seven point lead for Leave. Brian will not be sleeping easy tonight.

Wednesday, 15th June

I wake up at 7.40am, which might seem pretty early for a bloke who's busy doing nothing, but it's actually a bit late for a bloke who had planned to do something. I know two of the FAW chaps, the aforementioned Weeksy and another member of the medical staff, Dave Rowe, have been going out on a run every morning and I'd hoped to join them today. A flurry of texts are exchanged and it seems they're off out in 20 minutes but I'm still trying to unwrap myself from the duvet, still facing the challenge of getting the ladder hooked up so I can climb down from my rooftop abode.

I sort myself out then put on a bit of a sprint, okay fast jog, up to the hotel but I miss them. I don't know this at the time of course, so I hang around for a while. I'm wearing a Wales training top and matching Adidas shorts – some of the kit I get provided with when I host the media sessions for the A and Pro licence courses – I have to look the part, naturally. But then I wonder if the cops will think I'm actually dressing up to try and sneak in, like that bloke who used to pop up in team pictures before big games. Fearing the red laser dot again, I jog on. Now that I'm up and out, I might as well get on with it and have my first run in a week.

I follow the coastal path again. In contrast to yesterday, it's a fine morning, not exactly baking hot but at least the sun is shining and it's the first time we've seen it for a while. This is a great way to start the day, it has to be said, and I envy the guys the chance to do this every morning. Then, right on cue, they appear, already running back towards the hotel. Dave Weeks appears first, fiddling with the stopwatch on his wrist as he stops to talk. Dave Rowe follows a few paces later. I'm guessing these lads are a bit serious about this stuff, maybe PB's are involved. I run because I enjoy it and it goes a little way to counteract the impact of beer and burgers. The last time I saw these two, bizarrely, I was lying face down on a physio's bench at the team hotel in Cardiff and Weeksy was trying to rebuild my feet after I'd wrecked them doing a sponsored walk. Dave Rowe was watching on, wincing as another huge blister was popped and pus squirted out like a fountain.

That's the sort of blokes they are. In my hour of need, even though it was match day and they had loads to do, they were more than happy to help. It's that whole Together Stronger ethos. Everybody pitches in and everyone feels part of the team. On that basis, they're keen to know what the experience has been like for me 'on the outside'? I can only enthuse about everything I've seen so far. Dave Rowe's one of the few who's been involved since I first started covering Wales. If he wasn't working, I know he'd be out here as a fan. Weeksy is a relative newcomer and an Anglo, but he's completely bought into it. If there were Welsh passports, he'd have been granted one by now.

We discuss Bordeaux and the elation inside and outside the FAW group following the win. Apparently, the players and the staff were on such a massive high in the immediate aftermath, but then plunged into a deep low once the euphoria had worn off. After a flat day or two, Ian Mitchell – the team psychologist – stepped in with a 'kangaroo court' to lift everyone's spirits again. An activity designed to get everyone laughing, and it worked. These are the new challenges of tournament football, short gaps between key games, where the mental side is every bit as important as the physical.

We talk about the security around the team, a subject that inevitably leads to discussion of the upcoming game and the concerns around it. They've been told the French police have a different approach to their British counterparts, who are over here to act only in an advisory role. The British strategy is to keep an eye on ringleaders then nip trouble in the bud before it has time to develop into something bigger. The French prefer to wait until something starts, then pile in with everything. That tallies with reports of vans full of police sitting outside the stadium in Marseille as the Russians started the trouble inside it.

Weeksy's got one on eye on the stopwatch again so I shouldn't detain them any longer, they've probably got work to do! We say our goodbyes and they promise to look out for me and give me a wave in Lens. They head back to the hotel whilst I head on towards Dinard, past the Hitchcock statue and back home via the route we took in the rain last night. When I return, Steve's sitting under the awning with a tea and a fag. There's some crazy talk about a swim in the sea but that's quickly discounted as a glance upwards suggests more rain. Instead, we pack up and settle up, our seafront pitch only setting us back about €17. Steve's just bought a caravan and he's already contemplating coming back here.

Back on the road, we have a four hour cross-country run to Amiens ahead of us. One of the highlights of the drive is the bridge crossing at Honfleur. It's an amazing structure, worth every cent of the additional toll charged to cross it, then we stop for lunch at a service station recommended by my app. We're carrying waste water and we drive round in search of the grid provided for the use of camper vans and lorries. It's obviously a popular stopping and emptying point as it looks and smells pretty unpleasant. I hold my nose, turn the pipe round and let it all pour out.

Back in my navigational role, I suffer something of a setback on the approach to the campsite in Amiens when Steve misses a satnav instruction, then goes solo for a while and before long we're heading in the opposite direction to where we want to be. I keep calm, preach the mantra of 'always trust the satnav' and thankfully we get back on track.

The campsite proves to be something of a Euro 2016 hub. As we drive towards our allocated pitch, we pass Swiss, Irish, English and Welsh flags. There's another hiatus as we park and then discover we haven't got an electric plug-in. I check the booking confirmation and it's my mistake, I didn't ask for one. The solution is simple, the woman on reception suggests a different plot and doesn't ask for any extra cash. We reposition the van next to a large motor home with GB plates that appears to have been abandoned in a hurry, it's parked diagonally across two pitches and there's no sign of anyone in it.

We get ourselves set-up again: awning out, bunting up and, as there are so many flags flying, I add the massive Welsh dragon, draped across the front of the camper van. We claim this plot for Gareth the Camper Van, Owain Glyndŵr and Wales!

We've missed the other game in the group whilst we've been on the road but Slovakia have beaten Russia by 2 goals to 1, which means we are still top. It also means the Russians know that nothing other than a win in the final game will get them through. We may already be there, if we can get something against England. If we win, we definitely finish top.

Over a cup of tea, I read online accounts of the build-up. It seems Gareth Bale and Aaron Ramsey have been winding things up a bit. Gareth's suggestion that Wales players have more passion than England's has caused some degree of consternation, both in the media and in the England camp. I'm a bit surprised as Gareth's usually pretty careful not to say anything controversial. In this instance, I'm guessing he's decided to enjoy himself a bit. He's learnt to handle himself in the hottest of hothouses, Madrid, so dealing with the world's media is something he does every week. I don't imagine he's chucked in a comment like that without being aware of the consequences. It doesn't sound 'off the cuff', so I suspect it's part of the pre-match strategy.

Is it true? I think it probably is. Gary Speed started it. He made it a priority to get the players to learn the anthem as soon as he took charge. The Welsh language is the one thing that makes Wales demonstrably different from England, where a lot of our team were born. Playing for England must feel quite a lot like playing for a Premier League club. Everything sounds the same and looks the same as it does at their clubs, and 'Englishness' is a difficult concept to define. What exactly are the England players playing for?

I think there's a related factor, in that a lot of the Welsh team play at a lower level. This means that international football is the big stage for them. Chris Gunter's spent time in the Premier League with Spurs and Reading but most of his football's been played in the Championship. To Chris, 26 years old and already heading for 70 caps, playing for Wales is a really big deal. It's given him opportunities to travel the world and pit himself against some of the world's best footballers.

One of the biggest aspects of the success of the national team in recent times was built on another aspect that Gary introduced; enjoyment. It seems straightforward. Players are playing football and they should always be enjoying themselves, shouldn't they? Not necessarily. It's a job and like every job, you have things you like and things you don't like. I love covering football matches but I'm not so keen on going out and doing vox pops but I do it because it's part of the role.

The players enjoy each other's company, they've been together as a group for a long time and the core members are good at assimilating others into that group. When you're playing with your mates, it means more, ask any Sunday League side. That aspect is something England must currently lack. They have a young squad that's inexperienced at international level. The difference between England and Wales here is that England are playing under the pressure of external expectation that won't take that factor into account. There's no pressure on Wales. The Welsh media is overwhelmingly supportive, at the moment at least, the players are loved by the fans and the squad's surrounded by positivity. That makes it easier for players to go and play, to express themselves, to relax in the international environment and most importantly to have a bit of fun. They're having more fun than almost any team I can ever remember encountering in the past. England certainly can't compete with that. They know if they blow it against Wales they're going to get pelters from their fans and the media, there's not much fun in that!

Before I retreat to the galley and cook, we have a wander round the site, checking out the flags. Closest to us, there's a St. George's cross with the words 'Bristol City – For club and country'. A little further away, draped over a couple of tents, there's a Tranmere Rovers flag and I resist the strong temptation to wander over and remind them of Wrexham's – won two, drawn one – record against them last season.

This has always been an aspect of following England, a bit like lower division players appearing for Wales. The fans of small clubs look on England trips as their chance to announce their presence on the international stage. Chelsea apart, it's very rare to see any of the big club's names on flags. It's not such a big thing amongst the Welsh fans, perhaps because there are fewer clubs, but I've seen many more banners proclaiming towns and villages, and increasingly in praise of players, amongst our support. One of my favourites being 'When God created Joe Allen, he was just showing off'. In its own small way, I suspect it highlights another difference in the mindset of the two sets of supporters. England fans sometimes seem almost resentful of the players, I guess it's that sense of constantly being let-down so they rally behind the flag and the badge. Without the weight of a World

Cup win 50 years ago, Wales have only the 'Spirit of '58' and a general sense of respect for just about anyone who's ever pulled on the red shirt, although I'm still not sure picking Vinnie Jones was ever a good idea and Gavin Maguire should never have played against Germany in Nuremberg.

With everyone mingling happily around the site, no matter what their flags proclaim, we head back to our base for tea. I'm looking forward to this one, it's the lentil *cassoulet* in the wonder bag. I'm going to add the last of yesterday's *saucisson*, some hunks of bread and all washed down with a nice bottle of Saumur. We catch the end of Romania v Switzerland then later we'll have France v Albania to watch on the telly as well. More middle-aged, motor home madness!

Whilst I'm preparing the food, Steve gets into conversation with one of our neighbours. He's Dutch with a German wife, and they're on their way back to their home in the Netherlands. He asks about the football, naturally curious as to how we'll all get on together on this site after all the reports of trouble. It's interesting how the media across Europe seems fixated on this one negative aspect of the tournament so far. He also asks about Brexit. I'm sure each EU country has it's issues but the people we've met seem puzzled as to why we're going down this route. Here we are, on a French campsite, drinking French wine, mingling happily with people from different countries. To me, this is the European ideal. This is what the Remain politicians should have been focusing on, the bit we all understand. The concept of going on holiday, meeting friendly people, eating and enjoying the local food and drink, being covered in the event of ill-health, being able to move about freely and sharing common ideals. Instead, it's been made about the economy on one side and immigration on the other – neither of which resonate with me and how I feel about being a part of Europe, about being a European.

As I serve my culinary delights, our Dutch friend comes across to wish us '*Bon appetit!*' and informs us that a new group has arrived next to his plot, lads in a car. He lowers his voice. "I think they are English," he says conspiratorially. "I think maybe you should make their tyres go down with a knife." He smiles a naughty smile.

Life would be just about idyllic at this point if it weren't for two factors: one, the temperature's dropped and it's actually pretty chilly now, and two, I am awaiting news of a taxi which might be coming to pick me up to take me to Lens in the morning.

The FAW Trust have another pre-match event planned in town ahead of the game. They've got the First Minister, Carwyn Jones, coming. Originally, they'd asked if I could host it as Fran Donovan, who did the first event, isn't going to be available. Now it appears she is, so I'm only needed to share the hosting role and to ask a few football questions at the end of the session. I've explained the logistical issues, Amiens is a fair way from Lens and we're already booked onto a fans coach that won't get me into town until after the event's started. I've offered to try and book a cab but one local firm I found on the internet hasn't responded to my email whilst another number I got from the receptionist at the campsite doesn't appear to work anymore. So, I have tried but we're not particularly close to the centre of Amiens either, so my options seem almost as limited as my French.

I explain this in another email to Neil, the organiser. I really want to help out, but not being close to Lens makes it tricky and the fact they've got a person to host it now takes the pressure off. He copies someone else into the exchange and they come back saying they'll investigate getting a car from their end. I'll be honest, I won't be distraught if it doesn't happen. I'm here to have fun and to go and do the stuff I don't usually get the chance to go and do before games like sitting in or outside of bars, chatting with other fans and friends and just generally enjoying the build-up.

Hosting events for the great and the good wasn't on the bucket list when I took the decision to watch the tournament in this way, that's a bit more like what I do normally. Doing something different is why I'm staying in a small camper van on a municipal campsite in Amiens rather than staying at a decent hotel somewhere a little closer to Lens.

In other news, France beat Albania 2-0 to ensure they're the first team through to the knockout stage of the competition. Our aim tomorrow is to join them.

Thursday, June 16th – Euro 2016 Match Day 2

I'm awake early to check emails. There's no word from anyone at the FAW so I'm now working on the assumption that I'm sticking with the original plan. That means we're getting on a coach at Amiens train station at 11am. It's been organised by a guy called Leigh James who I've got to know through bumping into him on numerous away trips, both as a supporter and a reporter. He has a background in the travel industry and he's combined his passion and his knowledge on numerous occasions to arrange transport and accommodation for Wales fans. He's a Cardiff fan but he's known throughout Wales now for organising this sort of stuff. He's working in conjunction with another well-known Cardiff fan, Wayne 'Dibs' Anderson. I first met 'Dibs' a long time ago on an eventful trip to watch Wales play Cyprus. It's a long story but I got beaten up and ended up in hospital. Dibs ended up flying back to the UK with me, staying at my parents house in north Wales before heading back down to Cardiff. I hadn't seen him since until I went to a book signing and a Q&A at an event he organised ahead of the Northern Ireland friendly in March. 'Dibs Tours' are well known amongst Cardiff fans and now he's extended his remit to cover internationals as well.

As we emerge into the new day, it appears I missed some action during the night. Our Dutch friend had cause to upbraid the new neighbours in the early hours of the morning, apparently they were talking loudly. We've already ascertained that they are, in fact, Welsh, so it's a good job we didn't follow his advice about the tyres.

As Steve and I sit outside the van, with a cup of tea and a bowl of Weetabix, we catch sight of one of our immediate neighbours for the first time. Apparently they came back late but I was sound asleep, ear plugs in, so I heard nothing. These lads are definitely English, a fact we deduce from the Cockney accent on the lad who says "Mornin" as he walks passed us, back towards the badly parked motor home. He's clutching a bottle of beer and he's either just coming back from a night out or he's started the next one remarkably early. He apologises for any noise there might have been. We shrug, what the heck, we're all on holiday.

The Dutch guy leaves, wishing us all the best in the football and the referendum, and then the rain starts to fall, just for a change. We dress accordingly. It's coats and jeans with, needless to say, another T-shirt from my vast SO58 collection, teamed with the bucket hat, naturally. I've even got a cagoule from my pals at Nicholas Deakins, a menswear company based in Leeds, that perfectly matches the daffodil yellow of the strip around the hat. A lot of thought still goes into my match day attire!

The plan from here into Amiens is to catch a bus from a stop outside the campsite. I've got a map, provided by the lady at reception, that shows where it's located but as we leave, others are already on their way as well and we tag along with three Swansea fans who know where they're going, having had a few drinks in the town centre last night. In turn, another group of England fans tag along with us, the chaps from the Bristol City camper van. The conversation soon turns to the game and our score predictions. I hate doing this, always feeling like it's bad karma, but others are not so reticent. Interestingly, none of the Welsh contingent go for anything other than a Welsh defeat. Steve reckons 2-0 to England. Now, if I were the English guys, I'd seek to rebalance things by predicting a Welsh victory but, they don't. They agree. They're not aggressive or arrogant about it, they just can't see any way Wales could beat England. I actually find this quite comforting. I think we're a far better international team than they're giving us credit for. They may have better individual players throughout the team but that isn't the key factor at this level. We've already won a game, against difficult opponents, the pressure is off our team and very much on theirs. I am emboldened and pipe up as we board the bus, "I think we'll draw 1-1". Believe me, this is what passes for rampant optimism on Planet Bryn.

There's method in my madness. I don't actually think England are that good. I see a lot of their players performing well in the Premier League but the Premier League isn't the best league in Europe, never mind the world. It's the biggest but it isn't the best. *La Liga* remains top and we have a player who's enjoyed another great season playing in that competition. He's also just won his second European Cup. None of the England lads can claim to have had anything like the same level of success and it's hard to work out just how good they are, or might be one day be – in the case of the likes of Rachford, Stones and Sterling – when we haven't seen them play at the toughest level. Although there's no real reason why we shouldn't contemplate Wales actually being a better team and winning the game, a draw would still be brilliant for us and not so good for England.

We chat with the Swansea lads on the bus, then everyone gets off together and heads for the station. It's nice to see England and Wales shirts walking alongside each other. There were some incidents in Lille last night it seems, I've seen a couple of clips on my phone, but it just looks like a group of Russians marauding around the city trying to pick fights, pursued by a bigger media mob, carrying cameras above their heads. There have also been reports of England and Wales fans standing together in the face of provocation, which all bodes well for the atmosphere today.

Although I was born in England, as was Steve and as was Evo – who'll be coming out for the next game – we all support the land of our fathers, or mother in my case. I, at least, did most of my growing up in north Wales after moving over the border at the age of nine, learning the language before leaving home and moving to Leeds for a new job in my early 20s. I used to have a fierce dislike of the English football team but I've mellowed considerably. I've two daughters and a wife who are all English for a start so it would seem a bit mad if I suddenly started having a pop at their national side. These days, I'm ambivalent. I see that England doing well is good for the game in general, and I earn my living from that game but that's head not heart. I could only ever support Wales. I wouldn't even be a GB fan if they ever tried to resurrect that awful idea.

There's a crowd gathered round a couple of coaches right outside Amiens station and people are already being checked off the list that 'Dibs' is holding by the door. We're not on his bus, we're on the other one and as I walk towards it, I spot someone I know: 'Knocker'. We're occasional teammates as he and I have played alongside each other at the football centre owned by our mutual pals, the Boore brothers, Gwilym, Rhys and Alun. They're all Cardiff born and bred, and they're all first language Welsh speakers, which used to be unusual before the advent of the numerous and very popular Welsh medium schools in the capital. The 2011 Census showed that there are over 54,000 Welsh speakers in Cardiff, more than in any other town or city in Wales. It's probably even more by now – a seismic cultural shift.

I love this crew of lads, they're all fanatical Wales fans and go everywhere but they've all got loads of other things going on as well. Gwilym and Rhys, who I know best, are staying in the abbey near Bordeaux. They've got all their family and mates with them in its 20-odd bedrooms. They own the Gôl centre, where we play football

83

but they also have a successful company publishing children's books in Welsh.

Knocker's come out with another pal of his, a top Chef who's worked for Marco Pierre White and who's parents now live in Beziers. So, they've flown up to Paris, then got a hire car to a hotel on the outskirts of Amiens. Their flight back is first thing tomorrow morning, which might seem a problem, as Knocker's clearly not had a lot of sleep. He's a bit pissed actually but fabulously entertaining on the way to Lens, recounting tales of trips past and characters he's encountered along the way. Two stories have me and Steve crying with laughter. One relates to a character who went by the nickname Dai Hooligan and his sudden 'pincer movement' order in a pub in Burnley. The story's about a guy they used to call Dai The Loon. A tale about him crashing his new motor scooter in front of a group of Cardiff fans, when trying to ride *and* 'Do the Ayatollah' has the tears rolling down our cheeks. His tale of a recent Wales away game Kiev involves the memorable description of drinking dirty 'street' vodka in the company of down and outs. For so many of these loyal away lads, the game's only one aspect of the adventure.

We're very much on a Cardiff bus here, that much is clear. The lads on the back seat are from the valleys but they're all lifelong Bluebirds. There are one or two songs they sing about Swansea still but, admirably, they pretty much stay off the subject. That would probably not have been the case until recently but events surrounding the national team have very much helped in bringing people together, even fierce rivals. The positive impact of the success for the national side is one but there's been tragedy as well. The last time Wales met England, at Wembley in 2011, a well-known Cardiff fan, Mikey Dye, was killed by a single punch outside the stadium. An England supporter was later convicted of his manslaughter. It was a shocking incident and, in its aftermath, former enemies from Cardiff and Swansea came together to stage a football match to raise money for his family. Ultimately, maybe some good came out of a senselessly tragic event.

One song that does entertain and amuse, to the tune of Yellow Submarine, is clearly one that's been dreamt up on the long trips to Cardiff away games, with the chorus 'we all live in a twisted valleys town, a twisted valleys town...'. Maesteg apparently being the 'twisted valleys town' in question.

There's all sorts of stuff going on around us and conversational subjects change with bewildering speed. Siôn's mate, the Chef, talks about the quality of the meat here in France and how a lot of UK meat is actually of a higher standard. There's talk about fine wines that have been sampled in *haute cuisine* restaurants, there's talk about politics, the Welsh language and a bloke from Maesteg who had no arms. It spins around us until finally things quieten down as we enter Lens.

There's an instant visual reminder of my home town of Wrexham, as we pass big slag heaps on the outskirts, just like the one we've got at Rhostyllen. In fact, there are real parallels. These slag heaps now stand as a monument to an industry that no longer exists in either town. Both towns relied on coal and, in Wrexham's case, steel for employment. Also both towns paid a high price for relatively high levels of employment. There was a human cost in terms of the dangerous nature of the work. Lens was the site of Europe's worst mining disaster, in March 1906, when over a thousand lives were lost in a massive explosion at the *Courrières* mine. In September 1934, 266 miners were killed in the Gresford colliery disaster in Wrexham. Then there was the economic devastation wrought on the communities when the mines and steelworks were shut down in the latter part of the twentieth century. These slag heaps stand as a grim reminder of all that's been lost. I'm sure the valley boys at the back of the bus recognise it as well.

Lens, like Wrexham, is a town that has little to distinguish it from any other, apart than the fact that it has a football team and the community supports that football team passionately. We get a brief glimpse of the stadium, it's capacity bigger than the size of the population, then it disappears from sight behind other buildings in the foreground. Now we're in the back streets, some England fans walk along the pavement and flash v signs in the direction of the coach – nobody responds – we turn this way and that until eventually the driver manoeuvres the bus into a car park. We're about to get off when a steward rushes over to shoo everyone back on, a look at the company details on all the other coaches already lined up explains why. They're all from England. Mostly West Ham buses apparently. I bet we'd get a warm post-match welcome!

The next half an hour is farcical as we exit one coach park but have to wait for a police escort before we're allowed to move on to the correct one. The coach has to stay at a set of traffic lights whilst we wait for this escort. I've not seen anyone drinking at all on the coach. The Lens booze ban was meant to include possible searches of vehicles so nobody's taken the chance and, in this instance, it's probably a really good job as being stuck for so long tests the patience and probably the bladders of many on board. Finally, a cheer goes up as two police bikes arrive – lights flashing – and our two-coach convoy gets back on the road.

There's still confusion as we arrive at the allocated parking place. Stewards on the gates don't seem to know what's going on but it's now two and a half hours since we left Amiens, just 60 kilometres away, and the lads on board force the issue by getting off anyway. Now the coaches will have to stay here. The stewards may have walkie-talkies and be wearing high-viz vests but their age and appearance – some youngsters and a middle-aged woman – remind me of people who look more like they should be organising the parking at a local Round Table gala rather than a high-risk category international football match. It's all been a bit of a shambles so far.

Lens is not a big place, it's population is smaller than Wrexham, and we pass a few houses – one all done up in flags and flowers for the host nation and the teams who'll be playing there – before we arrive at the edge of the town centre. Now there's a much bigger police presence, particularly outside an Irish pub on one side of the road that seems to have been colonised by Wales fans and one on the other that's home to England fans. Clearly there's plenty of beer for sale in these establishments. We keep walking and head on towards the stadium, following the UEFA signs. All the way along the street, there seem to be *cafés* and takeaways selling alcohol. We look into a *Tabac* and, as well as fags and magazines on offer, there's a long bar at the back of the shop. So, in the midst of this supposedly draconian 'booze ban', even the newsagent's selling beer! It's good beer too, as we discover when we pop in. Lens, being a mining town and not far from Belgium and Germany, means that beer's the drink, not your fine wines. It's also the cheapest *grande bière* we've yet come across on our travels.

We stand outside the shop, watching the crowds go by, drink in hand. The former Wrexham and Wales player Neil Roberts stops for a chat whilst Steve gets talking to an England fan who goes all around the world supporting the side. The atmosphere's fine, even the sun's come out, and fans are mingling happily on the approach to the ground. I've had any numbers of messages from friends to 'stay safe' over the last couple of days but this all feels fine, not quite the carnival of Bordeaux but maybe that's because Wales fans are outnumbered here.

We contemplate a second and final drink before heading for the ground but the barrel's being changed or something and it's already 2.10pm. With the standard security checks to negotiate I suggest it might be better to head in. Steve agrees. We were a bit more diligent in allowing plenty of time to get in at Bordeaux but everyone's that bit more relaxed here, perhaps it's because you can walk to the stadium, and as we pass through the first check I have my first concerns that maybe we've been a bit complacent. There are loads of people milling around outside, including Tim Williams, my pal and the man behind the Spirit of '58 gear that so many people are wearing. He must be chuffed to see how his idea of six years ago has grown into the merchandising phenomenon we can see around the ground today. His hats are everywhere! I pose for a pic with him and he manages to pour beer down the back of my – his – SO58 T-shirt. Like it's being officially launched.

We check our ticket. The only indication as to where we should enter is a colour coded stand with an arrow pointing at it but the signage outside is poor to nonexistent. Lots of people are wandering around looking confused and there's absolutely nobody around to ask. We head to where we think we should be, it's the last possible entry point on this side of the stadium and, as such, there's a huge crowd of people trying to gain access through it. This is the bit where they search the bags, so it all takes a while and all we can see ahead of us are literally thousands of people, waiting either to get through the bag check or on to the next part of the process. It's getting pretty tight around us as more people keep arriving. I get talking to an England fan from Bolton and we both have the feeling this isn't good, in fact, it's potentially dangerous. I keep checking my watch, kick-off is now just 20 minutes away and we haven't moved whilst behind us, more and more people are arriving. It's a complete bottleneck. It's the security checks causing this, plus maybe our late arrival, but the irony is that we now have a perfect situation for a suicide bomber. We're packed in with nowhere to go, and my other concern is the surge that could follow the roar that greets the teams coming out. At that point people will stop being patient, as they are – just about – at the moment. There appears to be absolutely nobody taking control, no stewards, no security, just a crowd of increasingly frustrated football fans.

It comes as a relief when Steve taps me on the shoulder and says he thinks we're in the wrong queue. I'm happy to back out, even if it means missing the kick-off. We head back to where we started and try that other entrance instead. It might be because kick-off is only 10 minutes away or perhaps because we're actually trying to get into a less populated Wales section now, but the queue is nothing like as bad and we actually get through the next two checks just before the teams emerge from the tunnel. We're in the corner of the stand that runs down the side of the pitch. To our left and around us, it's all red, and to our right, it's all white. It looks like a 3:1 ratio in favour of the Three Lions. Despite all the disappointments, 50 years of hurt and all that, the England fans do continue to back their team in huge numbers.

Still, if they have the numbers, we have the passion, just like Gareth said. The singing of the anthems proves it. We belt out *Hen Wlad Fy Nhadau*, and they do their best with *God Save The Queen* but it's just not an uplifting piece, even if you do agree with the sentiment. I wonder what would happen if a politician seriously proposed changing it to something like *Jerusalem*? Another referendum perhaps?

Then we're off, in the new 'coal and grass' change strip – green and 'sort of' charcoal. I'm not a big fan. Hennessey's back in goal and Ledley and Robson-Kanu are in for Edwards and Williams, it's our strongest line-up.

We're kicking towards the majority of the England fans behind Joe Hart's goal and the sun's pretty hot now, intense on our faces, and I'm grateful for the eminently practical nature of my Spirit of '58 hat. Things almost go dramatically wrong right from the kick-off. Rule changes mean you can go backwards now and Wales do, with Bale rolling it to Williams but he slips as he attempts to kick it and only succeeds in hacking it straight at Harry Kane. Defenders rush in to scramble it away but it reminds me of the start of the game against Slovakia, we're being just that little bit sloppy at the back.

Minutes later comes the first chance of the match, as Lallana leaves Neil Taylor for dust and gets into the box to square the ball for Sterling, who's sliding-in ahead of Williams. He makes contact, right in front of goal, but the ball's scooped up and over the bar. It's a let-off.

I guessed we'd be happy to sit back and attempt to hit England on the break, but at the moment, England are just swarming forward. Our heads sway, momentarily, to the right as a corner kick from a deflected Bale shot feels like some sort of progress. It's temporary however as England get a grip again and our heads sway back to the left. It feels a bit like we're hanging on despite the fact they don't create much. Rooney's the main man for them. His control of the game from his deeper lying-midfield role is obvious. You have to admire the guy, much derided in recent years but he's a proper player and he's one of those who clearly does appear to be playing for the shirt. He drops a free kick from wide onto the head of Cahill who's got away from Williams and I'm relieved to see it sail into Wayne Hennessey's hands.

Barry Horne talked about Neil Taylor's problems at left-back in the first game when we analysed it over a pint in Bordeaux. Today, things are even tougher for him. He's got Lallana and Walker coming at him in waves, as if England had noticed something as well, a weakness perhaps, in that first match.

As the half hour mark comes and goes, the pressure's building. The game's low on quality but high on endeavour, one for the interested only to be honest, but Wales don't need to worry
about that and we roar for them to keep fighting. England roar for a penalty as the ball hits Ben Davies somewhere near the hand but we can't be sure. We not getting big-screen replays of the controversial incidents in this game, unlike the match against Slovakia. Then Smalling gets on the end of a Rooney cross – he's got away from Williams – but plants his header wide. As we head past the 40 minute mark, I'd be more than happy to get in at 0-0. The first half has dragged.

Wales then mount a rare attack with Robson-Kanu getting away from Rooney for the first time and the England captain, frustrated perhaps, wrestles him to the ground. It's a free kick, dead central but miles out. Steve turns to me with a knowing look, I smile and feel confident in asserting that it's way too far out to do anything. It's 35 yards I'd guess. Others are more optimistic and the *Viva Gareth Bale* song starts again. These Bale free kicks do have something of the penalty feel about them, with a hush descending as he goes through his customary routine. He strides forward and strikes the ball and, again, he makes it rise then fall just over the heads of the players in the wall. Not only does it dip but it swerves, towards the right. Joe Hart's slow across his line and dives to stop a shot he should save but it brushes his fingertips and finds its way into the bottom corner of the net.

The madness returns – proper crazy, loco, bonkers madness. I went to watch Wrexham at Brighton in the third round of the cup a few years ago – we took a fantastic away following – and, after going a goal down, we equalised in the latter stages of the second half. I remember reading one Brighton fan's comment on a message board afterwards, when he said he was pleased we scored because it was great to see 'a proper mental' behind the goal when it went in. It's not the most PC description perhaps but I understand what he was getting at. That scene when a section of crowd just becomes a frenzied, wriggling, leaping mass of arms and occasionally legs. It's the moment that makes it all worthwhile: every defeat, every tricky trip, every good player sold, this is what it's all about. This is what keeps us coming back, the chance of experiencing this moment again. If you haven't done it, felt it, been in it, you might not understand it. It's primeval, the complete surrender of oneself to euphoria. It's a beautiful, beautiful thing and it can be witnessed across the entire Welsh section for 30 seconds, maybe more, after the moment we see the ball hit the net.

The last and only time I've ever previously seen Wales take the lead against England was when I was 14 years old, standing at the back of the Kop at The Racecourse in May 1984. Mark Hughes nodding in what proved to be the winner. So, a 32 year gap but well worth the wait and I can't have celebrated it any more energetically than I have today, despite the advancing years. The next four minutes pass in a blur and at half-time no one seems to leave their seat. The England fans boo their team off whilst the party gets into full swing where we are, as the first big chorus of *Don't Take Me Home* rings out from our end of the stadium. We've left that song alone a bit today, probably because England fans have also been singing it in France, but now it's reclaimed as our Euro anthem, gloriously, in the sunshine in Lens.

As the teams reappear, it's no great surprise to see changes for England but it must be embarrassing for Kane and Sterling to get hooked this early. That's the bit you wonder about in terms of their attempts to build a team long-term. How will Harry Kane feel about international football at this moment in time? Does it already feel like it's more trouble than it's worth? Sterling was copping some fearful stick even before being taken off. Still, Sturridge and Vardy to bring on so Hodgson's now packed his side with attacking players, it looks like a massive gamble.

Rooney's our tormentor-in-chief still and now, in Sturridge, he's got someone to work with. The captain produces England's best moment so far when he curls in a shot from the edge of the box and, for the first time this afternoon, our Wayne's forced into a real save at full stretch to tip it round the post. The pattern's set though, exemplified by the fact that it's Gareth Bale who heads clear from the corner. When I used to commentate on the radio with Norman Hunter, he had a phrase for a situation like this: 'what we have, we hold.' That becomes the priority. Except, we don't have it for much longer. Another cross gets looped into the box, it's not cleared properly and comes back in again. I see the ball loop up and then I see someone really close to our goal swing a boot at it and it goes in. Even from the far end, I'm expecting to see an offside flag but it doesn't come, instead I see the bandaged hand of Jamie Vardy raised in celebration as he runs away from the penalty box. Then, for the first time in this tournament, I get a glimpse of something different to what we've experienced so far. The tier above our heads is un-segregated, there are Wales and England fans leaning over the wall at the front. In front of me a woman jolts forward, her hands instinctively moving to protect her head. A plastic beer glass has just hit her and it spins away and drops to the ground. I look up and see England supporters staring back, aggressively gesturing in our direction. That's where it came from. It wasn't enough that they got their equaliser, they wanted revenge as well.

I send Barry a text about the goal and he quickly replies. It was onside, the ball came off Williams' head. He's played Vardy in, much the same as Nainggolan did when we he headed the ball to Gareth Bale to score when we beat Belgium in Cardiff. It's a blow but there's still an awful lot to play for. A point would be fantastic, we'd be all but through, with four of the best third-placed teams also qualifying behind the winners and runners-up.

At 1-1, the ship steadies and instead of a storm, we sail into calmer waters. England don't do much with all their possession, passes start going astray and it isn't long before the noise that greeted the goal has quietened with Welsh voices now being raised again. Joe Ledley gets a knock, which is a shame because he has to go off just when we seem to be getting a hold on midfield at last. David Edwards comes on to replace him, then Hal Robson-Kanu – who's been pretty much a spectator all afternoon – is replaced by Jonny Williams. I can't think that's a change that's going to worry the likes of Smalling and Cahill too much. I'd like to have see Sam Vokes sent on to rough them up a bit. The thing is, there still appears to be a game for the taking here.

England are in a rut. They've thrown lots of attackers on and Rashford comes to join them, briefly raising a cheer from the England fans, but Lallana has given Neil Taylor a tough afternoon and now the emphasis has switched to the other side, and Chris Gunter. That might allow Neil to finally start pushing forward. Except we seem stuck on the idea of settling for the draw, defending for the draw. Gareth Bale's playing behind the ball, working hard for the team when we're out of possession but I'd love to see him push up, maybe just waiting for a big punt out of defence to chase. He's not had a chance to run at the England defenders yet, that looks like England's weakest point yet we've given them an easy afternoon.

I have to say though, the game looks like petering out for the draw that we'll celebrate long into the night. As the clock ticks down, England realise they've got to do more but the Wales fans respond with a big chorus of *Men Of Harlech*, it's one of those renditions that feels like it's a celebration when you're feeling confident. The volume levels are increased as one of the TV cameras picks out a lad in the Wales end, tears streaming down his face. He's overcome with the enormity of what he's seeing. Wales on the brink of a brilliant point, on the brink of going through, still top of the group. England are now on the brink of potential elimination. We've already sung, 'You're going home, You're going home, You're going ... England's going home'. Then a header from an England corner goes over and we cheer it like a goal and, as the time board goes up, we're three minutes away from it happening. Now Wales have possession, in the England half. Neil Taylor is in space and elects to swing a cross in when he might have headed for the corner flag. England clear and the ball heads back into the Welsh half. We just need to get hold of it once more, twenty seconds of hanging onto it and we're there. Sturridge is still lively and England make menacing moves down the left, the ball pings around in the area and I see him stretch a leg and suddenly the net ripples and time stands still.

This is it, this is why I never allow myself to relax and enjoy it until Wales are three goals up with one minute to go. You can't let your guard down. You just get hurt more. Now, around three quarters of the stadium, there is as the Brighton fan would say, 'a proper mental'. All around me, Welsh fans stand in stunned silence, hands on heads. Down at the far end, the England players and management are all leaping on top of each other, even Joe Hart's run the full length of the pitch to join in. That's pure relief, that is.

There's still a chance for one more attack. A cross is played into the box, Gareth Bale gets across the defender and makes contact but his glancing header goes wide. Joe Hart, back on his line again, does a calming motion to indicate that he had it covered, unlike the free kick he let in earlier. By now, England have reclaimed *Don't Take Me Home* as their own anthem, more confident now that they'll be staying beyond the group stage's final fixture. Then the whistle goes and it's over. Never has the phrase, so near yet so far felt more appropriate. Steve and I turn to look at each other, having been locked in our own private worlds for much of the second half. "England deserved it," he suggests. "They dominated, we didn't really do much apart from the free kick." He's right, we didn't play well. We probably set-up to draw rather than to win the game and, having got in front, we looked to hang on. We created very little and yet, despite all that, we were seconds away from a fantastic result. We were close enough even for me to contemplate it, then, I dropped my gloves and whack!

The players look stunned as well but the fans aren't ready to chuck the towel in just yet and as the players come over, hands are raised above heads to applaud them, their effort could not be faulted, they've given it their all. Chris Gunter leads them, flapping the top side of his hand against the underside of his chin in a gesture that says, 'Chins up guys! We'll be back.' It's one of those little moments that feels so massive, the fans and the players are as one. We are them, they are us. We will be back.

We turn and head slowly towards the exits. I'm very much not looking forward to the walk back to the coach. We've been cocooned in a corner of Welshness in the stadium, now we're chucked out in the midst of the delirious English hordes. I'm not going to take my hat off, or hide who I support, it's time for shoulders back and march on, eyes fixed forward. In fairness, there's not too much evidence of triumphalism outside, not that I hear or see anyway. There are TV crews waiting with the unenviable task of stopping fans to talk, a job I always dread as verbal abuse is almost inevitable but it's not my concern today, I just want to get back on the coach, get back to Amiens and put it all behind me. We walk back to the car park, past several bars. I'd be happy with a couple of cans for the bus but, nothing doing, as there isn't a shop in sight.

We're amongst the first to return so I sit outside for a bit. I ring home and Rachel answers. She's been watching so she knows what's happened. Although she's English, she isn't a football fan so she won't be too cruel. The fact that I can hardly speak or hold a conversation relates less to the singing I've done and more to the fact that emotionally, I'm on the floor. Shattered.

I climb on board the bus and we wait for the stragglers who've sneaked in an extra pint. There are other fans heading for other coaches that are travelling straight back to Wales, I'm glad I'm not on one of those, that could be a long quiet trip. 'Dibs' comes aboard just before we're ready to depart to address his travellers. He describes the organisation today as having been hopeless, he says the authorities ordered the Paris bus to leave despite the fact that not everyone was on it. A headcount confirms we're all present and correct and we set off for Amiens. Siôn's down the front so it's much more low-key on the way back. I can see his lack of sleep has caught up with him as he dozes off and, next to me, Steve gets his head down as well. I'm checking my phone to make sure there's not been any trouble – there hasn't it would appear – but there's awful news from back home where the Batley and Spen MP, Jo Cox, has apparently been murdered by a man who attacked her on the street with a knife and gun.

Already social media's suggesting he has connections to a far right group and that he was shouting 'Britain first!' as he attacked her. Jo

Cox was a leading campaigner for the Remain campaign and I can't help but wonder whether the toxic nature of the debate to date may well prove to be a factor in her murder. This referendum is bringing out the worst in people. It puts the disappointment of my day in its proper, utterly insignificant context.

An hour later, Amiens' tall cathedral spire comes into sight and we return from whence we came, the station in the town centre. Food's a high priority for me and for Steve but we need to get some stuff for tomorrow as well, so baguettes and milk are purchased before we come across a bistro with outside seating. It's early evening and there aren't many people about, in fact the only two people seated seem to be the owner and her boyfriend. Still, she confirms they're open and whilst Steve goes off to try and find tobacco, I make sense of a fairly straightforward but very enticing menu. Beers are ordered, just our second of the day, then, when Steve comes back, he goes for chicken risotto and I do what I always do and go for the burger.

We're sitting outside under an umbrella which is a good job because, as the food's served, it starts raining again. Just as we're tucking in, a crowd of young guys walk past – Brummies by the sound of the accents – and one of them is wearing an England hat. They decide to have a beer at the same place and sit down at the next table and I implore them to be gentle with us. They're nice lads as it turns out. From the West Midlands – Coventry and Birmingham – and they hadn't got tickets so were planning on watching the game at the Lille fan zone but got put off by the lurid tales about Russian hooligans, so stayed in Amiens instead. Next up, they're off to Saint Etienne but only one of their number has a ticket for that one. As we're chatting, another young England fan walks past and he stops to join in. He spots me and asks me to report on the TV that not all England fans are hooligans. The evidence of the scene that presents itself here in Amiens certainly backs up his assertion. Even then, one of the other group says, "Yeah but we don't help ourselves though, do we?" and they start discussing the rights and wrongs in an eminently civilised manner. It's an ongoing debate that must take place anytime right-minded England fans gather together.

The rain falls more heavily, dripping spectacularly off the edge of the umbrella into Steve's beer glass. I think he thinks it's magically refilling but we order another just in case and stay put until it clears.

Our English pals head off into the night with instructions for us to head to the canal area as that's where the good bars are. We follow their advice and five minute's walk away we find it, a pretty street of restaurants on one side of the canal and bars down the other. In the middle of the canal itself, there is a statue of a man, very much like one of the Anthony Gormley's on Formby beach, except that someone's waded out to him and he's now wearing a Wales shirt!

Poland v Germany's about to start so we find a bar with a big screen and settle down for our second match of the day. A little while later, one of the lads from the bus trip comes over and asks if we mind if he joins us? He's clutching a plastic bag with a bottle of Rosé and a couple of cans in it. He introduces himself as 'Pridey', he's one of the Maesteg lads and we pull up a chair for him. He gets a round in and the football's heading towards a very dull stitch-up of a goalless draw, so we get him to teach us the words to the 'twisted valleys town' song. He's a nice chap and he's joined by 'Knocker', back on form again. We go back over this afternoon's tales and he ends up demonstrating the 'pincer movement' motions that Dai Hooligan tried to pass on to the next generation in that pub in Burnley. This involves standing up against a wall and doing a sort of crablike walk to the left and right. More laughter, we're over the defeat. Beer and good company wins the day. This is the Welsh way.

There's one more challenge awaiting us, that of getting home again. The buses have long since stopped running, the bar owner's tried without success to call us a cab so we head to the station on foot. *En route*, 'Knocker' pops out of a kebab shop, telling us the guy who runs it has got one coming for him now, so we can share it if we want? We have absolutely no idea where he is, in relation to where we are, but we're tired and it's late, so we go with the flow. A rather swish looking Mercedes people carrier arrives and we dive in. The young guy driving it speaks good English and drives like a maniac, even more so after he drops 'Knocker' off and then turns to us and says, "Do you mind if I drive fast now?" Ten minutes later, €25 lighter and five years older, we're back.

4

Toulouse
Russia v Wales

'The Russia game was extra special to me for obvious reasons. I've always been someone who enjoys trying to defend against some of the best and most talented players in the world and scoring goals has certainly never been one of my strengths. I was just really happy for my family and my children especially that they'd finally seen their dad do something other than taking a throw-in or blocking a cross! I wish the summer of 2016 had never ended and I'm sure there are a few people with me on that!'
Neil Taylor

Friday, June 17th

Not the best night's sleep ever. At 3am, someone, somewhere close-by started playing music, then they started singing along. Even the ear plugs can't keep that out so we're both groggy over the morning cup of tea. We contemplate visiting revenge on the instigators who are no doubt enjoying a bit of kip now but sadly, or happily, we don't know who it was. The London boys next door left really early so maybe they had a jolly good knees-up before they set off?

We're back on the road ourselves a little later, with the biggest trek of the lot now ahead of us – Amiens to Toulouse – 820 kilometres and about 8 hours drive. We've got plenty of time before the next game but we have an important appointment in the city 48 hours before we take on Russia:

Super Furry Animals!

They're headlining the Rio Loco festival tomorrow night, so I've identified Limoges as our destination today. I've done a bit of prep work and emailed a campsite just north of the town and for once, they've replied. We are good to go and have a pitch booked for this evening – with electrics! It's about 6 hours from Amiens so that leaves us a nice, easy run to Toulouse tomorrow morning. Needless to say, we leave under grey skies. Is this the worst summer's weather France has ever had?

Now, travelling north to south down the spine of the country presents one major challenge: Paris. I've driven round it before, on the *peripherique*, the dreaded ring road. As we get close to the capital, it's clear the satnav's sending us in that direction. It's a lesson in confusion with signs everywhere, crazy filter lanes, tunnels and you get to see the Eiffel Tower albeit from a distance.

When I did it previously, I was driving a car, so the one big issue doesn't really ring any alarm bells. It's Steve who starts ringing them – loudly and frantically – as we approach yet another slip lane with the route we're following on our left. There's a tunnel and we're heading towards it when Steve clocks the flaps hanging down from a chain that's slung across the carriageway just ahead of us. "That's a height restriction!" he suggests – a note of anxiety in his voice – "I can't go that way!" and he swerves back to the right and a route that takes us off the ring road.

This is where I have to step up to the plate. If I'm not going to drive, I have to at least navigate and soon I'm using two devices again to try and plot a route back to where we're meant to be going. I notice at one point that we're heading north again, then I spot the Seine and see that we can drive alongside it and then get back on track. It's at this point that the tension in the cockpit is lightened a little by the sighting of a lorry with the logo 'DAICYCLE' down the side of it's trailer. So, we've had Dai Hooligan, Dai The Loon and now Dai Cycle!

For a while we seem to be heading for Versailles – although we don't see the Palace – and after 15 nervy minutes we're heading in the right direction, as are a couple of car loads of Wales fans that pass us. All roads now lead to Toulouse!

It rains the whole way to Limoges, heavily at times, and the driving conditions briefly become pretty treacherous with standing water on the carriageway. It feels more like we're sailing south. Eventually, we see signs for our port in this storm. We're hoping to find a supermarket to stock up again but the campsite's in the countryside, very much on the outskirts of Limoges, so we're going to have to make do with what we've got on board – there's at least two bottles of wine, so we should survive.

I head into the reception to confirm our arrival. As I'm walking in a crowd of Welsh lads cross my path, small beer bottles in hand, it seems we aren't the only ones to discover this place. In fact, the owner suggests he's going to find a plot in *Le Quartier Gallois* – the Welsh Quarter. In fairness, this guy's good. Not only did he reply to my email swiftly but he asks questions about which satellite system we have on board our van. I'm a bit nonplussed and don't actually know the answer, he takes a guess, names a system and then all becomes clear. "You need to be east facing", he suggests. "So, I'll give you a pitch that should allow you to get a signal." Not only that but he offers free Wi-Fi as we're a bit far away and might struggle to pick it up. Then this denim-shirted dude has advice about Toulouse, "Watch out for Russians!" he suggests. "They are very bad people!"

We are directed to our pitch by his assistant and we click straight into the – by now – familiar routine of getting all systems to go. We pull the awning out so that we can sit outside but still be sheltered from the rain. We're an awful lot better off than the lads just across the path, from north Wales, who are staying in very small tents. One of them comes over for a chat; their clothes are wet and they can't get anything dry. The only place they have to sit where they can stay out of the rain is by the washing-up area in the toilet block, so they have set up a second base camp there. Chairs, small camping stove, cans of beer, the lot.

There's a brief break in the clouds and I take the opportunity to test the first Wi-Fi hook-up we've had since Cheesy's house. If I walk away from the van, it works, and I manage to contact home via FaceTime, giving Rachel and the girls a quick tour of the site. They have one or two tough questions that need answering, most notably the old chestnut of "When are you coming home?"

I still haven't booked anything, although I'm beginning to formulate a plan. Steve needs to be back in Leeds for an awards ceremony on the 24th, as a couple of films he's made have been nominated. I figure that if we deliver the van back to Bordeaux – as agreed – on 21st, we could drive home from there. I've had a look at crossing options. Overnight ones all seem to be booked up so I'm thinking of the Calais Dover route with an overnight stop somewhere on yet another long drive north. When Rachel asks whether I'll be around for her birthday, I have a lot less information to share. We could still finish anywhere from bottom to top in the group.

Thought of home prompts me to make contact with the third member of our party who'll be heading out to Toulouse on Sunday so I send a text to warn Evo that he definitely won't be able to kip in the camper van. He's booked a flight to Limoges, as it happens, then he's getting the train down to join us. He has one request, can we buy him an air bed? He suggests Decathlon, the French outdoor and sports gear shop, he even sends a link to the website with the model he favours. His plan is a simple one – he's going to sleep outside. I hope for his sake the weather improves.

Steve is cooking tonight. There's no game on our TV but earlier in the day, the Italians qualified by beating Sweden 1-0. Next up is Czech Republic v Croatia but it's on the Bein pay-TV channel and our satellite system can't access it, no oven, no pay TV; we're slumming it here. Instead, I sit with a glass of red wine and watch a bit of a debate on TV, in French, and the graphic across the bottom of the screen reads *Jo Cox Morte Pour Europe* – Jo Cox Died For Europe. So, the perception in France it appears, is that she was killed because of the Referendum. When I switch over to a news bulletin, there's a report on the funeral of a police officer and his wife near Paris, which is being described as another terrorist attack. It's depressing stuff, I need football as my escape from the harsh realities of this bad, mad world we seem to have created.

Luckily, our TV is now showing Spain v Turkey so we wrap up warm and watch the Spanish win easily. They play really well and probably look the best side I've seen so far. We shut everything down shortly after the final whistle – we need a good night's sleep tonight – so no singing people, there's a very big weekend ahead!

Saturday, June 18th

Great news! It's raining! As we go about our highly synchronised pre-departure procedure, the lads in the little tents shuffle past, *en route* to the toilet block. They don't look quite so well rested.

I once got a tent as a birthday present, probably round about my 6th birthday I guess? It had a picture of a soldier on the side of it – I was really into military stuff – and was very easy to assemble. I used to go into the back garden, put it up myself and sit in it for hours. I even slept in it on a couple of occasions, at least until I heard a scary noise and beat an undignified and probably tearful retreat back to the house and the comfort of my top bunk. There were loads of cub and scout camps after that, with night times spent desperately trying to get some sleep despite the presence of half a dozen other young lads, the rain, the cold, the owls etc etc. I think that may have had an impact on my opinion of tents as a nocturnal option: 'Not for me thanks'. My camping begins and ends with something with solid walls and a floor.

Today promises a more leisurely drive to our destination than we've become used to, it's no more than 3 hours to Toulouse, so we should have time to get settled in before the big gig. Only one hour into the journey however and we're already having to recalculate our arrival time as we find ourselves in a long, slow moving tailback. We're edging along at a few miles an hour when we're suddenly propelled forward, a sensation accompanied by the sound of a loud bang from the back of the van. We've just been rear-ended!

This was exactly the sort of situation I feared from the outset; foreign land, someone else's van, paperwork, hassle, garages, delays and all the rest of it. Steve's at the wheel, so he pulls on the handbrake and we both leap out the van, ready to see just how much they've hurt Gareth? It's a two footed tackle from behind!

As we arrive at the back, an elderly couple are extricating themselves a little more gingerly from the their black Citroen. They come and join us to assess the damage, already offering profuse apologies with much waving of hands and shaking of heads. There's a visible bump to the left side door but that apart, the front end of their car seems to have come off worse. It doesn't look like we're going to be forced to seek immediate repairs, which is the first relief, but there is still going to be all the insurance stuff to do, so Steve steers the van off the highway and we begin the drawn out process of exchanging details.

This is where it gets a bit more complicated because I suddenly realise that in the midst of the lengthy pre-departure explanations of how to operate waste water systems and build beds, I haven't got a clue where the vehicle documents are stashed. Trying to explain this and the ownership issue in my rudimentary French – that it's not our van – proves tricky to a septuagenarian couple, clearly flustered at having been involved in an accident. Steve takes a few pictures on his phone, both of the damage and of the whole scene being played out: well, he is a documentary film maker after all. It's not going to make the final cut in any 999 Lifesavers show, but there is some comedy value to the two old dears poring over the incident document I find tucked away in one of the cupboards that we haven't actually opened before.

The old boy's pretty shaky of hand, so the process of filling out the form is not a speedy one. He consults with his wife on several of the questions asked, in the meantime – when I haven't got my head in hands much in the style of the guy in Bordeaux – I'm trying to work out what exactly I should be doing? I can't find any forms regarding the insurance, there is a registration document with the actual owner's address on it, but that's it. I check the company website on my phone, it says there's a 24/7 helpline but no mention of a number. I seek guidance from the person from the hire company who contacted me about the collection. I try her mobile number but it goes to voicemail. I send an email explaining the circumstances but that's me out of ideas. Instead, I practise my Gallic shrug when I think I'm being asked for addresses, or indeed any form of useful information.

The bottom line is, as Steve and I discuss, that they're at fault so it's probably their details we need more than the other way round. Steve's been outside chatting with the old lady whilst I've been peering over the shoulder of her husband at his writing desk, who keeps stopping to shake his head and mutter *'Merde! Merde! Merde!'* Apparently they've got a new mobile phone and she asked him for help to work it whilst he was driving, and that's how our silver surfers ended up embedded in the back of our camper van, 'no further questions m'Lud'. The form filling takes quite a while but at the point where it seems there's no more information we can bleed from them – I've got inside leg measurements, pin numbers, the lot – we let them go. Actually, there's one more penance they have to perform. Steve asks if they'll pose for a picture with our big flag and, somewhat nonplussed, they agree. The frustrated drivers still edging along on the carriageway are now treated to the sight of two old people and a slightly younger chap holding up an 8'x5' Welsh dragon, on the hard shoulder, whilst another slightly younger chap takes a picture.

It's been nearly an hour since the big bang now and we've all got on rather well, if I didn't know the French for 'I'm sorry', I do now. We say fond farewells and *bon voyages* and rejoin the traffic jam.

In relative terms, the journey from this point onwards is uneventful. Our first destination is the Decathlon sports store where Evo's detailed instructions lead me straight to the blow up bed he's identified as a best buy. Then we head for the supermarket and a restock. I definitely plan to finally release my new foldaway barbecue from its bag in the next couple of days so I purchase a bag of coals to facilitate a bit of outdoor cooking. Rachel has made further demands from afar about a particular type of hand soap she always brings back from France, so I chuck in a couple of bottles of that and with beer, wine, bread and sausages; we're all done.

Steve takes us on a bit of a drive round the back streets *en route* to the nearby campsite after that, he's involved in a desperate search for the tobacco for his little rollups but it's Saturday and it's clear our base is very much on the scruffy outskirts – the bit of the city that's all DIY warehouses and car parts shops. I hope he's not going to go cold turkey on me, it's a bit tight in the van for that sort of carry-on.

When he's resigned himself to his fate, we return to the satnav and follow directions to the site. It's the only one I could find anywhere near Toulouse so I'm guessing it's going to be pretty busy. We cross a bridge over a canal, following signs for *Le Camping*. The first *Le Camping* we spy is not promising. Judging by the stripped skeletons of rusting cars, the bags of rubbish and the huts that appear to be made from old doors, I think this one may be aimed at a slightly different clientele. Dark skinned kids and scrawny dogs play amongst the puddles and the backdrop appears to be quite a large rubbish tip. I have read TripAdvisor reviews that mention the presence of a gypsy encampment in close proximity to our intended destination, I think this might be it.

A 100 metres further on, a big set of metal gates announce our arrival at *Camping Le Rupe*. They slide back as we approach. There's another camper van already to our rear and two more parked up in the reception area ahead – all with red shirts alighting and Welsh dragons flying – it would appear we won't be the only ones using this as our base for the final group game.

Reception's busy but efficient. They have two members of staff dealing with the queue of blokes waiting to find out where they've been placed. In the booking process, the initial online price of €15 a night looked very reasonable, but then it became clear that this just referred to the actual pitch, on top of which were a raft of additional charges. Extra people meant considerable extra expense.

In the queue ahead of me, the guy gets asked how many people are in the van he's trying to book in? Six, he replies, "But you've only booked for two", the woman responds. Ouch, it's going to be 4×€45 for every extra person. This is a three star campsite that's charging the same nightly rate as you'd pay at a decent hotel. I think we can call this the 'Euro 2016 effect'. They know there's nowhere else to pitch a tent or a camper van here, so they've got a monopoly and they're more than happy to exploit it. I guess I'm just an innocent abroad and, obviously, it's the first time I've attended a summer tournament, but the willingness on the part of our hosts to fleece us is something I find quite depressing. We're pumping millions into the French economy as it is! More teams means more games, with more fans travelling vast distances to more cities and we're all paying road tolls or train tickets and buying food and fuel and searching for accommodation – the whole lot. Clearly, this isn't enough. I would lay odds that the price for this campsite tumbles once we've all packed up and left.

We're directed to our pitch by a man in a golf caddy and, again, we have an end of the road spot, so neighbours on only one side; a shabby old caravan that appears to have taken root. I think it's fair to say there's not a massive difference between those of our new surroundings and the traveller site we passed on our way in. The prevailing impression isn't being helped by the dark clouds that are gathering overhead again. It seems we have enjoyed only a brief respite from the rain that's followed us around France.

Despite all that, people are out and enjoying themselves. It may be a little scruffy but *Camping Le Rupe* is an amazing sight with Wales flags flying everywhere and all parts of our nation represented. Across the path from us – hanging between two trees – is a huge *Draig Goch* with the phrase, 'In Honesty It's Been A While', emblazoned across it; lyrics from one of my favourite Super Furry tracks, *Hello Sunshine*. That's just spot on, good work chaps! In honesty, it really has, but now we're here and determined to make the most of it.

Despite the threat of precipitation, I'm determined that the barbecue's coming out. It's a thing of beauty, held in a flat nylon bag about a foot and a half long. I have already had a go at assembling it back home to check how it all fits together and I'm confident I can get it up in under 30 seconds. In fact, I'm so confident, I give Steve my phone – on the stopwatch setting – and ask him to time me. From the pulling back of the bag's zip, to the cooking trays being laid across it takes me 28 seconds; a triumph and a PB. I have found my Olympic event.

Clearly impressed, Steve wanders off for a shower whilst I get to work on rolling up the bits of newspaper, collecting twigs and branches and building the base for what will be the first barbecue of the Euros. I love making a fire. I was taught how to lay a coal fire by my *Taid* – my Welsh grandfather – in the back room of his little house in Llanllechid, a small village on the side of a mountain above Bangor in northwest Wales. He used to roll up the newspaper, twist it into a knot then lay the kindling on top and the coals on top of that. It was a pyramid shape that saw the fire catch underneath; paper first then wood, then the heat generated ensured the coals were soon alight. I have a coal fire at home and it's a technique I use to this day. I've been using it on family holidays for barbecues, more or less successfully, in recent years as well.

The key to it is creating enough heat at the heart of the fire to ensure the coals catch alight. The slight variable with the barbecue is that it's charcoal and it's outside and it needs to burn evenly so that all the coals give off enough heat. I prepare everything diligently after a forage around our pitch for dry twigs and branches. Appropriately, I'm using a copy of *L'Equipe* as my base firelighter. Twigs next, in a triangle, then my new coals laid across the top. It's an unusual coal, I have to say, not like the usual charcoal or briquettes. It's bigger, like lava, with holes in it. I set fire to the paper and go off to open a small bottle of beer and prepare the meat.

On my return, I'm disappointed not to be greeted by the sight of a roaring inferno. The paper's burnt, the twigs are burning but the coal looks exactly as it did when I left it. I collect more twigs, shift coals around and light more matches but, no improvement. I have a look at the bag for any clues or perhaps some instructions. It's all in French but one phrase does jump out, something about rocks for a *barbecue au gaz*. *Merde!* By the time Steve strolls back, towel over his arm, I'm in the camper van with a frying pan full of sausages in my hand. Plan B.

Once we've eaten, there's more planning needed with regards to our night out. It's clear the campsite isn't an easy walk into the city centre but it does boast a bus stop a few hundred metres from the front gate. I've found a Toulouse travel app and downloaded it onto my phone. A quick consultation with it suggests we'll be catching a bus first, the 59, and then hopping onto a metro train from *La Vache* station – the cow station?! After that, we have to cross the river that runs through the middle of the city to find the venue. We are good to go.

I know the bus times, I think, but we give ourselves plenty of time to get to the stop. We leave the camp via the security gate, which has a young woman dressed in SWAT gear guarding it. She's about 5'4" and petite but I'm guessing she must be a mixed martial arts expert: she'll need to be if she's going to keep the crazy Russians out when they launch their attack tonight. There's a keypad with a code which I've taken the precaution of writing down, fearing beer-induced memory loss on our return.

We walk past our neighbouring encampment, the sound of some sort of eastern folk music drifting out from one of the ramshackle huts that appears to be a family home, from which a woman exits with a large pile of laundry. A battered old car screeches round the corner ahead of us and then into the camp, windows down: the occupants shout a greeting to us as we dive into the ditch to avoid it. There's clearly great poverty here. This is nothing like the civic amenity sites provided for travellers in the UK. These people live on the very edge of the city but also, I'd guess, on the very edge of society. France seems to have many problems with groups of people that it's failed to integrate into French society, a fact borne out by the awful events that have befallen the country in the last few months.

We walk on, over the bridge that crosses the canal and then the railway line that runs parallel with it; the mainline into Toulouse. In theory, we could follow the canal path all the way in but we're about 4 miles out so it would be quite a hike. Mind you, when we get to the bus stop a minute later, we discover that we've got half an hour to wait for the next bus, so we opt to set off anyway, the metro station appears to be a couple of miles at most.

It's a tricky walk as it turns out, alongside a main road into the city. It's not what could be described as the most picturesque route either and we're badly served by pavements. At one stage, we have to climb over the crash barrier and into some shrubbery where the path disappears completely. That settles it and when we come upon another bus stop, we opt to sit it out and wait for our chariot to carry us on to 'The Cow'.

It's a better idea. I've packed a small bag with some bottles of beer so we crack a couple open and refresh ourselves before the #59 pulls up and spirits us the last mile or so to the metro. A ticket bought on the bus for €1.6 is enough to cover the entire journey. As we head into the metro, the ticket opens the automatic gate and we go down the escalator to the platform. This is all pretty space age by British standards. I can only get a bus into Leeds city centre from where I live, 5 miles out. There's one an hour. There's no other public transport system. Getting into and out of the city by anything other than a car is very difficult.

Here, we're standing on the platform, separated from the train line by perspex glass doors that slide open as the train pulls up moments later. We get on, close to the front and I get a bit giddy because there's no driver! At the front of the carriage, there's nothing but a window, an almost unsettling experience. It feels more like a roller coaster ride than an underground train as we pull off. We travel through half a dozen stations to our destination without ever seeing a member of staff. It's a completely automated system, ticket machines, barriers, trains and one person somewhere, perhaps surrounding by blinking lights, occasionally pushing buttons as he or she plays with the ultimate train set.

So far, so impressive, but now it's down to humans again as we have to walk the last part of the journey to the festival site. Unhelpfully, there are no big signs pointing us in the right direction as we emerge from the Metro stop, Palais De Justice. That seems a bit remiss as I know many Wales fans are making the same musical pilgrimage. Still, I've got Google maps running on my phone, so what could possibly go wrong? I have a sense that the Metro station is pretty close to the park where the festival's being staged. So, when we're still walking twenty minutes later, it's clear something's not right. A cloudy afternoon has turned into a rainy evening and I'm getting wet again. Steve's sensibly opted for a proper waterproof – I have a lighter jacket and it's soaked. The anticipation is being washed away as we tramp the streets in an area of town that probably isn't on the usual tourist trail. There is one notable building we pass, an ugly, gloomy place that looks every inch the jail that once held *Résistance* fighters. For many, a plaque on the wall tells us, this was the final place of residence. It's a museum now. Normally, I'd be interested in ascertaining opening times but now though, I'm in search of something a little more uplifting and I can't find it. There's now a clear gap between me and Steve as I stare down at my phone and mutter. Needless to say, we don't take the simple step of asking someone for directions, we're blokes. We plough on.

It's only when I spot the football stadium at the end of the end of the road we're walking down that I can make a dramatic and yet somehow all too predictable deduction. For the last twenty minutes we've been walking in the opposite direction to where we want to go! I know a French word for this....

On the one hand, it's a relief to finally work out where we are and where we need to be, but on the other hand, it's a crushing realisation that we've got to go back and do the same walk again and we're only going to end up where we started from. Coming on the back of the barbecue coals disaster, my 'Team Leader' badge is losing its shine. I admit my error to Steve, we both mutter and swear, and then we turn round and walk back the way we've just come.

Needless to say, we arrive back at the Metro station to discover that it was, indeed, just a short walk from the concert site. At least it was if you turned left out of the station, rather than right. In fact, we're not the only ones heading in that direction. There's a group of lads ahead, wrapped in Welsh dragons. We're re-energised by the actual sight and sounds from the Rio Loco festival on the far bank as we cross the wide bridge over the Garonne river. There's a bounce back in the step again and I point out to Steve that the good news is we get a free drink with our tickets. I read it on the booking page as I was ordering online, something about an extra euro on top of the standard price but that covered a free drink. So, after presenting our tickets, I head for the info desk just inside the entrance and ask where we need to go for our free drink. The woman behind the counter looks a little puzzled, "Free drink?"she responds in English. "Yes", I reply pointing at my ticket. "No, that is the booking fee", she explains. My hat trick of cock-ups is now successfully achieved. Don't ask me why I thought we got a free drink, in hindsight I have no idea.

Anyway, forget all that, we're in – we've made it – another stop on the itinerary reached with only a few hiccups on the way. We head off towards the sound of music. In the near distance, there's a stage with a band performing and between us and them, beneath the trees, there are stalls selling food, drink and Celtic-themed products. The Celtic world is the theme of the annual Rio Loco festival this year, that's why they've invited the Super Furries to headline the last night.

I have an idea. There's another info desk nearby so I bowl up and ask one of the two young women behind it if I can have a festival poster, "*Comme un souvenir?*" Again, they reply in English, "Maybe, but we're not supposed to give them out yet. You should come back later." I plead. "Okay, but don't let anybody else see..", she orders conspiratorially, and I call Steve and his rucksack over. I promise to be extremely discreet and she rolls a poster up, I pass Steve's bag over and she looks left and right before quickly pushing the poster in. To anyone actually watching, it must look like a major drug deal going down, rather than a poster changing hands, but once the transaction's done, we nod and slip away into the night, checking over our shoulder to make sure we've not been followed.

There's one more transaction to enact before we emerge from the trees and into the light – the little bottles were finished a long time since – we need a beer. It's not Celtic ale unfortunately, it's your standard Heineken or Kronenburg, but it'll do for tonight. There's also a fee to pay on the plastic beer cups, adding considerably to the outlay on our first two drinks. I have to suck it up, I was the one promising free drinks after all, on top of every other one of today's shortcomings.

There's a big band playing on the nearest stage – lots of brass – an unusual combination of swing and folk. I think they're from Brittany but it's not the usual Breton bagpipes I associate with music from there.

As we're heading off in search of the main stage, still half an hour or so before the Furries are due on, I hear my name called and look over to see a familiar face from my childhood. In fact, two familiar faces. Steff and Tommy Evans used to live across the road from us in Ruabon. They're both a bit younger than me but everybody used to play out together, ride bikes, kick a ball, climb trees and all the rest of it. Their dad, John, taught at the same school as my mum so the two families did a lot together. We went away on a couple of long summer holidays, in convoy with them and some other friends, caravans behind the cars.

Both the lads, like me and my brother, have moved away from home but they retain their ties to the old country and they're here to support the national team as well. They've been travelling round together and we swap stories as we sup beer. It's a bit bizarre really, this reunion by the sides of a river in the south of France, but it's that sort of trip. Everyone I know from Wales is out in France and plenty that I don't.

Another group of lads from Cardiff stop and ask for a picture and we get chatting. I ask one of them how he's enjoying it, the Euro experience? He lowers his voice, throws a glance towards his travelling pals and says, "It's been great, but we're all staying in a camper van and I'm ready to go home now to be honest. It's hard when there's six of you – all blokes – packed in together...". There's a look of the Vietnam vet in his eyes, I think he's seen things he wishes he hadn't. I know what he's on about though. Just as the players haven't experienced this tournament football before, neither have we. We're used to fly-in, watch game, fly-out. There's some stamina required to come over and do this as a fan. Respect to the Germans, they stick it out for pretty much the duration every couple of years. We're ten days or so in and we're flagging, I hope the players aren't in the same state of mind! As show time approaches, we say our farewells, and head towards the main stage. I'd seen lots of Welsh people walking past as we stood and talked, now it's clear just how many fans have made this gig a 'must see' in the midst of the Euro experience. There's a sea of bucket hats, the red, yellow, green and the red, white and green products of Tim's creative genius. He's a massive fan of the Furries but he can't be here tonight, he's still with his family in Paris. He'd love this sight. It gets better as well as the band emerge to a huge roar. Cian's wearing his Spirit of '58 hat, brim turned up. *"Wales! Wales! Wales!"* the chant goes up as the lads take their places on stage.

This is fantastic, the perfect combination of the two things I've loved most all my life – family apart of course – music and football, and this is the band that I more closely associate with football than any other. The video for one of their early singles, Play It Cool, involves the band becoming part of a PlayStation football game between Wales and Brazil. Gruff helps turn a 3-1 deficit into a 4-3 win. I still remember seeing the video for the first time, on the Saturday morning chart show on ITV and being blown away. The national side was really in the doldrums at the time and yet, here we were, beating Brazil; it was certainly the best result of the Bobby Gould era.

There are so many connections for me. Playing the track *The Undefeated* on the way to and from the first four games of the qualification campaign for Portugal 2004 when, we were indeed, undefeated. Then having to turn it off as I drove back to Leeds from Cardiff late at night after a draw in the penultimate game that meant we couldn't qualify automatically anymore and, most recently, celebrating with the lads in the stadium in Bordeaux. Super Furry Animals are my Welsh football soundtrack. I've seen them live so many times, in all sorts of venues, but this is the best, in a park on a chilly summer's evening by the side of Garonne river in Toulouse. This is the best.

I've often found myself wondering whether I don't enjoy music more than football these days? There's so much wrong in the game, not least with my team Wrexham, condemned to play at a lowly level by uncaring authorities and trying to compete with egotistical millionaire owners who treat the game as some sort of personal plaything. Yet here tonight, in the midst of a wonderful footballing experience, I get to celebrate both. I'm 47 in a few days time. I leap around and sing and dance as wildly as I did when I went to my first gig on 9 April 1983 (The Undertones supported by Cook Da Books in case you're curious).

In between each track, the singing off stage replaces the singing on it, and then it all comes together, gloriously as the band launch into *Bing Bong*, the track they released ahead of the tournament. It's not really a football song, not in the traditional sense, but it has a deliberately inane chorus – it's Eurovision on steroids, like Germany being represented by Kraftwerk – I love it. It's the first time I've seen them perform this track live and in the middle of the song, up behind the keyboards, Cian starts the Hal Robson-Kanu chant. The crowd responds and the name of our versatile attacker booms back from the swaying bucket-hatted masses: bemused French people joining in, 'Who eez theese Al RobsonKanu?'

They want to know about the hats as well. I try to explain about *Esprit de '58* but it's hard when you're jumping around with a plastic beer glass in one hand and your other arm thrown around a French person you've never met before. We swap chants, 'Allez Les Bleus!' first, then 'Allez Les Rouges!'. This is a real party.

I've never taken drugs – nothing – not even a sneaky joint at college, so I can only imagine this is what a state of prolonged ecstasy feels like. It's different from the game. That's a sudden hit, a moment that suddenly overwhelms and transports you. This is something that grows inside you until you feel your heart soaring, your spirit lifting up and out of your body, out of the tips of your fingers stretched high up in the night sky. I'm in a field with lots of people but it feels like being alone, amazing.

The set finishes, inevitably, with the traditional extended wig-out version of *The Man Don't Give a F*#k*. The band depart but Cian remains, playing with buttons, lifting the tempo, adding squeaks and beeps, then he's gone and the noise stops. The crowd remains. They've done an encore – there won't be another – but nobody's going home, not the bucket hat brigade anyway. The locals clap heartily then head off into the night. We stay. *'Don't take me home, please don't take me home...'* rings out. The stage is empty but still we sing. Cian reappears, punching the air, and heads back up to the mic in time to join in with a rendition of *Hen Wlad Fy Nhadau*, what better way to end a festival of Celtic music?

I'm not ready to be taken home just yet, neither is Steve, it's time for a beer and it's time for a catch up with the world's greatest rock 'n' roll band. I send Gruff a text to see if there's anything happening backstage. A text pings back almost immediately. He'll come and meet us at the backstage entrance. The stewards want to get us off the site by now, so I have to use a bit of French to explain to one beefy bloke with a walkie-talkie and an aggressive attitude why I need to go the opposite way to the direction in which he's intent on forcing me. I'm helped by another Welsh guy who stops to ask for a selfie and then explains to the bouncer in excellent French that I work on the TV. This seems to help legitimise my claim to be 'meeting the band' and our man becomes quite helpful, pointing us in the direction of the VIP gate.

There's another security guard there, a muscle-bound black guy who's really friendly. We have a bit of chat about the football and, in between my feeble attempts at conversational French, he radios the backstage area to let them know we're there. My phone's battery is about to die but I get one more text from Gruff to say he's on his way with two passes before it splutters and dies.

Our man emerges from the darkness, as good as his word, and we share big hugs and I offer hearty congratulations on a magnificent show. Apparently there were lots of technical issues – half the time Cian was seconds behind the rest or something – but that's the accomplished musician talking, I'm just a fan and from where I was standing, it was brilliant. We make our way back stage, which is quite literally that. Behind the stage, there's a small caravan selling beer, some chairs and tables, fairy lights strung across the trees with the lights on the Pont Saint Michel reflecting off the river. If only I had my easel. If only I could paint.

I see the rest of the band and approach with arms spread wide, a grin stretched across my face in recognition of the thing I have just witnessed; a religious experience. I want them to know just how much I've enjoyed it, just how much pleasure they've given me over the last hour and a bit, how much I've loved everything they've ever done and how much gratitude I feel for all the marvellous music they've made for me. I probably fail. They're all grinning as well though – I'm sure this gig must have been a bit special – if only because we're all off to see if Wales can qualify for the knockout stage of the European Championships in less than 48 hours.

Steve and I find seats amongst the group of band members, partners and tour crew. Beers appear, and we chat and draw our zips up against the chill of the night. It appears the shower issue was sorted without the need to call on the camper van, as they've been using a local hotel where Guto's staying. The rest of the lads seem to have been sleeping on the tour bus which is parked a couple of hundred metres away. The organisers have allowed them to keep it on site until after the game, so they've got a very handy base just a mile or so up river from the stadium.

As we're chatting, we hear the strains – drifting across the river – of another chorus of *Don't Take me Home*, followed by another and another. As idyllic as this place is, we're drawn towards the noise like moths are drawn towards the light. Cian's headed off already, in search of the night's vibe. As a group, we leave the backstage area and cross the bridge, towards the noise. There's a crowd of Wales fans outside a pub but as we're approaching we can see the shutters are coming down and the lights are going off. Dylan Llewellyn's there, my old friend, another who tries to combine a serious career in TV football coverage with acting the giddy goat on Wales' away trips. Dylan's a proper fan as well, rarely if ever misses a game, home or away. He's been at the gig – he's a massive Furries fan – we embrace heartily, barely able to take it all in. It's true. It's almost surreal. My team, my band, my mates. Dylan's been staying in the abbey in Bordeaux with his regular travel companions but he's flown the nest, intent on seeing a bit more of the host cities, rather than just travelling in on the day. Also, lured away by the attraction of seeing the gig tonight.

On cue, Gruff's arrival causes a stir, he's a proper hero to so many Welsh football fans, especially those who 'support' SFA in much the same way they support the national team. He's one of them, one of us, they all are. Then Cian staggers into view, he's been celebrating! He's with Sonny Coleman, Chris's son. Like Cian, Sonny's wearing his SO58 bucket hat. Apparently he managed to blag his way backstage and the band have been looking after him ever since. Cian says he's off to bed and weaves off in the direction of the bridge, the river and, assuming he successfully makes it across both, the tour bus.

We say our farewells too, it's late, way past Metro train time so we need to find ourselves a taxi. It's one of those nights you don't want to end. In younger days, I would have gone looking for the next venue, the bar that serves until the sun comes up, but now the camper van looks the best option. We have Evo's arrival to look forward to.

We walk back to the station we arrived at. There aren't many cabs around so we're drawn towards a bar that appears to still be open. As we approach, a guy appears and starts folding up the chairs lined up outside. It's a blow and he apologises, in English. It's a shame because it looks like a good place for a drink. He promises to try and call us a cab and we promise to bring our custom tomorrow and on the day of the game. He says he's not going to be opening, he's too worried about the prospect of trouble. We haven't seen a single Russian, good vibes abound and yet, still there's the fear. Despite his best efforts, he draws a blank on the taxi front as well, apparently they're all busy, so we wander off to a busier road to wait and hope.

It's a frustrating exercise. My phone being flat isn't helping as it means I can't order an Uber so we have to resort to a very old fashioned system of waving at cars. He goes to one end of the street, I go to the other. It looks like Steve has won when a car stops near him but some other people pile into that – I think there may have been a bit of a row – in the meantime I finally come out on top. A taxi stops for me and I shout to Steve to run before anyone steals this one from us. I jump in the back and ask him to take us to Camping Le Rupe, he seems a bit confused, so I ask Steve to get the address up on his phone and show it to the driver, he took a picture of the address before we set off for just such an eventuality as this; drunk in a strange city. Steve doesn't respond, so I ask him again. Still nothing. One more attempt and he barks back, "Alright, I'm doing it!" It's 4am, 19 June, and we've just had our first cross word!

Ten minutes and €20 later, we're back at base. We're not going to be creeping back in it appears, there are cabs turning up constantly with Welsh lads tumbling out of them. The security guard dispenses with the formality of checking the wristbands they issued to us on arrival, intent to get us in and off the street as quickly as possible.

This has been one of the great nights.

Sunday, June 19th

A late start to Father's Day, the first Father's Day I think I've ever been away from my family. It's noon before anything stirs inside Gareth. No discernible hangover however, which is a bonus, I suspect tolerance levels are increasing the longer the tournament goes on. It's a rare day this, no driving to do for the first time in over a week, our only journey's going to be into town to meet up with our new team member but that isn't until this evening.

The weather's indifferent again but the afternoon passes pleasantly enough sitting under the awning, I've got a card and a small gift to open, pre-packed by my thoughtful wife. We sip cups of tea and chat before I finally feel ready to embark upon a mission to get the barbecue going. I venture off-site to a service station I've spotted: they always sell coals don't they? Yes, as it turns out. I carry my bag back to base, ready for another crack at creating an alternative culinary option. I build my base – same technique as before – it lights quickly and soon there's that reassuring orange glow from my fuel. At the risk of getting boring, something I may have long since achieved, in contrast to yesterday, this is quality charcoal and we're quickly up to cooking heat. More meat gets thrown on whilst Steve sorts a salad and does some potatoes. The first bottle of wine gets opened and all is well with the world.

Around us, the same scenes are being enacted outside pretty much every camper van and tent. The wisps of smoke rise above the campsite. There's a pleasant low level chatter, occasional laughter and somewhere on the site we can hear the whoops and shouts of a game of football. The Red Army is enjoying some R&R before we all go into big game mode again.

A text confirms that 'the Evo has landed' and is now on a train to Toulouse. He's due in at 8pm so I suggest a meet up at a Metro station near the station. As we head through the camp to the exit, we pass a single camper van draped in the red, white and blue Russian flag – not much of a Trojan horse then. I wonder how they felt as they pulled in through the gates and realised they arrived in the Welsh ghetto, Toulouse? We've worked the timetables out better this evening and we're joined at the stop by a few more lads heading into town to see what's on offer the night before the biggest game in the history of Welsh football.

The metro's much busier tonight, there are lots of Wales shirts around but lots of French shirts as well as the host nation are playing their final group game. Many I'm sure will be heading to the fan zone to watch the game on the huge screens. As we exit the station, the heightened state of security is quickly apparent. There are throngs of fans outside a number of the bars in the vicinity and facing them there are ranks of riot police. This must be the impact of the Russian presence, but the big crowds of French fans heading for the fan zone must be causing concern as well, a fact reinforced as we walk towards a patrol of heavily armed soldiers. Evo must wonder what he's let himself in for as he makes his way up from the station?

We catch sight of him early, he's a big bloke, and waste little time with our greetings before setting about finding somewhere suitable to sit down and watch the game. Off the main drag, we spot a restaurant with tables outside and we claim one, perching ourselves on the high stools. There's a screen inside showing the football that we can see, although the well-heeled crowd here don't appear to be taking much notice of it. Bizarrely, they seem more interested in eating and chatting with each other? The sense that we're probably not in the right place grows as no one comes to serve us, so we give up and leave, heading back to the main street. All the outside tables in this part of the city seem to be taken and as we peer into each one looking for an inside table, I spot some more friends from home. Ceri was one of my best mates at school. We did loads of Wrexham away games together and he was the guy who made the stencil and spray-painted the Welsh flag we took on my first ever Wales trip to Nuremburg in 1993. He'd sprayed the flag round the back of his mum and dad's house, unaware that the paint had gone through the flag, leaving his parent's patio emblazoned with message 'Duke Ruabon On Tour'. Ceri's with another former travelling companion, Chris 'Twin'. He's 'Twin' because he has a twin. He was also briefly known as 'The General' as he used to organise all our Wrexham away trips. Often, we piled into the back of a transit van: for big games we'd have a coach or two. We called ourselves The Binline, a spoof on the Wrexham hooligan firm, The Frontline. Our motto was 'Too pissed to fight.' The football was often rubbish but, heck, we were in the Football League in those days! We had some cracking trips and people still ask 'Who took the OO out of Hoole Hall?' The answer, as any self-respecting Binliner will tell you is, 'Bonk did'.

After a chat and a catch up, we move on and then someone else I know wanders over for a chat. Actually, Evo and I both know him, as he's a former BBC Radio Leeds employee and we all worked together. It's Danny Savage who is now the network's North of England correspondent. He's a little off his regular patch but he is at work as we quickly guess. He's left a group sitting at a table drinking cups of coffee – that's a clue in itself – they are the only coffee drinkers as far as the eye can see. They are keeping a clear head as they're all on duty.

Danny confirms our immediate suspicions – they are on 'hooligan watch'. In their party, there will be a cameraman, a sound recordist possibly, a producer and a security guard. Danny's wearing his 'hooligan watch' outfit which consists of a polo shirt, a pair of those black hiking trousers with lots of zips and pockets and sturdy walking boots. They're all basically wearing the same outfit, as if they want to look like the police. They stand out like a sore thumb, in fact, with their stern faces, they look more like hooligans than any of the cheery beer-swilling crowds they're watching so intently. Danny's a nice guy and he's clearly a bit embarrassed given that he's effectively here to keep an eye on me, Evo and Steve, as we are 'fans' and therefore potential 'hooligans'. I watched some footage of hordes of cameras and reporters who were chasing after the Russians chasing after England fans in Lille and the media pack outnumbered either of the other two groups. It's fair to say news channels love a bit of scrapping. This peace, love and harmony will not get reported. 'News' appears to only be a negative these days. In this instance, I confidently predict that Danny and his crew are in for a long and quiet night, lots of singing apart. Even as we're talking, a coach load of Russian fans drives along the road, in between bars packed with Wales fans, there's some waving but basically, nobody takes any notice. We move on.

The France game's underway now so the need to find somewhere to call home is pressing. Still on the main street, but beyond the most popular venues, we come upon a smaller bar, it looks pretty busy but we push our way in and squeeze into a suitable space in the middle of the room. The game's on at the end of the room but we have a high table to lean on and soon we have beer to drink. The place is predominantly full of Welsh but there are one or two Russians as well and a few French. If the French score, everyone will celebrate together I'm sure but they don't and neither do Switzerland. It's a dull and rather predictable 0-0. Predictable as the result suits both sides and ensures the Swiss, France's friendly neighbours, make it through to the knockout stages. Still, the bar unites in a chorus of *Allez Les Bleus* before the air's filled with a fabulous rendition of *Calon Lân*. The popular hymn is becoming a firm favourite with Welsh fans now. It was previously the property of the rugby fans, but their repertoire has shrunk rapidly as the game's become less of a sporting event and more of an excuse for a weekend away. The football crowd has the youth, the ingenuity and the imagination: we wear bucket hats on our heads, they wear foam Daffodils. We eschew the stereotypes, they revel in them.

With the atmosphere building nicely in this packed little bar, Evo brings bottles and bad news. They've run out of beer! We've drunk it all! The bottles are all they've got left. Fail to prepare, prepare to fail. How could you run out of beer tonight of all nights?! We want to stay here, drinking all the beer, but we can't because it's all gone! With supplies exhausted and having had to sup some strange Mexican brew because it's all they had, we decide it's time to head off into the night.

The streets outside are thronging with fans, French, Welsh and some Russians. Still watching are the lines of the riot cops but they know the way the night's going now, there are now some smiles with Wales fans are going over to shake their hands and have pictures taken. I don't know what they were expecting, I hope they're pleasantly surprised. The mood is extremely good. I also hope Danny and his brave BBC band are tucked up in bed, the only thing likely to keep them awake the amount of caffeine they've consumed.

We catch the Metro back to La Vache but we've missed the last bus so I get to do my Uber thing. A car's ordered via the app on my phone. I think our driver's quite new at this lark, Uber drivers definitely don't have to do 'the knowledge', and our bloke gets lost. I can see his car going round and round in circles on the handy map you get to plot your car's progress on your phone. He calls me twice to try and ascertain our location. He's got a nice car and he's wearing a smart shirt and slacks when he finally arrives, I think his day job is probably in IT.

Back at base, we manage to smuggle Evo past the security guard despite the fact he's not wearing a wristband. The camp's clearly not ready to call it a day yet. There's a bar and it's busy, it's lure proves too great and we park ourselves at a table. My presence is noted by a group of lads from Wrexham at the next table. One of them starts to sing 'Bryn Law's on fire, Barry Horne is terrified' and, unsurprisingly, it doesn't catch on. There's another bloke who looks like a pirate; he has a grey beard, a red face and the brim of his bucket hat turned up at the front. I think it's fair to say he's had a few. He keeps coming back again and again for a chat, until his mates drag him away. It's all a great laugh, then an Irish guy comes over. He's very intense, some sort of football coach or scout and he talks very seriously at us about various young players that he's attempting to sign up with English clubs. It's tiring just listening to him so, we sup up, and head home.

The night's not over however as Evo fancies a bit of cheese and wine, both of which we have. We sit out, under the awning with the *fromage et vin*, before deciding to call it a day. Now, the final task. Evo breaks out his survival bag, whilst I start to inflate his airbed. He takes a turn as I start to hyperventilate but between us, we get it done. He lays it out under the awning, gets inside his sleeping bag, then puts the sleeping bag inside the survival bag, and settles down for the night. As I climb up to my bunk, I realise that I've forgotten to cancel the hotel I'd originally booked for tomorrow night. I needed to cancel 24 hours in advance to get a refund, so, it looks like Evo will have the chance to sleep on a real bed tomorrow after all. He can have the top bunk, I must confess, I quite fancy the idea of a real bed and an en-suite bathroom and a break from Steve's snoring.

Monday, 20th June – Euro 2016 Match Day 3

After a poor night's kip, my hotel plan seems more attractive than ever, a sense enhanced by the fact that Evo's first up, claiming the best night's sleep he's had in weeks. I suspect the fact he's got two energetic young sons may have something to do with that, plus the fact that he ditched the big plastic bag fairly soon after settling down, apparently he was too hot inside it. The upshot of this is that he's happy to forego the hotel room or even the top bunk in favour of another night under the stars. He's hardcore 'Camper Man'.

It seems the sun gods are shining on our new guest as the sky is clear and blue for the first time in weeks and we can enjoy our *petit déjeuner* under the awning and hatch a plan for the day. Thankfully, it's quite a simple one. We'll head into the city this afternoon, I'll go and check into my overnight accommodation, then we'll go and drink beer. It's our first experience of a 9pm kick-off so we're aware that in terms of alcoholic intake, today should be regarded as a marathon, not a sprint.

The final round of games in the group stage start simultaneously so we'll playing at the same time as England v Slovakia. The outcome of that could be crucial to our hopes and we digest our Weetabix and croissant with the team news from the other game. It's being reported that Roy Hodgson has decided to field a much changed side and that may not be helpful. Slovakia have also won one game, so they are our closest rivals for what looks like the second automatic qualification slot. Third place means waiting and hoping. We could do with England beating them to guarantee top spot, then we only need a draw to ensure we finish second. Even finishing on level points with Slovakia means we go above them – we beat them in Bordeaux – and we're through.

It does look a little bit arrogant though, to effectively rest players before qualification has been sorted out. Rooney's one of a reported six changes that are going to be made to the team that played in Lens and I thought he was their man of the match in that one. I'm pretty sure the Wales side will look very similar. Gareth Bale's already sounded the rallying cry, beat Russia and go we'll through, no matter what happens elsewhere.

I'm doing a bit of forward planning myself at this stage. Steve wants to be back in Leeds for that awards ceremony on Friday and Evo's flying back to the UK from Bordeaux as we have to get the van back there tomorrow by noon, so we'll leave early, do the swap and then go our separate ways: Evo to the airport and Steve and I will drive back north to get a ferry. The overnight crossings are all booked up, or extremely expensive, so I opt for a Calais boat instead. It's a heck of a drive from Bordeaux, too long to do in one go, so I look on the map for somewhere suitable to stay tomorrow. Rouen seems an option, especially as there's a budget hotel chain I've used many times before there, Hotel B+B. I've often booked them when I'm driving with the family on holidays. They do a good family room option, with a mezzanine level and a decent breakfast for a few euros extra. I know, I know, I'm Alan Partridge, AHa!

Anyway, whatever happens tonight, I will be home on my birthday in two days time. After that, who knows? I'll be waiting to see whether I can also celebrate my wife's birthday, also dependent on this evening's outcome. It's Paris on Saturday night for the group winners, Nice on Monday night for the runners-up and who knows if, where or when for the third placed side? If we finish 4th, it's straightforward. I'll be waking up to watch my wife unwrap her presents.

Travel plans in place, it's time to concentrate on enjoying the next few hours as if they were our last, which they might well be. We shall eat, drink and be merry! Working through the list, I'm right up for another run out for the barbecue, after all I've got most of a bagful of charcoal still to get through and this is our last chance to eat all the food we've got left. So, we chuck it all in. Steve sorts the last of the potatoes, then fries some eggs we picked up along the way, I do the inevitable sausages, some burgers, there's a jar of coleslaw, big beef tomatoes, baguettes, the lot. A bottle of wine gets opened, I make fire and I'm as happy as Larry, standing in the sunshine, sipping a chilled rosé and turning over sizzling pieces of meat. I've also got the music going on my little wireless speaker, a specially prepared playlist of some quality tunes. All around us, similar scenes are being enacted. You can feel the blissed-out atmosphere, underneath the Dragons, beside our tents and vans, we're all living our dream.

It seems bizarre that in the midst of this anyone could even contemplate the possibility of violence but we're all aware, I guess, that our campsite might be something of a sanctuary. I suggest that instead of eating hot dogs and drinking wine, we should all be in training in preparation for the moment when we venture out through the gates of our castle. The Russian hooligans have, apparently, been displaying their Mixed Martial Arts prowess by beating up middle-aged, overweight Englishmen. The internet is awash with footage of their fights in France, including material filmed on the small gopro cameras that can be attached to a body harness.

Social media, Twitter, Facebook, Youtube, etc etc give nutters of all persuasions the chance to achieve the notoriety they crave. They gain further exposure from the fact the 'mainstream media' are now happy to replay much of this material – lending a dangerous credibility to the perpetrators – taking them beyond the realms of the internet and into everyone's front room. If we got all the Welsh lads together, mocked-up an unarmed combat training session, then filmed it and posted it on YouTube, someone, somewhere would think it was real and pretty soon, I'd lay odds that the deception would become 'fact'.

If we actually went through with it and pulled it off, we could claim it as a work of art: we'd probably win the Turner Prize. A couple of glasses in, I'm content to limber up with Dai Hooligan's 'pincer movement', which would make a good name for a band. It's Evo's first experience of this so we quickly get him up to speed – he's a big unit – me and Steve can hide behind him if the bum-bagged hordes attack. After a shower, I've got to decide on my own match day attire. No bumbag, although I have got a small blue rucksack that contains the stuff I'll need for my overnight 'offsite'. Then there are certain items I can't wear. The brown New Balance trainers and jeans are out because I wore them in Lens and we lost. I can't really revert to my Bordeaux gear because the Adidas trainers I wore there I appear to have left there, plus it was mild there and hot here, so jeans aren't a viable option. On that basis, my grey Reebok Paris trainers get their first international call-up, matched with grey shorts and my favourite Spirit of '58 T-shirt, the one based on the cover of Pink Floyd's *Dark Side Of The Moon* album, where the prism is a football and the light that emerges from it is red, yellow and green. It's been designed by a Cardiff chap who works under the name of 'A Guy Called Minty', one of a host of cool, talented people who've turned their hands to producing Wales gear, providing an exciting alternative to the overpriced nylon football shirts that will still predominate in the stadium this evening: I prefer a bit of cotton next to my skin. On my head, needless to say, I will be wearing my bucket hat, the one I've worn for both the games so far. The bucket is exempt from all the usual lucky charm rules. Tim's talent is to have created the ultimate manifestation of all that it means to be a Wales fan in the form of a hat. Genius that.

Departure time is 3pm and there's a bus at 3.20, so we get to the stop with a few minutes to spare. There's a good crowd already assembled at the bus stop as we arrive – cars and lorries hoot their horns and wave as they pass on the road. It looks like the lads have been here for a while, as they've hung a big Wales and Wrexham flag on the mesh fence, bearing the proud motif of the Gwersyllt Reds, some of the club's most loyal fans. The lads come over for a chat and to ask if I'll have a picture taken with the flag. By the time they've got the flag off the fence and then sorted out the photo settings on someone's phone, the bus arrives and we're the last to get on. We squeeze on and pay for tickets. For me, it's a one way journey. I've got my little overnight bag with me, the hotel's going to be the first stop before the build-up really begins.

From the Jean Jaurès metro station, it's a short walk to my abode for the evening. It's a small hotel down a side street, I get checked in, head up to the room and drop my bag off, then straight back down to rejoin the chaps. Steve's off on a beer-scouting mission and he returns to report the discovery of a great looking bar close by.

We follow him down a street and into a small square, at the corner of which there is a sign for a *Tabac*, which is probably what drew Steve in this direction in the first place. From the outside, it looks like a shop, but like Lens, when we follow him in, it turns out that there's a little bar opposite the shop counter. It's obvious what's caught his eye; all the fixtures and fittings appear to date back to the 1960s. There's some great Formica furniture and a fantastic mirror behind the bar, exotic looking bottles on shelves and the walls and tables are a light green. A middle-aged woman beams out from behind the bar, and takes great pride in pouring out the three beers we order. It literally feels like we've stepped back in time.

We sit at a green Formica topped table and marvel at the way this has all been preserved. Our host explains, in French, that the tobacconists and bar has been in her family for a hundred years. On the wall behind the bar she proudly points to an old beer tap. She says it's the original pump dating from 1910. European countries seem to do a far better job of protecting small businesses and independent operators like this. I think back to the fantastic restaurant we visited in Brussels prior to the Euro qualifier in 2014 that was over a hundred years old. In the UK, the chain is king and if it doesn't turn a decent profit, it gets turned into flats.

A ruddy-faced old guy pops in for a beer. It looks like he's a regular, as the lady greets him and immediately starts pouring. He takes a long sip and leans on the bar, then turns to survey the late afternoon clientele. When he hears us talking, he's interested. In French, he asks where we're from? I answer, "*Pays de Galles*." It turns out our man knows *Pays de Galles*, or at least a small bit of it. Evo and I listen intently, put our rudimentary French into practice, and piece together a tale that begins with a coach trip over to Cardiff to support the French rugby team in the 1970's. Things begin to get really interesting when he begins to recount the memories of his stay in Monmouth before and after the game. It's tricky to keep a grip on the narrative but with skilful questioning – we're both journalists after all – and lots of mime, we ascertain that there was a woman involved. The mime bit comes in especially handy with this part of the tale, as he goes into a full-on routine involving puckered lips and that thing where you turn around, put your hands on your own shoulders and it looks like you're snogging. I'm not sure how we get onto an interrogation about how far things went with this Welsh woman but he makes it clear that kissing was the extent of his activity, *"Je suis un homme d'honneur!"* he emphatically declares, 'I am a man of honour!'

From there, the conversation moves onto his massive TV and how he likes to sit in front of it and watch sport – all sport – all day. He says he was a rugby player himself but we'd already worked this out from the flattened state of his nose, a fly half apparently and he played at a reasonable level. Nowadays, he works for the post office. He finishes his drink, we have pictures taken and vow to try and find his long lost love in Monmouth before saying *au revoir*. It's been a fabulously French start to our pre-match build-up.

We head off towards the city centre where the streets and bars are much busier. It's red, red, red everywhere as we enter another square. We find the Welsh Fans Embassy here and, on the next stall, a young woman invites us to have our picture taken. It's the Visit Toulouse team offering free photos with a backdrop of the city. It's computerised, so you can choose which one you want. They also have a box of props and fancy dress you can use. Steve dives straight in and comes out wearing a glittery cap and a clipon French flag tie, Evo opts for a big, blue, curly hair wig. Boringly, I don't opt for anything flamboyant other than a French flag on a stick, and I was the one who studied drama at Uni.

We have a photo each and I agree to keep them in my small packaway rucksack, but opening it up seems to trigger something in my head. I had the match tickets, I know I had them, so where are they now? Throughout the tournament, I'd kept each game's tickets in the original envelope I'd received, ready for distribution at the stadium. They're not in the bag, they're not in my pocket, they must still be in the hotel. I'm 90% certain they're there – I saw them on the bed before I set off – but I'm still gripped by something of a state of panic. It's the sort of occurrence that I dread; getting to the stadium, no tickets, the nightmare scenario. Attempting to remain as calm as possible, I inform the lads that I need to return to the hotel. Don't panic!

I rush up the three floors to the room. I know they are there and yet there's still that doubt isn't there? Maybe the cleaner's been in and chucked the envelope away. Maybe I imagined the whole thing. No, I didn't, they're there on the bed. I sweep them up, both cursing myself for being so slack and celebrating the fact that I have, after all, now got them.

A flicker of relief passes over the face of Steve and Evo, even as they affect a nonchalant 'never doubted you' outlook as I return to reception – a telltale grin across my face. I've cut into valuable drinking time with my foolishness so there's an extra sense of purpose now as we stride out, heading for the river side and the bars we spotted on our post-gig walkabout on Saturday night. *En route*, we bump into our first group of Russian fans. There are no bumbags, no black T-shirts and we don't feel the need to adopt the 'pincer movement'. In fact, we exchange greetings and handshakes and pose for photos.

All the bars we pass seem to be full of Welsh fans, many of whom are in full voice already, still four hours before kick-off. Seeking a swift route to the bar and therefore to more beer, we bypass the busy places and alight instead on a quieter looking establishment directly opposite the river, right at the end of the bridge we crossed with the Furries at the weekend. There's a decent range of beers, beyond the Kronenburg/Heineken axis and a sign on the wall promises happy hour between six and seven. Steve goes off to join the queue for the facilities whilst I purchase pints and take them out of the bar and over the road to the pavement opposite, overlooking the river. The road runs parallel with the river, directly towards the stadium which is actually on an island in the middle of the Garonne, accessible by bridge. Across on the far bank, we can see the festival site and, still parked up alongside it, the Super Furries tour bus.

We've chosen a fine vantage point for people watching. Already, crowds of fans are beginning to make their way towards the stadium, passing us as we lean against the stone wall and sip beer in the sunshine. Steve returns with horror tales of the toilet, only one apparently, and clearly suffering from an influx of full-bladdered football fans. As ever though, no matter how much ale's been drunk, there's nothing other than peace and love in the air. There's some singing, chatting and laughing but nobody overstepping the line; no aggression, it's joyous.

I don't know where the massed ranks of riot police have positioned themselves and, most certainly, they're here somewhere but from where I'm standing, they aren't going to be needed tonight. Groups of Russians pass through the crowds gathered outside the bar and along the pavement and all the way they're offered hands to shake or asked to stop for pictures. Steve's particularly active in this area. He keeps nipping off and coming back with great pictures of smiling Russians in strange hats. So much so, that Evo and I begin to speculate that he may be working on behalf of the Foreign Office or British Council. My guess, even if the hooligans are still here, what would they gain from ruining this? Putin may have all but condoned their actions but I'm sure the vast majority of their compatriots were embarrassed, maybe even worried about the potential for payback against another British team this evening? It won't happen. This is a party and everyone's invited.

Talking of parties, Cian appears, still wearing his bucket hat, brim turned up. The last time we saw him, he was heading off across the bridge ready to return to the tour bus. Except, as he recounts, he opted to make the trans-Garonne crossing by balancing on the narrow ledge on the outer side of the bridge, rather than the pavement. Needless to say, if he'd slipped there would be at least one empty seat in the stadium this evening.

It's Steve's turn to get a round in now, he's managed to time it so Happy Hour's just beginning but he returns a little later looking a little less than happy. It looks like they've miscalculated on beer stocks again and not only is there not a Happy Hour tonight but there's no beer either! Levels are running low, rationing has been introduced and, as a result, we're drinking a hybrid half beer/half white wine concoction. It's an unlikely combination, I'm not convinced it's going to catch on but it certainly packs a bit of a punch. So much so that when I'm offered another, I politely decline. In the old days, watching Wales was all about drinking enough to dull the pain, but now things are different and I want to make sure I remember as much as possible for as long as possible. We might never have this opportunity again.

There are some fantastic sights as well as the crowds heading for the ground begin to swell. Two Russian guys appear in what look like cavalry officer's jackets from the mid-nineteenth century. One in red and black with lots of gold braid and extravagant epaulettes. His mate wears a large conical hat with a single red star on the front, the 1917 equivalent of a Spirit of '58 bucket hat?

With 90 minutes or so to go before kick-off, we finish our drinks and join the general drift to the stadium. It's one of the more spectacular walks to a ground, firstly alongside, then over the river, through the trees and a park. All the way along, I'm overwhelmed by the atmosphere. It's just brilliant, such great excitement, such anticipation. It's a feeling – a mood – like I've not experienced for a long, long time. There's a tremendous innocence about this, a naïvety perhaps. We got to the quarter-finals in Sweden in our only World Cup appearance in 1958 but I wouldn't imagine there were even a handful of Welsh supporters out in Sweden. There are tens of thousands here in Toulouse, all heading towards the stadium and a date with destiny. It's such a privilege to be in their midst that I get quite emotional, even more so when we bump into a group of Scots guys who've come along to support Wales. They're wearing kilts, of course, and look like paid-up members of the Tartan Army, a huge fan group that's become synonymous with boisterous but well-behaved, self-policed support of the national side. They're being stopped every few yards for pictures with Wales fans and Russian fans. I can't resist a wee dig, we've been in their shadow for so long, "Hey, are you lads lost?" I ask. They groan collectively. I'd guess it's the hundredth time they've heard something along those lines today given their side's failure to qualify. We stop for a chat, a photo and more handshakes.

The crowds build towards the first security checkpoint but we've learnt our lesson from Lens and allowed plenty of time to get in. Through the second check and then ticket turnstiles and we're swept into the concourse around the outside of the ground. Evo and I are both on a present buying mission before we take our seats. There are UEFA concession stands selling a range of items; T-shirts, caps, bags, scarves and the like. The prices are fairly reasonable, mind you, they don't need to add much of a mark up given the price of the ruddy tickets. I get tops for Megan and Millie but choice is limited as stocks are running low, a theme of our visit to Toulouse it would seem.

Elsewhere, there are queues for food and drink but the beer's really weak and we can't be bothered joining the line for anything else. Before we go in we stop for more pictures with two big Russian blokes wearing traditional smocks, baggy trousers and those Cossack-style boots with the pointy toes. If there's one thing Wales lacks, it's a male national costume. I've seen a chap in a full dragon suit but apart from that, we haven't got any equivalent of the Scots in their kilts or the Dutch in their orange costumes and huge wooden clogs. Actually, we have a contender for our new national costume: the Wales football shirt and bucket hat combination's in evidence all around. It's being displayed by a group of four men having pictures taken close by, I get talking to one of them. He tells me he's followed Wales on rugby tours so he's used to the experience of being away from home for a long time, he's happy to stay on in France for a while longer yet. It's proof positive that the round ball game's attracting people who've previously followed the oval ball game, or 'The Egg' as many Welsh football fans refer to it.

We enter the stadium, a single tier bowl, through a tunnel and emerge into a splash of colour and light. There's the bright green of the pitch then, to our right and left, a solid block of red. As the seats sweep round beyond the halfway line, there's a preponderance of white but even in its midst, there are small pockets of red. The far side looks like the neutral section but, again, there are Dragons draped over any surrounding walls or barriers. In other words – like Bordeaux, we've got loads more fans than the other lot. I guess it's not surprising given the relative distances involved but we're talking a country with a population of nearly 150 million people, fifty times the size of Wales.

Our seats are in the same sort of position as the two previous games, almost level with the corner flag on the opposite side of the ground to the tunnel and the dug outs. We're at the very end of the row, like Bordeaux, a few rows closer to the pitch than Alex Gage. He calls out, fully up to date with team news again, because he's on duty and I'm not. There's one change, Sam Vokes starts in place of Hal Robson-Kanu.

It's one of those little surprise selections we've encountered throughout this Euro journey. I thought Hal was first choice frontman these days but 'in Cookie we trust', so Sam it is. I'm really pleased for him, having known him a long time, since he came into the Under-21 setup as one of Brian Flynn's 'discoveries'. He's been totally committed to the cause ever since, even whilst his club career has taken dips. Now he's back in the top division with Burnley and he's getting his first start at a major international championships, a good summer for Sam!

There's another stage of the Gage pre-match ritual that we now have to go through, "These are rubbish, I've seen both their games. Rubbish! You'll win this..", he opines emphatically. When it comes to football, Alex is one of the most knowledgeable cameramen I've worked with. His opinion is not to be dismissed, however, it doesn't tally with my ultra cautious approach to watching Wales. If you offered me a draw, I'd take it – right here, right now. I admonish him for his dangerous, carefree optimism. Actually, it's not carefree, because he may be a Black Country boy but he's spent so much time around the Welsh squad and been to so many games, that he's a fan now. He's certainly spent enough time in Cardiff to be able to claim dual nationality.

He's making his prediction based on what he's seen, all I've got to go on is the second half of the game against England, the one we watched whilst devouring a triple level burger in the apartment in Bordeaux. I've heard it said that England should have been well ahead by half-time, that Russia were worse in the second game, against Slovakia, but I didn't see any of that one – we were driving to Amiens. I have had a look down the list of their players and it's hard to pick out a danger man given that they all play in Russia. If there's any encouragement to draw from that it's that Russian clubs haven't done anything in European competitions for a while. Reasons to be cheerful? Maybe.

To be honest, my outlook is pretty sunny. It's been such a great day that I don't honestly feel any anxiety about the game. We've won a game, we've scored some goals, we've had a laugh, I didn't ask for any more from this experience than that. If it all ends in two hours time, I won't be sad. Still, I'm extra vigilant about trying to take everything in, the sights and the sounds and I follow the entire UEFA pre-match presentation with a keen eye. It's a beautiful, warm evening, the stadium's full and the noise levels rise as the two teams emerge. *Hen Wlad Fy Nhadau* is the first anthem sung and we sing lustily, aware that this might be the last time Europe and the world gets to hear this for quite a while. The Russian one is nowhere near as stirring, their fans struggle to make their voices heard, even inside this compact stadium.

The players complete the formalities, the high fives and the handshakes, the captains exchange pennants and then we're off – Wales kicking towards our end. Straightaway, they're in action right front of us. Joe Allen snaps into a challenge in our half and carries the ball forward at pace, playing-in Gareth Bale who powers up to the edge of the area and fires off a shot. Akinfeev beats it away but only into the path of Sam Vokes who's following in but he mishits it and the chance is lost. The assistant ref on our side has his flag up anyway, for offside, but that was for Vokes not Bale. Inside 60 seconds and we've made a chance. It's a clear statement of Wales' intent as the red shirts seize immediate control. If England was ponderous, a little cautious, this is very different. We need a win and we're going for a win – right from the off!

The band strikes up. The Barry Horns again providing the stirring soundtrack, enhancing the upbeat tempo to the atmosphere. We take our cue from them and *Don't Take Me Home* is the plea from twenty thousand voices. It seems the players are intent on ensuring we stay.

The two full-backs are pushed right up, the three central defenders base themselves no further back than the halfway line and it's there that James Chester once more shows great anticipation to nip in and win possession ahead of an opponent. He does the sensible thing and rolls the ball to Joe Allen and he looks up and plays a pass in between two defenders. It's one of those moments when everything slows down, the blur of a bleached blonde head – Ramsey – emerges from between them; clean through, dead centre, edge of the area. The 'keeper races out and slides across the turf to block but what happens next is beautiful. Players like to call this a 'dink'. It's a little flick under the ball that lifts it up and forward – Ian Rush used to be brilliant at it. Aaron's mastered it as well, as the keeper's body approaches, he performs the 'dink' and the deft chip carries the ball over Akinfeev; there's only one place it's going. I turn to celebrate with Evo before it even hits the net. All around us, people are tumbling over seats, over each other, punching the air, hugging, ten minutes gone in a game we need to win and we're winning.

I don't think it's relief that pours off the away end, I think it's expectation, a final realisation that this team is different. Welsh football isn't like it was before. We've always been crushed by the burden of expectation in the past, like the last time we played Russia in a play-off second leg game, all square from the first game in Moscow, a full house at the Millennium Stadium and we lost 1-0. This team embraces expectation and thrives on the pressure. One goal up, now going for more – angrily buzzing around any Russian who has the temerity to try and take possession of the ball.

The fans go through a full repertoire now, including a couple of personal favourites, *1-0 to the Sheepshaggers* – to the tune of the Pet Shop Boys track *Go West* – and 'We know what we are, We know what we are, Sheepshagging bastards, We know what we are!" – to The Beach Boys' 'Sloop John B'. This is then followed by a round of baa-ing, much to the bemusement of many foreign observers. Those of us who follow the Welsh clubs that play in English league competitions have been taunted about our supposed bestial preferences for as long as we've been going to games. These responses have been developed in celebration of the stereotype – they're not subtle but it's better than getting angry. It's funnier too.

To further underline the differences between 'us and them', the next anthem to rise from the red end is *Calon Lân*. I've always loved this hymn – we sang it at my wedding – because it isn't really about God and I'm not really a believer. It's much more about 'the self' than that, about being a good person for the sake of being a good person, rather than to satisfy a higher being. To be able to belt it out – arms wide – in celebration of this wonderful experience is to be somewhere close to having that *Calon Lân* – that 'Pure Heart'. This is our church, this is our religion. These are our Gods.

Ben Davies breaks up another attack in our half and plays the ball to Ramsey, who carries it forward then links up with Bale. Russian defenders panic and all race towards him yet somehow he appears to divert the ball left; a deflection maybe? If it came off one of those panic stricken Russian players, worse is to come because the ball goes straight to Neil Taylor who's all alone on the left side of the penalty area. Neil Taylor?! Neil's never scored for Wales, he had a great chance in the qualifier in Cyprus, was even closer to goal than this and he missed it. I'm not confident and, sure enough, history repeats itself as the 'keeper again races off his line and blocks the shot – but the ball spins back to Neil who has another go, with the 'keeper down and

Months in the planning, departure day finally arrives and the packing's done. I have my essential items to hand; socks, passport and Spirit of '58 bucket hat.

The first stop on a complicated journey took me across Leeds to collect my travelling companion and fellow Wales fan, Steve. The only part of the journey I hadn't planned for was the return trip. We didn't know when we'd be coming home!

Hang out the bunting! It looked and felt like Bordeaux had been taken over by Wales fans and we wasted no time in letting the neighbourhood know we'd arrived.

It was clear France was on a high state of alert, with a real fear the tournament would be a terrorist target. Despite that, whilst they patrolled, we partied. This was a joyful invasion.

Only here for the *bière!* *Zombie Nation Awakes* told the story of qualification from my perspective as a reporter but I wanted a different experience in France. I've always enjoyed the chance to follow Wales away as a fan and this was one trip I didn't want to miss out on! It was a summer of sightseeing and singing I had on my agenda, rather than interviews and injury updates.

Smile please! There must have been a million selfies taken during the course of the campaign. One of the things I enjoyed most about France was meeting fans from all over Wales but also Europe and beyond.

I was constantly bumping into childhood friends, former neighbours and even legends like Ian Rush. I was happy to help capture the moment for my pal Iwan and his son.

The final few steps before the moment when it all became real. Ticket in hand and about to enter the stadium to finally see the dream come true – Wales playing in a summer tournament.

One of the first people I saw inside the ground was Alex, the cameraman who's been with me all the way covering Wales games for Sky. He was working at Euro 2016 but made sure he was at every Wales game. He was as excited as me!

No matter how hard the Slovakian's fought this was always going to be our day, and what a day it was. The Red Wall was born and the adventure of our dreams was underway – *Bienvenue Le pays de Galles.*

When I'm working on Wales games, I have to appear cool, calm and collected no matter what I've just witnessed. At full-time in Bordeaux, I was free to go mad!

The Barry Horns have done a great job in lifting the atmosphere at Wales games and they were brilliant in France. When things went a bit quiet after Slovakia's equaliser, they got the fans going again so, at full-time, I made sure I went to say 'thank you for the music!'

I was wearing a very different look on my face when I took the wheel of the camper van for the first time as we headed up to Brittany and a reunion with our pal Brian. Steve quickly worked out I was probably a better navigator and he did most of the driving from then on, as we covered thousands of kilometres on our own *Tour de France*.

I was happier on two wheels, even adopting the correct costume as we went exploring the coastline near Brian's house. All I lacked were the onions across the handlebars.

Taking *le petit-déjeuner* in Dinard, with 'Gareth' – our camper van – behind me. This was a rare dry spell in between the downpours.

Despite what the sign says, we didn't feel welcome enough to try and get through the police cordon around the team hotel, but the town and the Breton nation really took the team to their hearts – the Celtic connection between Wales and Brittany coming to the fore.

All aboard! We swapped the camper van for a coach for the final leg of the trip to Lens. Getting into town proved tricky but getting a beer proved to be much easier, despite a so-called alcohol ban. As you can see from the magazines behind us, even the newsagents had a bar!

Increased security checks made for chaotic scenes outside a number of the grounds, particularly Lens. It could have provoked clashes but everyone got on okay outside. Inside, we were clearly outnumbered but never out-sung!

It was a real blow to see Wales let a crucial point slip in the final few seconds but most of our fans acknowledged we didn't play particularly well.

It was a quieter night back in Amiens, where someone had clearly gone to great lengths (and depths!) to add this statue to the Red Wall.

Toulouse, and two great nights. The Super Furry Animals gig a couple of days before we met Russia was every bit as memorable as any of the games. Even better, I managed to get backstage afterwards and share a beer with my favourite ever band.

Another member of the small but select band of North Leeds Reds arrived in time for the final group game. Evo's a big lad and there was no room for him in our little mobile abode, so he slept under the stars for a couple of nights.

Despite all the dire warnings about Russian hooligans, the pre-match atmosphere in Toulouse was every bit as good as it had been in Bordeaux. Maybe the bad lads had gone home because everyone we met was friendly.

'Football Before Education' says the flag, as this lot missed quite a bit of school to follow the national team. So many fans had always hoped that one day they'd be able to share this experience with their children and what a positive experience it turned out to be, for Wales fans of all ages.

A result, performance and atmosphere the like of which we'd never witnessed before. The football Wales played was breathtaking; the best I've ever seen in nearly 40 years following the national side.

Guto and Gruff from the Super Furry Animals were at every game. Can you guess which of the pair slept in a hotel during their extended stay in Toulouse and which of them slept on the tour bus parked just up the river from the stadium?

Mission accomplished. We'd qualified and the celebrations got even wilder when it was announced that England had only drawn, meaning Wales finished top of Group B. The party after the game went on long into the night and the scenes outside the stadium were utterly joyous.

I didn't know it at the time, but the guy on the right had already become something of a star during the game when TV cameras had caught him weeping with happiness as the final whistle approached. I could empathise completely; I'd shed a few tears myself in that second half.

Next stop Paris, via a quick detour to Leeds to get my washing done. I dived off the metro *en route* to the ground to make sure I could at least say I'd seen the *La tour Eiffel*. Needless to say, there was a Red Wall around it!

Before, during and after, there was a great mood between the two sets of supporters, the Northern Irish fans bringing great humour and their famous *Will Grigg's On Fire* to the party.

Everyone seemed to hike their prices up for the duration of the tournament, not least Parisian bar owners, so the cake shop round the corner from this one did a roaring trade in 'off-sales'.

The game came just a day after the result of the EU referendum had been announced. It seems the outcome was as big as shock in France as it was in the UK. Lots of questions, and still not many answers!

I wore this hat to every game and I needed it's protection from the fierce sun inside the Parc des Princes.

A legendary stadium hosted a less than memorable game, but who cares? We won!

To be in the last eight was as much as anyone could have hoped for, and to be in Paris celebrating was even more special. Welsh music was again well represented with Euros Childs and H. Hawkline amongst the travelling support.

After racing home to celebrate my wife's birthday, I was soon back on a flight from Doncaster to Paris. Steve and his son Fergus were with me and we stopped, on the drive from Paris to Lille, to visit the Welsh memorial at Mametz Wood. One hundred years since the start of the Battle of the Somme, it was a poignant and necessary detour: Lest we forget.

The scenes that greeted us as we arrived in Lille city centre on match day were unlike anything I've ever witnessed before. It was full-on craziness from the minute we stepped out of the metro station. I've never seen so many deliriously happy people gathered together in such enormous numbers before!

I think there was a flag from pretty much every town and village in Wales on show in France through the summer, including plenty from my hometown. I found a window ledge above this balcony and used it as a viewing point for the incredible scenes taking place in the square below.

In Lille's *Grand Place* I bumped into a crowd of pals from my own home village, including Andrew, seen here chatting with a Belgian fan. One of the greatest aspects of the whole Euro experience was meeting fans from all over the world, all brought together by football. I've never felt happier than I did that day.

No event in history has ever united the Welsh nation like this one. North and south are separated by a terrible transport network and it took a trip to France to bring everyone together. It was an event that also helped raise global awareness of the very existence of a place called Wales.

I think these kids were probably trying to tap us up for a few Euros before the game but Steve and Fergus invited them to join our party and they were soon having a great laugh together. It was all so uplifting.

Inside the ground we were in a minority, but the Belgians seemed to have left a lot of their energy in the *Grand Place* as Welsh voices soon filled the stadium on an incredible night.

It was hard to take in at times. Here we were, winning a quarter-final tie against the side ranked second in the world. There will never be another night like Lille. I'm so glad I wasn't working – being professionally detached – so that I could stand on my seat, shout, sing and just completely enjoy it.

Oh, what a feeling! The moment when Sam Vokes' header hit the net is my single most favourite football moment so far. That was when we knew we'd win – no more heartbreak – we were into the semi-finals!

What an incredible group of people – players and staff. There was a genuine bond between them and us that just got stronger and stronger as the tournament went on. I've never experienced anything like it.

I hunted high and low to find a copy of *L'Équipe*, the famous French sports paper, at Charles de Gaulle airport the next morning. The headline shouts 'What Madness' and who could disagree?

Back on the Doncaster-Paris commute before catching the TGV to Lyon. Match ticket prices were raised even higher and precious days-off negotiated, but still we came in huge numbers. Lyon was red all over and the Elephant and Castle became the latest pub to enjoy a bumper day!

Just around the corner from the party at the Elephant & Castle, I had time for a quick radio interview with Ellis James, the talented actor, comedian and self-confessed 'Welsh football obsessive', who was recording a series of programmes on the Euros, from a fan's perspective, for BBC Radio Wales.

Our view for the semi-final. I'd got tickets for me and Evo from a Swiss bloke. They were in the upper tier but at the wrong end of the ground as it turned out. Around us, the evidence of the overpricing of tickets was clear; loads of empty seats.

The end of the road. Nobody wanted to leave the ground afterwards because that meant going back to life – back to reality. We could have lived this experience for ever. This was the greatest summer of my life.

defenders racing over to cover him on the goal line. As cool as you like, Neil flicks out his left foot and sends the half-volley through all the bodies and into the back of the net, NEIL TAYLORRRRRRRRR!!!!!!!!! Neil Taylor makes it 2-0 and there are barely twenty minutes gone! AAAAAAAGGGGGHHHHHHHHHH!!!!!!

It's joy unconfined now because we're not just beating Russia, we're battering them. Our full-back, who's never scored for Swansea, who started his career playing non-league football at Wrexham, has just finished off another sweeping forward move by this so-called 'one man team'. 'Bales' they've called us in the English media. First goal – Ramsey. Second goal – Taylor. England are still drawing with Slovakia, Wales are currently top of the group!

It's the realisation of all this that begins to overwhelm me a bit at this stage. I can't stop shaking my head. I rest my hands on top of my bucket hat, pull the brim back a bit, puff my cheeks and blow out. It's hard to take in. We've been hardwired for failure, now we're being rewired for success. I say 'we', and by that I mean the generations of us who've seen Wales fall short time after time. I'm happy to report there are many amongst us in the stadium who don't carry that mental burden, some even young enough to think this is what it's always like following Wales! It isn't, it really isn't. Twenty-five years of trips and I can count on the fingers of one hand the number of times I've been present with Wales 2-0 ahead in a competitive game away from home.

Because of that history, I won't relax, one Russian goal could yet change everything and they almost get it when a long punt from the goalie catches Ashley Williams and the striker stretches out a leg to make contact and try and direct the ball past Wayne Hennessey, who has to make his first save and pushes the ball round the post, then catches the corner.

Russia enjoy their first prolonged spell of possession so far but Wales are brilliantly set-up and disciplined. They keep reshaping, getting those two lines of players back behind the ball, then targeting the player in possession in little snapping packs. Joe Allen is simply magnificent again. There's no way through for the opposition and they fear the consequences of throwing too many men forwards. Gareth sets off on a gallop that leaves defenders trailing in his wake before he again forces Akinfeev to save, the ball spinning off the 'keeper and into the path of Sam Vokes on the edge of the area. Sam should score but his shot goes just wide.

It's the cue for another flurry of attacks. Ramsey fires in a fierce shot that's saved. Bale has another long range crack and again Akinfeev has to get his body behind it. One more goal surely finishes it and the players look like they're going for it before half-time. A Russian attack breaks down and Gareth races away with the ball, pursued by two white shirts, gets up to the edge of the area and tries to shoot across the 'keeper but he gets down to save. I can't remember a game against decent opposition when Wales have created so many chances, we could soon be out of sight.

As half-time approaches, the anthem rings out again, this time almost in a musical 'round' with our section a few seconds behind the fans behind the goal. It's like a choral performance now, as their 'Gwlad! Gwlad!' starts and we follow. It's beautiful. Then it's Chrissie Coleman's Barmy Army, over and over again. It reminds me of the campaign when we almost qualified for the USA '94 World Cup – when Bodin's penalty hit the bar. We used to chant "Terry Yorath's red and white army!" clap, clap, clap, clap "Terry Yorath's red and white army!" again and again, for about twenty minutes. During the away game in Cyprus I remember feeling drained with the exertion of it, especially in the heat of that Limassol evening but we couldn't stop. Every time the volume dipped, we'd redouble our efforts and keep it going. It worked, we won.

There's the same intensity to it this evening although it doesn't go on anything like as long but we've got more songs to sing these days for a start! The players keep going as well and even as the time board goes up, we're attacking. Bale's racing away again, playing in Ramsey but Aaron delays and the chance to shoot is gone. Russia have time to respond with a shot of their own but it goes wide. It's still a warning and I'm happy when the whistle goes to bring an end to an exhilarating and exhausting half of football.

The interval is as much a break for us as it is for the players. I'm still at the head shaking stage to be honest. Two up and cruising is not the Welsh way. Gagey appears at my shoulder, "Told you they were rubbish!" he exclaims. "This'll be 4-0, no problem!" I have to mount a rearguard action to fight my inclination to finally agree with one of his wild predictions, now is not the time for getting complacent, keep it together Bryn. I fall back on the defence I used when he said the same at half-time in Haifa, with Wales one up in the qualifier, "They can't be as bad as that again in the second half." He dismisses my feeble attempt. "4-0, bet you!"

As it stands, with England and Slovakia still at 0-0, even a draw's good enough to get us through in second place and it takes something of a leap of imagination to see the Russia we've seen in the first half actually pulling that off, never mind getting the win. Still, one more Welsh goal and I'll dare to dream.

It seems our heroes have the same objective because they rip into Russia again, right from the off. Bale has yet another shot, then Gunter gallops up from the back to pick up a pass and deliver a near post cross that's hacked clear. If anything, the first five minutes of the second period suggest Russia's race is run. Bale has a fine chance to wrap it up after another great through ball from Aaron Ramsey. He gets beyond the last defender and for the umpteenth time, Akinfeev has to race out. Like Aaron, Gareth lifts the ball over him but this time the angle's trickier and, as we hold our breath in anticipation of the goal, the ball drops a yard wide of the far post.

Still, Wales are in complete control. First to everything, confidence oozing through every pass and move. I remember watching Aaron Ramsey warming up for an Under-21 international once, many moons ago, and he was flicking the ball up – juggling it, doing tricks – with a broad smile on his face as his teammates watched on. It struck me then that this was a player who loved football, who loved to play football, to entertain, and I'm seeing the same thing in Aaron now. He's all tricks and extravagant turns, he's revelling in the chance to show what he can do. Footballers so rarely seem to enjoy playing these days. If they do, they don't dare show it, but here's Aaron on the biggest stage, loving every minute of it.

The new Chris Coleman song booms out, again using that *Sloop John B* tune, "Chris Coleman had a dream, To build a national team, He had no strikers so he played five at the back ... five at the back, With Bale in attack, With Bale in attack, Watch out Europe, We're on our way back!' Sam Vokes and Simon Church might take issue with the no strikers suggestion and the 'on our way back' bit suggests the people of Europe still recall with awe our appearance in the 1958 World Cup in Sweden but still, it's a good song.

The game moves past the hour mark and Wayne Hennessey still hasn't touched the ball in this half, that's how tight the grip we have on the game is. As England continue to struggle against Slovakia, the 'We are top of the league' chant starts up again. I'm half an hour away from a trip to Paris now and there is a sense that the game's moving towards an inevitable conclusion.

Wales have not let up, Joe Allen epitomises that by holding possession under heavy pressure from two Russian players, deep in their half. He loses the ball then dives into a tackle to win it back again. Frustrations get the better of the Russian players as he receives his punishment for such persistence, a sneaky forearm block as he jogs back to the halfway line. Joe reacts furiously but the ref's seen it and the Russian is shown a yellow card. The fans love the commitment and "One Joe Allen, there's only one Joey Allen!" rings out from the red corner.

Joe Ledley's had a fine game as well, winning possession back frequently, then looking to mount attacks with a swift pass forward. He picks out a run forward from Chris Gunter with a long diagonal ball and Gunter gives it back to Aaron just outside the penalty area. Sam Vokes is standing just on the edge of the box, our furthest man forward – and offside – but the pass isn't aimed at Sam because Aaron's spotted yet another late run from Bale, coming in from a wide position. The Russians have stepped up, expecting the flag but Sam's not 'active' – not interfering with play – and Gareth receives the ball, all alone bar the keeper, eight yards out. Has Akinfeev ever had a busier game than this? Once again, he's off his line smartly to try and stop it but, as he arrives, even though the ball's really on his right side, Gareth does something clever with his left foot, and he manages to get the ball across the keeper's body, beyond his reach and inside the far post, 3-0, game over, job done!

Now, now, now, I can relax. Now I can enjoy it, really, really enjoy it. No tension, no fear. Just joy, happiness, and a prolonged jump up and down in the arms of my comrades. I've been so utterly fixated on the game, in fact on all three games, that I've been in a bubble. The two previous games have been close, hard fought and nail-biting right to the end; this is different. I've now got twenty lovely minutes to take it all in, to enjoy this utterly incredible experience. To marvel at what we're watching; a Welsh football team playing terrific football

– proper, top quality international standard football – in a vital game against a country fifty times the size of our own. It's hard not to get emotional, tears start to roll down my cheeks. I think of my *Taid*. He's a lot of what I'm about, I've got his DNA. I think of Gary Speed, his name is chanted again this evening. They'll both be enjoying this, somewhere.

I had these feelings of elation in Israel when we were 3-0 up in the qualifier with twenty minutes to go but then I was sitting by the touchline and next to the away dugout – suit on, at work – elation internalised. Tonight, I'm just a fan, in my bucket hat, trainers and shorts. I can sing and dance and stand on my chair and hug the people around me. This is what I came for. We all know now, we're going through.

The only question is whether we go through as winners or runners-up. I'm not that concerned. The aim at the start of the tournament was to get beyond the group stage, nothing more. We're going to do that. Song after song, chant after chant roars out from every Welsh throat in the stadium. As the clock ticks down, the manager can start to think about that next match. There'll plenty of recovery time if we're second and playing in Nice on Monday but what if it's Paris on Saturday? The board goes up for Joe Allen to come off and there's a huge ovation from the fans. What a performance! His name rings out again, then it's the Joe Ledley song, as his turn for a rest comes around, *Ain't nobody, Like Joe Ledley...*, we groove along with the funky brass sounds of The Barry Horns, 'Makes me happy, Makes me feel this way...' The truth is, it's the whole team that makes me happy, that makes me feel this way. On cue, as I experience something like pure happiness, we sing about having a pure heart again.

The last ten minutes fly by. Wales compound Russia's humiliation by keeping possession of the ball for most of those minutes. Every pass is greeted with a cheer, the rare Russian touches with a boo. There's even a first chance of the game for the men in white, as their fans stream towards the exits. They finally work space for a cross but Ben Davies steps in front of the one striker and in doing so probably just does enough to put him off. Right in front of goal, Dzyuba can only divert the ball over the bar and they're denied even that consolation. I can only imagine what the reaction to this result is going to be back home for these lads, I suspect a transfer to Lokomotiv Siberia awaits!

Bale's next to get the call, three goals in three games for him but he'll be as pleased as anyone tonight that Wales have proved this is much more than a 'one man team'. I'm happy to see Simon Church come on for his first taste of tournament football. He's another loyal servant, another I've followed since I got to know him as an Under-21 international. Like Sam, Simon's English-born but totally committed to Wales. He's had a tough season of club football, been moved around and in and out the team, this is his reward for such sterling service to the national team.

The board goes up, Aaron has one more crack at matching Gagey's half-time prediction but we're not going to be greedy, 3-0 is fine thanks. Somebody behind me taps me on the shoulder to ask for a selfie and as I'm smiling into the camera phone, I miss the final whistle.

The players head over – triumphant – and we stay exactly where we are to salute them. It's probably the greatest Welsh performance I've ever seen. I was there when we beat Germany and Italy in qualifiers, even Belgium in the last campaign but it wasn't like this. We nicked it against them, won by an odd goal, rode our luck. In this game we dominated from start to finish and we comprehensively outplayed the opposition. The type of football we played was way beyond anything I've witnessed with Wales before.

As the players dance around in front of us with Joe Ledley demonstrating some exciting new moves, the PA announcer offers congratulations to the Wales team for getting through, then there's another big cheer as the graphic showing the final group table goes up on the big screen at our end. England's game has finished 0-0, 'We are top of the league, We are top of the league!

We came hoping to see a goal, we saw that. We came hoping to see a win, we saw that. We came hoping to see Wales go through, we saw that. We came never daring to dream Wales could win the group but look, that big screen, see that? Played 3, won 2, lost 1, for 6, against 3. Group B winners, Wales!

I do have a quick think about how this is going to impact upon my wife's birthday plans as the players and coaching staff continue to celebrate with the fans? Getting to Paris should be okay, it's the getting back that's the challenge. Still, it's Paris, a major capital, there'll be a way.

We stay in the stadium for ages, still singing and soaking it all in.

I spy Gruff and Guto from the Furries – they look knackered – maybe it's been a bit noisy on the tour bus? Bunff from the band's there as well and I stride over towards him, clutching my plastic UEFA bag with the girls' T-shirts in it. We do a little jig. Seeing the SFA lads just brings home how this has turned into the absolutely perfect music and football weekend.

Finally, some fans start to drift away and as we make our way towards the exit, some of the FAW staff are now over in our corner. I see the masseur, Chris Senior, and he shouts and waves. He's carrying an expensive looking camera and firing off shots of all the players and the celebrations, he beckons me over and points the lens in my direction so I give him a big smile and a clenched fist. Chris is typical of the backroom staff, dedicated to the Welsh cause despite being from Huddersfield – a team player – as thrilled to witness this as any of us. I can't wait to see his album from this one.

Osian Roberts has also come over to meet members of his family or friends and lots of fans congregate round him, shake his hand, ask for pictures. He's happy to oblige. A Welsh speaking Welshman, I know just how much it means to him to see the national team succeed, he's dedicated his life to improving the game in the country. Tonight's success has a lot to do with that work and, going forward, should be further enhanced by what's been achieved in Toulouse this evening. I manage a quick word and a shake of the hand before he disappears into the crowd. Beyond Osh, Mark Evans is also enjoying the moment. He's another man who, like me, would describe himself as a fan first and foremost, just one who got lucky. We're used to pacing up and down nervously alongside each other in the tunnel at various stadia across Europe, tonight I'm back on the other side of the fence but Mark knows how much it means, we embrace across the actual barrier that divides us.

Then we're up the tunnel, out of the stadium and it's clear the party's just getting started. There's a band playing – not The Barry Horns – some local guys but there's a lot of brass involved and Wales fans are whirling each other around, dancing wild jigs: Joe Ledley would love it. I bump into lots of friends in the midst of this crazy hoedown. The lads who've been staying in the Abbey, Gwilym, Rhys and Alun Boore, Gary Pritchard and his wife Mari. Their children are with them too, school having been taken off the curriculum for a couple of weeks. In fact, the kids are holding up a Welsh flag with the legend, *Pêl-droed Cyn Addysg* written across it in large letters: 'Football Before Education'. Gary's daughter is in the middle of her GCSE's so she's going to have to go home but I'm not sure the rest of the youthful posse will be back behind a desk before next Monday. Dylan Llewelyn's there as well, almost speechless. It's almost that time when the old boys like us are feeling drained. We've spent a lifetime waiting for this. It's hard to find the words. It's just great to watch new generations of Wales fans having the time of their lives – *pêl-droed cyn addysg* – the optimistic, energetic future of Welsh football.

Reluctantly we leave the stadium, the band still playing. It's getting late and we've actually got an early start, plus the lads have bought tickets for the last metro train back to La Vache and a shuttle bus that the campsite's organised to get everyone home. We head off into the night. Across the road from the stadium, a fine smell drifts towards us. It's the smell of food cooking. We haven't eaten since lunchtime and the sight of a big grill covered in sausages – yes, more sausages – cannot be ignored. It's a double spicy sausage hot dog and *frites* all round, best €6 I've ever spent! We eat as we walk.

We're following signs to the city centre and Steve and I recognise the street as the one we walked down and then back up in our attempt to find the festival site on Saturday. We remember there's a pub a little further up and, sure enough, we spot the crowd outside. *Bar L'Evasion* is proving to be a popular watering hole on the walk back towards the Palais De Justice station. It's been a long time since the last beer, so this is to be savoured. There's more singing, of course, but as we stand and chat, the Anglesey pirate from last night approaches. He seems pleased to see us. He's panicking about getting back to the camp – him and his mate both reckon they won't be able to do it alone, they'll get lost – I think this may have happened to them before. Steve and Andy promise to look after them, to make sure they get back to base safely, the lads look genuinely grateful.

Our small party makes a move after one beer as time is ticking on, it's well past midnight now, and we make the short walk to the station. From there, I hop off at Jean Jaurès, saying my farewells quickly before the perspex doors slide back shut and my pals head off into the night. I've got a short walk back to the hotel. If I'd passed a bar that was open, I might just have been tempted but I don't, not before I reach the front door of the hotel – central Toulouse appears to have closed down for the night – so ring the bell for admittance. There's no bar here, but I'm not going to be entirely thwarted. I spot a sign behind the reception desk that suggests bottles of water and beer are available to purchase. I order one of each.

Back up in my room, adrenaline still flowing through me, I get the chance to recharge my flat phone and as the power flows through it, it pings away with all the text messages coming in, it seems a lot of people have shared in our success tonight. My mind turns to what comes next and I start to check flights to Paris. Can I get there and back from Leeds? Can I get back on Saturday night? If not, how early can I get back on Sunday, the big day? It would seem the answer to questions one and two is no. It's 2am and I still haven't got a plan. I've got to be up and out in a little over six hours, so I set the alarm, switch off the light, and lay my head down, with a broad smile across my face.

Tuesday, 21st June

I'm up and awake and down in the breakfast room all too soon. I don't really think I've taken full advantage of having a proper bed to sleep in but, with my bag already packed, at least I can dive in the shower before I go down for breakfast.

There's a copy of *L'Equipe* on the table by the dining room door. I pick it up on my way out and sneak it into my bag before I pass reception. I'm tired, my head's full of Paris and I suffer a mini travel disaster at the Metro station. I buy a ticket, put it in the machine and it disappears. I look on in despair. There's no one to tell, no staff, just an old security guy who can't work out my problem. I can do nothing but go back and buy another ticket.

Despite this hiatus, I reach La Vache just in time to hop aboard the bus back to the stop near the camp site. I share the ride with a south Walian chap who looks like he's also heading to the same place and who has spent the night in a French woman's apartment. She apparently took pity on him when he got a bit 'tired and emotional' and couldn't work out where he was anymore. I wonder if he was an *homme d'honneur*? He's not really a football fan, he admits, he's more into surf boarding but he's come over for 'the experience'.

Off the bus and back towards the campsite, where there's lot of activity, it seems many people are heading home today. One of the vans leaving the site's being driven by Dan, who works in the Wrexham club shop. Actually, it's not a camper van, it's an actual transit with the back loaded with mattresses and camping equipment: that must have been interesting for the 3 intrepid travellers. I stop for a chat and, like me, these lads are wondering just how they're going to get themselves home and then back again in time for Saturday?

I walk back through the site. Some fans are still sleeping off the celebrations, others preparing for the next stage of this *Tour de France*, my pals included. Fair play, they're just about ready for departure but it appears the big pack up hasn't been without it's issues. Well, one major issue involving a leaking toilet. Apparently they awoke to a flood and had to quickly mount a mop up operation that's cost the lives of several tea towels. We'd had no problems previously – the toilet 'cartridge' has been emptied regularly and we've been operating a 'no solids' policy since after that first night spent in the car park where the cartridge emptying operation proved particularly unpleasant, or so Steve tells me, I missed that one...

We give the van one last wipe down – there's still a vague whiff of urine in the air it has to be said – then climb aboard. Steve's at the wheel, Evo's in the passenger seat and I've opted to sit at the table behind them. I have some work to do; Mission Paris begins in earnest between here and Bordeaux. We have to get Gareth back by 12 noon, so we leave Toulouse on schedule at 9.30am, which is good going when you consider the long day we had yesterday. It's a pretty straight run, 140 miles or so, and when a call comes from the lady at the camper van company to check on our return, I'm able to confirm we'll be there at the agreed time. They have a base in Bordeaux so she's going to come and meet us when we hand it back.

We're soon on the *autoroute* and cruising. In the back, however, whilst searching for cheap flights, I'm also keeping one eye on the floor. There are still puddles and every time the van brakes a little, a surge of liquid breaks like a wave from under the bathroom door. I leap up with the last remaining tea towel to try and soak it up. I have a theory that this may be connected to the rear end shunt, there may yet be more than that dent to knock out when the insurance claim goes in.

We have one last fuel stop as we need to return the van with the same amount in the tank as there was when we collected it. This proves to be troublesome. There's a designated area of the station forecourt for vans and larger vehicles and we join a queue behind another camper van, with UK plates. In fact, both available pumps are occupied. Except, there's nobody using the pumps and no sign of anybody in the vans. We sit and wait for movement for about five minutes and nothing happens. More people pull up behind us. Steve's getting angry now. He jumps out to go and investigate and he's even angrier when he comes back. The lads in the vans have all gone to get something to eat! They're Wales fans so I can't be too judgemental, Steve is less forgiving. The message must have reached the drivers and their mates in the service station *café* as they suddenly appear, clutching baguettes, keeping their eyes firmly fixed on the ground as they jog back to their vehicles so as to avoid the angry stares.

Back on the road, Evo sets about translating the sports paper headline, '*Les Etonnants Gallois!*' It's fairly straightforward as it turns out, 'The Amazing Welshmen!' I like that! I don't like the flights I'm coming up with for Paris though. The aim of the exercise is seemingly a simple one, find a flight that gets me back home as soon as possible on Rachel's birthday. The problem is, there aren't many flights back on a Sunday morning. I don't suppose there's much call for them, if you go to Paris for a weekend, you want to make the most of it and fly back later. Somewhere like Heathrow has the most choice and early options but that involves a three to four hour drive home tagged on the end, so even if I fly back first thing on Sunday morning, it'll be early afternoon before I get home. I suppose I could drive down and straight back but we've done thousands of miles on the road in the last fortnight and that prospect doesn't really appeal – get home, unpack, mow the lawn, repack, drive to France again – *Non, merci.*

Talking of mowing the lawn, Rachel's had a crack at it whilst I've been away. It hasn't gone well – apparently she's broken the lawnmower. Clearly my presence is required urgently, systems are starting to fail in my absence. When I'm away covering Wales for work, I often get a phone call from my wife, usually right in the middle of doing an interview or something important, with a plaintive voice on the other end of the line saying, "Hiya, I can't get the telly to work...", or "The hamster's dead."

We roll into Bordeaux just about on time and follow the satnav directions back to the college where we first met the owner before being whizzed off into the suburbs. Evo's got time to go for a look around Bordeaux before his flight back. He's keen to buy some cheese to take home as a gift so we wish him a fond farewell, a little jealous of the fact that he'll be back in the UK this evening, whereas we have another long drive ahead of us. I go and collect my car from the car park, which all goes smoothly. As I hit the *Sortie* button on the parking app, the gate opens and I'm free.

As I emerge onto the street, the lady from the rental company comes over and introduces herself, having spotted the camper van. We all head back to where this epic journey began, ready to give Gareth back and to move all our stuff from van to car.

As we're transporting bags and barbecues from one vehicle to the other, the owner appears. She's never seemed particularly happy in our presence but now she's positively scowling. She barely offers a greeting and walks round the back to survey the damage before going to sit in the back. She summons Camille, the rental company rep, and talks at her in a low voice. Camille then comes back over to where I'm standing on the pavement. She has two issues to discuss. She wants to know if it will be alright for her to record my thoughts on the experience of renting the van through her company? They've only been going a short time and they'd value the feedback from a British customer as they're keen on offering their services more widely in the UK. That's fine. Oh, and the owner is not happy, she says the van should have been cleaned and it's dirty. That's not fine.

A pretty bizarre episode then plays out on the pavement as Camille points her camera phone at me, pushes record and I automatically go into full-on veteran broadcaster mode to deliver a report on the camper van experience. It's all done in one take as I make some general suggestions, one or two criticisms but overall rate the experience as being positive. No sooner have I finished this than Camille is back to tell me the owner wants to know what I'm going to do about the fact her van is dirty, could I go and clean it now? We're in the middle of Bordeaux, we still have to drive 5 hours north to Rouen, this option is rejected out of hand. It was in the contract, apparently, that the van be returned in the same state it was handed over.

Steve's getting pretty exasperated by this stage as well. We left the campsite first thing this morning, when were we meant to clean it? All these observations are relayed back across the road and into the camper van to the angry looking owner. I feel sorry for Camille, she's doing the UN peacekeeping role between two factions who seem increasingly intent on war. I can see where this is going. "Okay, tell her we don't have time to get the van cleaned but I'll give her €20 to go and get it done herself." Camille nods solemnly and crosses back over to the van to deliver my offer. She returns. "Yes, she says that is acceptable." War is averted.

Steve keeps it together sufficiently to wave an *au revoir* at the scowling figure still sitting hunched over the table in the van. I walk across – pretty livid by now – and silently chuck a €20 note onto the table in front of her. It's a poor show I know but it's not as if we damaged her van, someone drove into us and if we'd known it needed cleaning, we'd have cleaned it. When we picked it up, the guy explained what we needed to do before returning it and we've done all those things. As I walk back to my car, I figure now probably isn't the best time to mention the leaking toilet. The whole episode's left a bit of a bad taste in the mouth, and a bad whiff in the van.

I'm back at the wheel now and I point the car north; we should be in Rouen by early evening. Steve dozes off and I tune the radio to a very weak BBC signal to get a crackly commentary on Germany v Northern Ireland. The Germans score early and look set for a big win but the Northern Ireland keeper, Michael McGovern, makes a string of top class saves to deny them another goal. That's two defeats for the Irish but their one group win means they finish third, and they'll now have to wait to see if that will be good enough for them to go through. It seems a bit mad to lose two out of three games and still go through but that's the result of the expanded tournament that helped Wales qualify, so I'm not complaining.

We reach our destination, a small hotel on an industrial park on the edge of Rouen, at about 6.30pm. It's not a mezzanine as it turns out, the three beds in this family room are all in line on the same floor. We dump our overnight bags and Steve has to perform emergency repairs on his reading glasses which are now in a worse state than the camper van toilet. He's using small bits of tape to try and hold them together. The appearance created is very 'Jack Duckworth' (kids, ask your dad).

We have Wi-Fi now so it's a chance to do a bit more work on Paris which now involves Steve, as he weighs up whether he will be making the return trip. The awards ceremony he's attending means he can't go on Friday so he's investigating Saturday options. He comes up with an interesting suggestion – Doncaster – early on Saturday and there's a flight back early on Sunday. Doncaster! Forty-five minutes from my front door! Why didn't I think of that?

I'm mulling this one over in my mind as we head over the road to the 'Buffalo Grill' for tea. As the name suggests, there isn't a vegetarian option. We order and as we await the arrival of a plate of onion rings, I check the exact details and the prices of the Paris trip. It'll be £300 but it'll get me back to Doncaster by 10.30am on Sunday and I'd be home before lunch on my wife's big day. There's a party planned but it isn't until late afternoon. Next step – I check my hotel booking app. A workable plan is being hatched. Fly out Saturday morning, get a hotel at the airport, drop my bag off, into Paris, watch the match, back to the airport hotel then up and out for the return flight at 10.05am. In the circumstances, that seems just about spot on. I quickly find a fairly cheap hotel which offers a free shuttle service to and from the airport. I book it. Then, as the main course appears, I book the flights. My match ticket's already sorted as I'd ticked the box, for the next two rounds after the group stage, on the order form from the FAW. So now I'm all set, 'Que sera sera, Whatever will be, will be, I'm going to gay Paree'. I remind myself to ring Rachel once we're back in the hotel and I won't be cross about the lawnmower.

There's another game to watch this evening, Spain v Croatia, but there's nothing resembling a bar where we're staying so we head back to the room to watch it and a general catch-up via the Wi-Fi. The news is full of the Brexit referendum build-up and reports from Calais of trouble around the refugee camps, with suggestions that cars with GB plates have been targeted by protesters.

There's no mention of any of this on the BBC News website as far as I can see, but a couple of the Leave supporting news sites are going big on it. I guess the inference is, do you really want these people coming in? Needless to say, I mention this to Steve. We're driving to Calais tomorrow morning, having avoided any aggro anywhere for the last fortnight and we're keen to make sure we don't run into a riot just as we're about to leave France.

I make FaceTime contact with the family, so I can deliver news of my travel plans in a more 'personal' manner. I think it works. I get an okay and I offer commiserations about the lawnmower situation. I'll be back tomorrow and, truth be told, I'm very much looking forward to it. If I didn't have Steve with me, I'd have contemplated hanging on in France but it would be tough on my own for a few days and budget hotels on the edge of town are probably about all I could afford given the way everyone's hiked up their prices for the tournament. So, home seems the best option, quick recharge, proper sleep, then back out.

As we settle down for the night, it seems that despite waving him off at midday, Evo isn't yet at the point of putting his head on the pillow. His text messages recount a tale of travel woe that began with his cheese being confiscated by customs for being 'too soft', this after an Irish couple in the queue ahead of him had their set of *boules* confiscated for being 'too hard'. It's not over either, he's currently stuck in Piccadilly station as all trains across the Pennines have been cancelled for some reason. It's even more complicated than that. He's been sent from one station to another in Manchester, only to keep being told 'There aren't any trains from here, try the other one'. It's a travel saga of Barry Horne proportions.

My last task of the day, before lights out, is to see whether there's any clue as to who we'll actually be playing in Paris? The only update is that it could be Northern Ireland as, with Turkey beating the Czech Republic 2-0, they squeeze through as one of the four best third-placed teams. It's down to three now, the Irish, Turkey or Albania. Of the three options, I'd take the latter.

5

Paris
Wales v Northern Ireland

'I've got used to Bryn going away to watch Wales over the last 18 years or so. He missed his very first wedding anniversary for a trip to Finland and I don't think he's been home for one since! So, I was fairly relaxed about him clearing off to France, for two weeks at least. I don't really understand football but I do understand that going meant a lot to him. I became a bit more concerned when he tried to explain the implications of Wales doing well and the possibility that he might not be home after two weeks after all. My concerns grew when he warned me that Wales going through from their group might well mean he'd miss my 'significant' birthday. I had to warn him, if that was the case, it might not be worth him coming home from France at all.'
Rachel Law (Long-suffering wife)

Wednesday, 22nd June

It's my 47th birthday and it's the first time, since we got married and had children, that I haven't been at home for it. It's a strange feeling, usually everyone gathers in the bedroom for present opening before they go off to school or work. Today it's just me and Steve, who clearly hasn't got me anything – nor actually remembered – as I get nothing more than a "Morning!" as a greeting before we head down for breakfast.

There's not a lot of time to kill before we need to be back on the road.

The ferry's at midday and we've got 200 more miles to do, the last bit of which may be a bit slow due to flying rocks and angry Afghans.

In fact, we hit a delay much closer to home. We came off the *autoroute* a few minutes away from the hotel but the satnav directs us back onto it via Rouen itself and we get caught up in the morning rush hour. It's the not the start to my birthday I'd have wanted. It's a bit fraught until we finally emerge from the city and get back on the open road. The journey thereafter goes smoothly, but Steve's checking for any more reports of trouble at our destination. The obvious place to look – the Daily Mail website – has nothing new to say. Steve's also wrestling with the thorny issue of whether or not to travel to Paris. He hasn't got a ticket yet and I'd initially only ordered one, although I offer to check if there might be any more available.

We approach Calais with a sense of trepidation. It's quite a while since I've been here. We used to cross to and from Dover regularly on family holidays but, in recent years, we've been sailing from Portsmouth. It's obvious a lot has happened in the meantime. The approach road to Calais – all the areas at the side of the road – is bordered by high metal fences. As we get closer to the ferry port, we can see one of the vast refugee camps, then police vans parked on the hard shoulder, with officers in riot gear standing idle by the side of the road. The prospect of the UK closing the door to these people permanently will surely have an impact on this roadside city.

It's hard not to think that the whole Referendum issue basically centres on what's happened here. The images of hordes of refugees, desperately trying to get into the UK, jumping onto lorries and the like, have been widely reported. It can't be a coincidence that something close to a mainstream anti-immigration party has emerged in Britain in the last few years. First it was 'Sangatte', the camp that was closed in 2002, whilst more recently it's been 'The Jungle' that's been the subject of so much coverage. Much of the discussion and campaigning has been about the financial impact of being in or out, or lawmaking, or straight bananas but I think, to many people, the EU question is who do we have to let in? But the EU's 'free movement' policy does not apply to refugees and migrants from Africa or the Middle East – these are not Polish plumbers or Latvian lorry drivers – these desperate people wouldn't be waiting in squalid conditions hoping to sneak into the UK in the back of a truck if they could just hop on a ferry.

Whether the UK is in or out of the EU there will probably still be refugees, and some will still make an effort to get across the Channel. The only difference is that the EU may see the chance to shift the problem across the channel and have the UK border checks at Dover instead.

Our final approach to the ferry port is unhindered and we join the line for an earlier crossing than the one I'd booked. As we board, it's clear the exodus of football fans is well underway, with lots of national shirts on display in the bars and restaurants. I have more orders to follow as far as the onboard shop's concerned, Rachel has tasked me with bringing back bargain booze for her party, so I buy boxes of red, white and rose and transport them with some difficulty to a table. From there I send an email to the FAW asking if there might be another Paris ticket, for Steve. A reply comes back quite quickly, 'yes, no problem, we'll add it to your order'. They've already got my credit card details, so they can just use those to make the purchase. This appears to be good news but only if Steve actually wants to go, if not I'm about to be charged for a ticket I don't need. There's no sign of Steve so I attempt to make contact by phone and text. After a few minutes he appears and I pass on the good news. He still hasn't made his mind up though and the flight price has gone up, presumably as more Wales fans have cottoned onto this potential route over? It's up to £400 now. He's not sure whether he wants to pay that much. If he doesn't want the ticket, I feel a need to retract the request fairly swiftly, before they've processed it. The poor bloke's in a real quandary and I've put him on the spot. He decides not to do it so I send the email that says I won't need an extra ticket after all.

After a short ferry crossing, there's the inevitable long drive home. The long, empty stretches of well-maintained roads we enjoyed in France are replaced by the crowded, crumbling motorways of England. We started the journey with rush hour in Rouen and we end it with rush hour in Leeds – no less frustrating but at least I know where I'm going. I deliver Steve to his front door and help to unload his gear. We have a hug and bring an end to an excellent adventure. I've enjoyed his company, he's been an invaluable asset on the driving front and I think we've both had two weeks we'll remember for the rest of our lives. I'm sure Andrew approves, he's been with us all the way. I head across town and home, pulling onto the drive at 6.15pm, fourteen days and five hours after I pulled off it. Quite a bit's happened in between, not least the fact that I'm a year older.

The dog races out to greet me as the front door opens. Rachel's next, with a big hug and a kiss, but the girls are both out, socialising or something. I eat my birthday tea outside and have a chat with my wife. Megan comes back briefly, before heading out again to someone else's party, then Millie appears. So, we're briefly all together, enough time for me to distribute my gifts to them – the only bad news being that the chocolate bar sprinkled in gold dust from Dinard has broken in transit. The *brocante* items from Bordeaux go down well with Rachel, as – needless to say – does the wine and the two Euro 2016 T-shirts both fit the girls. A set of nail varnishes each from the ferry is also well received by both daughters. In return, there are a few birthday gifts for me and cards to read. With the present swap complete, I retire to the lounge to watch Ireland v Italy.

Millie joins me, explaining that she's really got into watching the tournament and she's been keeping up with Wales. She watched Monday's game on her own at home, most of it anyway, missed the first two goals but jumped up to cheer when Gareth got the third. Given that she's Leeds born and bred, this is progress. She qualifies for Wales through her *Nain*, her Welsh Grandmother. The England game was on in the classroom whilst she was in a cookery lesson at school and she promises me she didn't celebrate when Sturridge scored.

There's late drama in the game we're watching now as well, with the Republic scoring in the last few minutes to win and guarantee their progress to the knockout stage. I'm sure my pal from behind the bar in Bowes pub in Dublin is enjoying his trip as much as I enjoyed mine. Other scores from the evening mean we now know our opponents as well, it'll be Northern Ireland on Saturday. I'm glad I booked early, the price of flights from the UK to Paris is about to climb even higher. Finally – football over, eyes heavy – climbing into my own bed feels like the best gift of the day, a decent night's sleep will be the second best. This, I really have missed.

Thursday, June 23rd

Mission accomplished on the sleep front, I feel energised enough to go out for a dog walk with Megan and we talk through the GCSE's

I've missed since I've been away. Her overall assessment is positive, although she's not about to get carried away, which is good. It's like me with Wales, caution is the watchword but I know it will be fine.

Back home, I'm aware that there's an important job to do, I'm reminded of it every time I look out of the back window. I head off to the garage, get the lawnmower going again, and reduce the height of the grass to a more respectable length.

Once that's done, I feel I deserve a treat, so I sit down to watch a recording of the Slovakia game, the S4C version with Nic Parri's commentary and Malcolm Allen shouting a lot alongside him. *Ardderchog*! as we say in Welsh!

Steve's back in touch later, on the hunt for tickets again. It seems that when he told his wife he'd turned down a ticket, she said, "Why did you that?! It's a once in a lifetime opportunity." My chances of helping out are now slim so I refer him to the UEFA ticket portal. It's the place they'll be sticking any spare tickets. The other option is to take a gamble and just go and try and pick one up outside but he's reluctant to try that given the cost of the flight out.

Talking of big decisions about Europe, Rachel comes home from work and we walk up to the polling booth together to cast our vote.

There's no game today, a break between the group stage and the knockout. The only Euro coverage is tonight and revolves around the Referendum, the only result that matters is whether we stay or go. We aren't due to find out until the early hours of tomorrow morning. I'm still catching up with sleep so I decide to call it a day before David Dimbleby's had a chance to say much more than, 'Hello, good evening and welcome..', or was that someone else? There's a last check on the internet before I go to sleep, the markets are up which suggests the City of London clearly feels confident, and I read a quote from Nigel Farage that says he believes there will be a narrow margin in favour of Remain. Reassured, I sleep well.

Friday, 24th June

I awake just after 7am, at roughly the same time as my wife. She mutters, "What's the result?" and I reach down to the side of the bed to pick up my iPad. I only need to press on the screen to know, as there are notifications of social media messages I've received whilst the tablet's been inactive. The tone of them tells the story. It's Leave. I go from slumber to wide awake in an instant. I let Rachel know, even as I'm seeking final confirmation from the news websites and, there it is, we're out!

We head downstairs together to watch the news. The markets are opening and the pound's crashed. We have a holiday in Portugal planned for next month, luckily most of it is paid for, but I suggest we're going to be eating in a lot. Rachel always has a good question for a time like this, one that you hadn't considered: "Will we still be in the Eurovision song contest?" Our removal would be one of the few benefits I could identify but sadly, I think the answer is "Yes".

My two daughters are watching the news with us. Both have spent lots of summer holidays in France or Spain, we've had exchange student visits and school trips to Berlin and Paris, they know 'Europe' and both seem a bit nonplussed about suddenly not being 'part of it'. I'm exactly the same. I've travelled around most of Europe – I like it a lot – in fact I have never really had a desire to travel further afield, to Asia or America, as everything I want is here.

I know I won't be stopped from crossing the channel just yet, which is a good job as I'm booked on a flight to Paris in less than 24 hours, but it will feel strange being perceived as 'British' rather than 'European'. It doesn't feel like progress.

The fact that I'm heading back over so soon definitely adds to my sense of bewilderment. The figures show that Wales voted in favour of Leave. This I find staggering. I'm no expert but I know EU money supports many projects in Wales, particularly in areas where it's hard to attract investment because of their relative isolation. Is that investment going to be matched by a government in London? It seems a big gamble.

I would guess immigration has played a large part in the vote but it's a complex issue in Wales. Many people I know, particularly from the west of the country – both north and south, the Welsh speaking areas – would say that it's the people coming in from England who bring the greatest threat in terms of changing the culture, and not being able to or even wanting to speak the native language. On the other hand, the town I grew up in, Wrexham, is home to a large Polish population now, and there are lots of Portuguese people there as well. So much so that Wrexham Council recently suggested that Welsh was now the 4th most popular language in the Borough, behind English, Polish and Portuguese. I can see why people think that doesn't seem right in terms of the impact on a small town.

What makes it even harder to work out is what I've just seen with my own eyes over the last fortnight. Tens of thousands of Welsh people enjoying 'Europe', putting up with the problems patiently, embracing the local population and mixing happily with people from other countries. It doesn't seem to tally with that vote, and yet not everyone who's been going to the games can have voted Remain, not by any stretch of the imagination. I find myself wondering whether I've been sitting next to people who voted Leave? It's a strange train of thought but I feel perplexed at having seemingly got this one so wrong.

It's a sense that only grows as I see that Northern Ireland voted in favour of Remain. Maybe I'm only thinking about this in simplistic football terms, but Northern Ireland supporters are usually associated with strong support of 'the Union'. At games they sing *God Save The Queen* and fly the Union Jack alongside the Red Hand of Ulster flag. Wales fans fly the Welsh dragon, emphasising a 'difference', yet it's Northern Ireland that's voted in favour of maintaining ties with Europe over going it alone with Britain. Scotland did the same, so it's England and Wales who want out?

It's a very strange day. Life goes on and I go out and do some shopping, to get Rachel some birthday gifts and a card, so she'll have some more stuff to open on Sunday. As I walk around, I find myself trying to work out who's voted what, and will we be split on these lines forever? I pick Megan up from an exam and vow to try and do nothing but focus on family then football. It's hard though, especially as Megan declares that as a result of the vote, she's going to move to Canada. One other statistic the day's produced suggests young people voted overwhelmingly in favour of Remain. I guess it's more likely to be people of their grandparents' age who voted for Leave. This generational split does not bode well for future harmony. My head's a mess. I should be so excited about the biggest game I've ever been to but I'm not. It seems the last two weeks were the final carefree, halcyon days. I view the future with trepidation. We haven't had a big war for a while, are people bored with peace?

After tea, I pack a small bag and prepare to settle down in the guest room as I don't want to wake up everybody when I get up. I wrap the gifts, write the card and switch the light off. I'm up at 4.30am.

Saturday, 25th June – Euro 2016 Match Day 4

Actually, I'm awake three hours ahead of the alarm and immediately my head's full of the EU vote again. I wrestle with it, manage to doze off again and secure a couple more hours kip before I get up with the first rays of the sun pushing through the blinds. Still, I can't see a lot in the dark and I stagger around getting my clothes on and trying to find my phone, my wallet and my camera. The latter proves elusive and an extensive and increasingly frantic search fails to find it. In the end, I have to enter our bedroom and shuffle things around, lift things up and generally create a low-level rumpus that inevitably wakes Rachel up. I mumble an apology as I check various pockets. My hand wraps round the offending article and I slip out again, damage done.

There's still time for breakfast before I set off. If ever there was a good time to drive down the A1, this is it, Saturday at 4.45am. I've never actually been to what's officially called Robin Hood Doncaster airport before so I've set the satnav to help me find it. It's a new airport, opened a little more than 10 years ago, but the approach roads appear to be much newer than that as they don't actually appear on the map screen on the dashboard, which is indicating that I'm currently speeding across green fields.

Less than an hour after leaving home, I'm parked up in the short stay zone – the long stay was shut – and walking towards the terminal building. It's not a big site so it's not a long walk. I like that. From car park to departures in two minutes: my kind of airport! It doesn't appear to be very busy either, the doors slide open and I enter the building, already checked-in, so I follow signs to a small desk where a guy greets me, scans my boarding pass and directs me on to the bag check.

There's a short queue, which gives me time to remove the belt I'm wearing, the belt that holds up the same grey shorts I wore in Toulouse, combined with another special SO58 T-shirt – the one with the Eiffel Tower on the front – the same Reebok Paris trainers – appropriately – and, naturally, the bucket hat, although it's in my bag just for now. In other words, I'm wearing almost everything I wore for Russia. Everything has been washed though, I hope that doesn't affect their lucky powers?

As I get everything ready to ensure a swift move through the scanner area, I glance up at the wall and, level with my head, there's a plaque. It's the blue European Union flag and it records the fact that this airport was opened in 2005 with the assistance of EU investment. I can't imagine the staff are feeling too confident about their long-term prospects this morning either, WizzAir use this as a base for flights to Eastern Europe, Poland in particular.

No beeps and I'm straight into the main hall. There's a Wetherspoon's at its heart and there are one or two people sitting at tables nursing a pint, even at this ungodly hour. Too early for me, I'm not sure real ale would mix well with the porridge I'm still digesting.

I'm expecting to see a few red shirts around but there don't seem to be any, surprisingly however there are some England shirts around. There's a flight out to Malaga before ours but even after that's been called, the shirts with the three lions are still dotted around, and they join the Paris queue when it's our turn. I get chatting with a chap in front of me. He's had an earlier start than I have, he's flown in from the Falklands! He's meeting his mates in Paris, as they'd expected England to qualify top of the group, but instead they're now having to make their way down to Nice.

Now I get it, and it becomes even clearer when we board. The ticket prices were high but the plane's only about a third full. The pilot confirms it as he makes his pre-flight announcement, "We're supposed to be full according to the manifest but it looks like a lot of passengers haven't turned up...". England fans have got in early and bought the seats when the flights were much cheaper, expecting to win the group, but didn't, so haven't bothered turning up.

There's plenty of room to spread out and, once we're up in the air, I claw back some of the sleep I lost to the EU last night. I awake with the plane already on the approach to Charles de Gaulle. The next trip, on the shuttle bus, from where the plane's stopped to arrivals, is almost as long as the flight but I'm straight off to passport control, joining the short EU line with an anxious glance over at the long queues up to the non-EU desk: got to enjoy it while it lasts!

The next stage of the journey should be straight-forward. I want to get the bus to my hotel, drop my bag off and return to the airport so I can get the train into Paris. I don't like leaving things to chance and have researched the route I need to follow. I turn left confidently, following the airport hotel signs. *En route*, it's clear Charles de Gaulle is a bit like Leicester Forest East motorway services on a Saturday lunchtime, a hub for football fans from all over. I see Croatia shirts, Republic of Ireland, Northern Ireland and, of course, lots of Wales shirts.

I find the stop for my bus exactly as described and, after a bit of a wait, I get picked up and taken to the hotel. I get there five minutes before the driver's due to head back to the airport, so I check-in, race up to the room, drop my bag in and head back. I get to the lift before I realise I've left my bucket hat in the bag. I have ten seconds to make a decision. If I miss the bus, it'll be another half an hour off my pre-match beer but, if I leave it and we lose..? I race back down the corridor, grab it and run back to the lift. The driver's just walking out of reception as I get down – hat on. Ok 'drive', let's go!

Back at the airport, I want a one day travel pass – not available from the machines – so I join the queue in the ticket office and then jog off to the right platform as there's a train due to depart for the city centre shortly.

The guy on the desk gave me a map of the train system, incorporating overland and underground lines. It's a pretty complicated piece of work, on both sides of the sheet he's given me. I'm used to the London Underground and it's map which is a brilliant exercise in simplifying something that could appear unfathomable. I'm relatively new to this system having only had one afternoon in Paris previously, many years ago, but I'm not sure I'm going to get to grips with this by the time I'm heading home tonight. I do the first bit successfully. I find the RER line and the train takes 40 minutes or so to wind it's way into town. We're entertained *en route* by a couple of rappers who do their thing to a backing track as they make their way through the carriage. They're good at it as well, French hip hop and rap is something I know a bit about, there's quite a bit in my music collection. France's cultural mix of North African influences often gets skilfully interwoven with Jazz and dance to make cool rap music. It's is the sound of the urban suburbs, the *banlieues*, the same suburbs now being identified as the breeding ground for radicalised Islamic youth. One of the best gigs I've ever been to was a Parisian hiphop collective called 1995 performing at night on a beach near St Tropez. I chuck a couple of Euros into their hat as the lads move past.

I need the map again after our arrival at my destination station, Gare Du Nord. Before I do anything else, I want to get my hands on my ticket. I also have more tickets to pick up as my friend, Alun Llwyd, has asked me to collect the five he's ordered. He and his pals aren't getting into Paris until later and the FAW hotel is some distance from the stadium so, if there's any delay in their arrival, they could be in trouble. Alun has helped me out many times in the past so this is a small thing I can do in return.

Finding the hotel is my next challenge. I'm switching from the overland service to one of the underground lines now and I'm wandering around with the map, trying to identify the right exit to take from the station concourse. I need the green line to Les Halles, then a change onto the red line to Porte Maillot. In between lines I get pretty confused and end up travelling along one of those flat escalators, only to get all the way to the end and realise I need to go all the way back. The place is packed with travellers but there's nobody to ask for directions so I press on, feeling very much the bewildered tourist.

I get it right the next time and the last bit of this journey is straightforward, a short walk from the Metro to the hotel, *Le Méridien Etoile*. The lobby's thronging with people and many of them are wearing Wales shirts, presumably doing the same thing I'm doing. I head downstairs to the distribution centre. Dylan Llewelyn's down there with his son, trying to sort out tickets for his mum and dad who have made a last-minute decision to come out. He's only managed to get one ticket so his father's out and about approaching touts somewhere in the city. He looks a little fraught. This is just the reason why I wasn't keen to end up with a spare ticket and the hassle of trying to offload it.

I join the short queue and enter the brightly lit meeting room that's being used by the FAW team. I spot Lucy, a familiar face to the Wales away regulars and someone who goes out of her way to help when and if she can – she's a very popular figure – and I make sure to thank her for all her efforts on my behalf over the last few weeks. The envelope with six tickets is handed over and I feel like I should be leaving the hotel with an armed guard, given my precious cargo. On my way back out, I bump into Cian again, hat still on, brim still turned up. He's finally escaped from Toulouse and the tour bus. He heads off for a drink, I need to eat. I've been travelling since quarter to five and it's 1 o'clock now. Out of the hotel and back towards the Metro there's a restaurant advertising *moules et frites* plus a beer for €13 – in Paris – that has the look of a bargain. I'm in!

The waiter seats me at an outside table. It's a little overcast but the day's warm enough. I don't need to see a menu, I can point to the picture on the sign by the entrance. It turns out that I've taken a prominent position, as Wales fans pass me on their way to and from the hotel. Laura McAllister comes into view, she's a former Welsh international footballer, now Professor of Governance at Liverpool University, another of those incredibly well-rounded, well-read people who follow the national team. We've met before at events in Cardiff and she stops for a chat as my big bowl of *moules* arrives. She has tales of travel troubles, luckily not her own. Some friends were due to fly out from Heathrow but there's been an air traffic controllers strike and they arrived at the airport to be told their flight was cancelled. They won't be able to get out in time for the game now and they've got two tickets waiting for collection at the hotel. Imagine that?! How angry would you be? Not at the loss of the money even, though that would be bad given the price of the tickets, but more at the missing of the game.

Next to pass, mid-*moules*, is one of the FAW security lads. I won't reveal his identity as he's sneaked away from base, desperate for a McDonald's, as he's grown a little weary of the hotel cuisine. He's clutching the familiar brown bag to his chest. I reassure him that his secret's safe with me.

My own meal's hit the spot as well, breakfast in Leeds and lunch in Paris seems very cosmopolitan, and I contemplate another beer before deciding against it. I want to get stuck into the real pre-match build-up as soon as possible and time's ticking on. I head back to the Metro and make contact with Gary Pritchard to see where he and the chaps are going to be doing their drinking. He gives me the name of a bar and a location, which I forward to Alun as our ticket handover point as well. It's close to the stadium apparently. So, I get the map out again and try and work out my best route. There is a change, close to the Eiffel Tower and I need to see the Eiffel Tower. I can't come to Paris without saying I've seen at least one of the sights can I?

I descend into the Metro station and try to work out what to do next. There are two young people wearing blue bibs who appear to be on hand to offer advice. I approach one of them and ask him which way I need to go *"pour Le tour Eiffel?"* He seems a bit confused. I would have thought this was an easy one for a person whose job it is to offer guidance to people trying to find their way around the city, but it proves beyond him. He starts an explanation, then stops and needs the help of his female colleague, who tells me I need to follow the long corridor to a connected station.

It's a couple more stops there and I leave the station, camera at the ready. I'm walking behind three lads in Arsenal shirts – looks like they went a bit early with their flight bookings as well. There's a bar up ahead with a big crowd of Wales fans outside, clearly I'm not the only one who's had this idea. On the approach to it, there are the African guys you often see walking up and down the beach in France and Spain, selling sunglasses and ethnic jewellery and ornaments. Only here, they're selling flags of the competing nations and the dragon's obviously today's hot item. This is brilliant. This is one those sights that make you realise just how much more the world now knows about Wales. It's a striking flag but, until recently, very few people beyond the UK will have recognised it. Thanks to Gareth and the gang, that's very different now. In a world of global markets, this is brand recognition.

A little further down the road, another striking sight, as a guy carries a long pole festooned with alternative Welsh and Breton flags. I wonder if he's travelled with the team from Dinard? It would be great to think he's travelled to support his Celtic brothers.

Then things get even more surreal, as another chorus of *Don't Take Me Home* rises from the crowds on the pavement and a group of Japanese tourists stop on the opposite pavement and whip out their cameras and phones to record the scenes. They all file past, pointing them towards the fans. What's amazing about this, is that behind the bar, clearly visible, looms the Eiffel Tower, one of the most recognisable tourist landmarks in the world but these visitors only have eyes for the boys in red!

I cross over to get my own picture and the big building behind us is definitely going to feature. I am wearing my bucket hat and in front of the Eiffel Tower, as is the lad depicted on my T-shirt. Life mirrors art and all that. The sun's behind me as well though and I'm struggling to sort out a decent selfie. One of the three Arsenal chaps notices my predicament and very kindly offers to do it for me. This is the spirit of Euro 2016.

My sightseeing mission accomplished, I'm back on the ale trail and I work out a route to where Gary is now. It seems I can walk some of the way at least – alongside the Seine – all part of that Paris experience! Ten minutes south and having passed many Poles, I reach a metro station that should take me to our meeting place. I can tell I'm going in the right direction by the number of Wales and Northern Ireland fans milling about. We all pile onto the next train and travel to the station nearest to the stadium. At this point, the train all but empties but I stay on. I've been talking to a Welsh family: father, mother and two young children, who've come over on spec, hoping to find tickets and so far they've not had any luck. They're trying at the ground instead. I wish them all the best in their search as they get off.

Two stops further is the end of the line. So I leave the station in search of the bar. The seasoned travellers tend to like to find somewhere a bit quieter and this area appears to fit the bill on that basis, as there's pretty much no one around, no fans, no locals. I have a detailed description of the bar's location and this doesn't quite tally with it. I begin to have my doubts so I consult the internet. I got off at Boulogne Saint Cloud and the bar I want is at Place de Saint Cloud. They sound like they should be quite close. They aren't. Even as the penny's dropping and I'm staring at my map, a French lady stops and asks if I need help. She's the first person to offer assistance during the entire tournament and I feel quite overcome with gratitude. As visitors, it has felt a little like we're being left to our own devices, no signs, no guides, none of those volunteers that were on hand in London during the Olympics. She outlines my options; there's a bus from across the road, or back on the Metro and retrace my route. As she explains, the bus in question goes past so I figure the next one might be a while. I go for option two.

As I'd pulled into the station, I sent Gary a message saying I'd be there in a minute – that was 20 minutes ago. I need to confess my latest cock-up before they send out a search party. Heading back in the direction of the Parc des Princes again, I find my latest connection station and finally head in the right direction. The second train I get on is full of fans – both sets – and the Northern Irish lads start singing a song in praise of their manager, Michael O'Neill. This upsets the bloke sitting near me with a couple of mates. None of them are wearing any 'colours' which is very unusual on an occasion like this. He gets to his feet and starts singing 'No surrender, no surrender, no surrender to the IRA!' This is wrong on a number of levels and I feel obliged to speak up.

Given that the majority of the Northern Irish supporters are almost certainly Protestant – the Catholics tend to follow the Republic – he's not really taunting the right crowd and that's the point I make as I ask him to stop. He seems a bit taken aback, then angry, "It's just a bit of banter isn't it, they're singing so I'm singing back!" he snaps back in what I think is a Cardiff accent. "Yeah" I say "but you're trying to wind them up. There's been no trouble for two weeks, let's not start now eh?" He makes his own assumption about my accent, correctly as it happens. "You know about it in Wrexham do you? I've been supporting this shit for years." I'm confused now. It seems a strange way to describe a team that's just got to the last 16 of the European Championships for the first time. I ask him what he means by that, but I think the discussion is boring him already so he heads back to his mates. My station helps bring an end to the first moment of aggression I've witnessed since I looked up to see the sneers of the England fans on the upper tier in Lens.

Finally, I've made it to the right place. The scene that greets me is exactly as Gary described in his text. *Les Fontaines* is opposite the station, easily spotted as there's a large crowd of people assembled under its awning and out on the pavements around it. The lads are all there, with their families, gathered around a couple of tables near the bar. There's a bottle of wine on one of them, a tower of empty plastic glasses and a couple of full ones. After the usual pleasantries, they have a suggestion, it seems the owner of this bar has pushed the usual price of a pint up from €4 to €10, so I'm directed to the little *Patisserie* next door. As well as pastries and cakes, they sell cans of beer. I resist an *éclair* and opt for some Heineken instead.

I spirit it back into the bar next door and Rhys Boore peels one of the plastic glasses from the tower and passes it to me. Now I see what they're for! Under the cover of the table top, I transfer my beer from can to glass. Let the games begin! I have a referendum vote to try and blitz from my brain. Gary and the lads were in Paris last night, singing pro-EU songs on the metro, which apparently earned them a round of applause from their fellow travellers.

Then, Alun Llwyd and his group arrive, the party includes his record label business partner, Kev, 'Indie Rock God', Euros Childs and Huw Evans, better known in music circles as H. Hawkline. Euros I've met before, we had a very good night out in Cardiff after the Welsh Music Awards presentation a couple of years ago. He's the brother-in-law of Alun, my pal, although he isn't signed to Turnstile. Also with them is Gruff, Alun's former business partner in the legendary Welsh record label, Ankst. They form an orderly queue and I pass out the tickets before dispatching Kev to the *patisserie*, after he'd promised me beer in return for my collection service.

It's gone 3pm now, according to my watch, and I'm thinking we probably have less than an hour before we need to head to the stadium, until I hear someone mention that it's four hours until the 6pm kick-off, and I realise I've been working on UK timings. We've got another hour! Result!

Nobody's drunk enough yet to forget what happened yesterday. I'm in the midst of avowed Remainers. They're all first language Welsh speakers and, as such, probably wouldn't describe themselves as British. They'd be Welsh and European. Those who support the concept of an independent Wales would argue that it could survive and prosper within a supportive federation, like the EU, as the Scots are now suggesting, given that they voted overwhelmingly in favour of staying in the EU. The arts in Wales, in which all these people are or have been involved in, have benefitted from EU grant funding. Great uncertainty lies ahead. The EU exit may lead to a strengthening of the call for a Welsh exit from the UK in nationalist circles, despite the majority voting in favour. Ah jeez, more beers please...

It's a time to talk football. It's time to assess the task that lies ahead. It's clear we are all conflicted. We all see this as an eminently winnable tie, but none of us want the Euro experience to end with defeat to Northern Ireland. We want a glorious end to the journey, going out to Germany or France, not a team representing a population smaller than our own.

The two teams met in a friendly in March. I was a bit distracted by the fact that I'd destroyed my feet on Jeff Stelling's sponsored walk a couple of days earlier and, despite Weeksy's best efforts, I was still in so much pain that night that I left before the penalty that Wales got to equalise. From what I saw, the two teams looked well-matched, although that Welsh team was missing it's star names. With them back, we should have enough but there are players in the Northern Ireland side I've never seen play, and I do get to watch a lot of football!

More cans are required at this stage and Euros is delegated to go and fetch them. He's sent on his way with very careful instructions. From what I've seen of him, Euros is a lovely chap but he comes across as being a bit detached from normal, humdrum life. He's incredibly creative and makes fantastic music – he's otherworldly – so the instructions are quite detailed. Five minutes later he returns to the group: no cans. The *patisserie*'s run out, but there's another shop further up, and Euros heads off again. This time he's successful.

All the time, beer's being drunk and the atmosphere gets more and more ebullient. There's a wide roundabout in front of our bar, that also passes another bar which is even more crowded, with a man dressed in a Santa suit riding round it on a three-wheeled bike, decorated with tinsel and baubles. After a couple of circuits, he disappears into the midst of the crowd at the bar opposite and then emerges with two more people hanging off his bike, they appear to be Wales fans. There's a big cheer. There's singing as well, not so much in our bar but the one opposite, with both sets of fans running through their favourite anthems. For the Northern Ireland supporters, that means the *Will Grigg's On Fire* song. It's not all football fans though, there are French people eating and drinking where we are, so the atmosphere can't be threatening. There are police but they're staying right back, their presence all but unnecessary when everyone's intent on getting on together. There appear to be a lot more Welsh fans than there are Northern Irish but nobody's claiming territory, flags are hung side by side.

There's time for one more drink before we head off to the stadium. There's no great hike here, we're a couple of minutes away from the first cordon. I manage to lose Alun and the rest, but I'm not sitting with them anyway so I'm probably entering via different gate. The Parc des Princes then appears ahead of us, fairly low so not quite as imposing as many modern stadia. I haven't been before but it's obviously a legendary venue to many Welsh rugby fans as it was the site of many Five Nations clashes, when even the great teams of the 1970s often came a cropper here but, for the Welsh football team, it's a first ever visit.

I'm still struggling to find any decent signposting outside the stadium and, as usual, there appears to be nobody to ask, so I end up doing almost a full circuit before I find the right entrance. There's quite a scrum around the bag checkpoints – as we've seen at other grounds – but beyond that, on the concourse surrounding the stadium, things are a bit more relaxed.

It's clear now that the game being in Paris has attracted more neutrals than has previously been the case. I'm hearing a lot more French being spoken but there are people from other nations here as well. I see two Japanese guys in Wales T-shirts and stop them for a picture and a chat. They know about Gareth Bale, Wales is the team they're supporting and they're wearing the tops to prove it. Now you can see that this isn't just a big derby game between two 'British' teams, it's a big game at an international tournament that *happens* to be between two 'British' teams. This is the festival of football experience. I like it. This could be our last match, one of the two teams is heading home tonight, so everyone appears hell bent on having the best time possible. Who knows how long it'll be before we get another chance?

I head into the stadium. You can see that this is an old ground, and very different to Bordeaux for example, immediately after pushing through the turnstiles. It's pretty cramped and dark inside, and there are long queues for food, for drink and for the toilets. As I push through the crowds and climb the steps to the stand, I emerge into another bowl of a stadium. It holds just under 50,000 people so it's the biggest ground we've played in yet. My seat appears to be in the usual position, somewhere close to the corner flag, on the opposite side to the dugouts.

I move along the line to where my seat is – not that anyone's planning to sit down – and, as I turn to look at the pitch, I'm standing in the full glare of the sun. I'm immediately grateful for the decision to race back to my room for the bucket hat. The fan to my right has not come so well prepared and he's being admonished by his partner for coming out without his bucket hat, especially as she'd bought it for him as a gift. My neighbour has ginger hair and his face already has that slightly red look to it, that suggests he needs to go and find the shade, not sit out in the sun for the next two hours.

Next to him, I recognise his partner as Sarah Powell, whom I last saw speaking – very well – at the FAW Trust event in Bordeaux. An awful lot has happened since then, particularly in terms of what she was talking about, the ability of this event to raise the profile and participation levels of all sports in Wales. Her partner asks me for a score prediction, something I refuse to do. "I never predict scores in Wales games," I respond to his evident surprise. "Why not?" he persists, "Go on, what do you think?" "Okay," I concede. "The reason I don't do predictions is because I don't generally feel very optimistic about Wales' chances, my generation has see too much failure to get carried away." Now Sarah joins the discussion, "That's an attitude we've got to change!" she says – and she's right – but I think mine is a lost generation and I declare that to be the case, adding that she'll have no problems of that sort with the younger people who are experiencing all this. "Come on. Prediction?" Sarah insists and I finally cave in. "Alright, 1-0 to Northern Ireland with Gareth McAuley to get a late winner." They both look a bit shocked. I'll leave the rampant optimism to the young folk.

It's noticeable that there are new faces around me, new voices as well. I may be a tiny bit paranoid but it sounds like there are more south Walians in my area of the stadium. In my mind at least, this suggests more 'eventers', the people who like to make a weekend of a Six Nations game. Converts are always welcome but I do get a bit uptight when people don't know the names of the players. The evidence for my supposition is supported by a small incident after the anthems, with the players lining up for the kick-off, when the chap to my left sits himself down and his wife sits down next to him. Needless to say, as has been the case throughout, nobody else does. So he gives the bloke in front a tap on the back, and asks him to sit down because he can't see. In fairness, the man in front does begin to lower himself before realising that he now needs to ask the bloke in front of him to sit down and so on all the way down to the front. Of course, the reality is, this isn't going to happen so, the man in front shrugs, turns back and stands to watch the match. The chap next to me looks unhappy, but he and his wife have no choice but to stand if they want to see the game. It's the way it is, the way it has been throughout the tournament. None shall sit.

Looking around the ground, it's full, which is great and there are far more red areas visible than green ones. In fact, even the predominantly green patches are surrounded by or even interspersed with red. Still, in the opening minutes, it's the minority that makes the majority of the noise. *Will Grigg's On Fire* gets them all very animated, even though he's on the bench again, in fact he hasn't yet played a minute at the tournament! Instead, Kyle Lafferty's starting up front and Wales line up as they did in Toulouse.

The boys in green make the better start to the game, with Dallas having a shot that forces Wayne into a full-length push around the post, and then immediately Wales go up the other end, where a Gareth Bale ball into the area drops just behind Aaron Ramsey.

The big worry about this game, particularly from the Welsh perspective, is that it might end up looking more like an FA cup tie. A 'battle' is likely to suit them more than us. They organise well, tackle fiercely and rely on set pieces for goals. The early signs aren't promising. It's scrappy, lots of fouls, misplaced passes and very little quality – I wonder what the neutrals are making of this?

There are brief flickers of excitement as Aaron bundles in a header from Sam Vokes, but he's offside, then as Jamie Ward has a shot for Northern Ireland that Wayne Hennessey has to tip over. That means he's already had to make more saves than he did in the entire evening in Toulouse. There are more fouls, lots of them on Welsh players. Martin Atkinson's the ref and he lets a lot go before he finally books Stuart Dallas for yet another lunge at Gareth Bale. That apart, there's not a lot to sing about, at either end, and the half-time whistle brings some relief and some disgruntlement, particularly around me. I've heard people discussing what Wales are doing wrong, which seems amazing to me, given the context of the game we're watching.

I head for the toilets, joining a long queue that snakes around the corner and only edges forward slowly. There's a low murmur of analysis around me, but there's not the buzz amongst the support that there's been in previous games. The big difference, of course, is that Wales have been ahead by half-time in all the previous matches. Can it really be the case that we've already got used to being in front? Up ahead, a south Walian accent pipes up. "Come on, what's wrong with you?! Lift it! We're drawing in the last 16 of the European Championships!" As a rallying cry, it's like a scene from *Zulu* down by the urinals.

When I return to my seat, there's a chance of another quick assessment with Sarah and her partner. I'm actually feeling a tad more confident now, having had a chance to see what Northern Ireland have to offer. I dare to suggest we've got the match winners because we've got the quality players, but I don't change my pre-match prediction however, that would be tempting fate. Then the second half gets underway, with our boys now kicking towards the official Welsh 'end'. This raises the volume, aided by a belated *Men Of Harlech* led by The Barry Horns.

They're good at judging when things need lifting, they know their football, and a full-blooded blast soon gets the crowd going, except for the lad in the row in front of me who's more intent on playing games on his phone. In fact, he's actually sitting down! He's got a Wales shirt on but he's with his parents, and I suspect he may have been told to wear it. To be fair to him, the game's poor but even so, it must offer more than *Angry Birds*?

After absorbing a bit of pressure, nothing too dangerous but I get very anxious whenever the Irish have the ball in our half, Gareth Bale picks up a ball midway inside their half and he swings a fantastic right footed cross into the box. Sam Vokes is the target, naturally, and he gets in ahead of Cathcart, the marking defender. I'm almost level with Sam – centre of goal, maybe 10 yards out – as he rises to meet the ball and heads it down, but he heads it wide. All around, hands go to heads. It's the first proper chance of the game for either side. I feel sorry for Sam, he had a good chance in that last match as well so he might come in for some stick but he's done really well in his lone striker role. That miss may have made some minds up on the bench, because a couple of minutes later the board goes up and he's replaced by Hal Robson-Kanu.

The substitution brings a big response from both the band and the fans. We're looking for a hero now, Hal's played that role against Slovakia already and we'd take another HRK intervention in Paris. Or a Gareth free kick, that would be good too.

Especially as he's hacked down again, a little outside the penalty area. Anticipation levels rise as he begins the familiar pre-kick routine.

He smashes the ball up and over the wall but McGovern's kept an eye on it and does a far better job with it than Joe Hart. He pushes it away from goal and the chance has gone.

There's another change to come, Ledley switches with Jonny Williams, and things begin to shift the way of Wales. The sun's still beating down and the temperatures are high inside this bowl. When I look at the Northern Irish lads, I sense they're beginning to tire. The substitutions seem well timed because both players will run at defenders, something Jonny immediately does to good effect. He's inevitably fouled, as he always is, but he'll do it again and again and, the two central defenders in particular, are beginning to look like they're feeling it. In fairness, Gareth McAuley is 36 and he's had a lot of high-intensity football in a short space of time. This is the tournament challenge isn't it? He's a very important player for Northern Ireland, at both ends, but does he need a rest? It's a big call for Michael O'Neill. Actually, Jonny Evans alongside him looks to be finding it hard as well. He takes a long time to retrieve a throw-in down in front of me, he seems to be breathing heavily, looking for a chance to take a rest.

The game's mainly being played in their half of the pitch now, yet Chester does a brilliant defensive job with one Lafferty break out, sliding out of the challenge in the box with the ball at his feet. What a tournament he's had so far! How can he not get a game at West Brom? Play moves back in to their half. It's been a long time since Wayne's had anything to do. I would suggest Northern Ireland would quite like to push this one into extra time now, although my prediction could yet come true?

Then comes the best period of pressure Wales have managed in the entire game. Bale stations himself out on the left side of the box and, having been continually closed down by two or three players every time he's picked the ball up, suddenly he's got a bit of space. Aaron feeds him the ball, he crosses into the box and it's cleared but we're winning all the second balls now, filling the midfield. Aaron's got the ball back and delivers the same ball wide to Gareth. He sets off towards the byline, and whips another cross in. I'm in line with it as it marks a curve across the area, beating the first defender, too far away from the keeper and McAuley's the last man back. Hal's racing in to meet it and McAuley sticks a leg out, sensing his presence. He makes contact, five yards out – the outcome's inevitable – the ball flies into the net and, in a millisecond, even the *Angry Birds* fan is up on his feet, seeing what all the fuss is about. Behind him, I'm hugging my red-faced friend, hugging Sarah, hugging anyone I can get my hands on basically! It's the sheer relief of it, the sheer beautiful, life-affirming relief of it.

I'll be honest, I think we've won this now. I think that will be enough. I've never thought like that before but this team keeps changing my mindset. Instead of throwing it away, they've got stronger, they've kept pressing and good substitutions have again helped. Northern Ireland's efforts have been expended in trying to keep Wales out, I can't see how they can change that now.

They give it a go, of course, but there's a real sense in the Welsh end that the game's ours. It's not an arrogance but a belief. Even Northern Ireland moves into the Welsh half don't induce a flicker of a drop in the volume, as *Don't Take Me Home* absolutely booms out from every Welsh fan in the Parc des Princes, over and over again. We're not going home, not yet. There's one moment of worry still, as the two Williams boys collide, chasing a ball in our half. Jonny has suffered too many injuries playing for Wales for anyone not to be concerned as he lies face down, but every bit as worrying is the sight of Ashley Williams, also face down, clutching his shoulder. James Collins gets stripped off and ready to come on. My mind's already on the next game, a quarter-final, will they both be missing? Jonny gets to his feet first, looks okay, then Ashley but I can see him clutching his arm. It doesn't look good. He seems to be waving at the bench but he's waving to keep the sub off, rather than call him on. He's a warrior.

Northern Ireland get the ball up and around the penalty area for the first time in this half but the massed red ranks stand firm, and even the captain manages to swing his foot at a ball to clear, despite the fact he's got one arm hanging limply at his side. The clock ticks down, the volume goes up and the anthem is heard for just about the first time since before kick-off: we're all 'eyes on the clock' now. We're into added time, deep into it as Ramsey runs the ball out from the area, loses it and then pushes his opponent. Martin Atkinson pulls the yellow card out. Northern Ireland have a last chance to throw the ball into the box and their fans find their voices again. Their goalkeeper sprints from one penalty box to the other whilst we stand – transfixed

– at the far end. If there is going to be heartbreak, it's going to be worse, far worse than England. The ball's swung in and there, at the back post, is the head of Gareth Bale to clear. There's a roar around me, then the whistle goes up to the ref's lips and our arms go up into the air. It's the most amazing release from the tension. It's been an awful game, probably the worst of the tournament to date, but that almost makes it even better, because the team came through it again; a different sort of challenge, the same outcome. I turn to my right. "Told you, 1-0, McAuley, late winner!"

The celebrations after this game are a bit different from Toulouse, if that makes any sense, it's a bit more relaxed. Almost as if we're getting used to this. We sing *Don't Take me Home* again and again, over and over as the players come over to the fans. They join in, then they do the huddle and soon after, their children come to join them. Gareth Bale's daughter runs across the pitch, chased by her dad. She's in full Welsh kit. He catches her and scoops her up and we cheer. She's seen a ball now, and kicks it towards the goal, more cheers. Sarah spoke about the potential legacy of Euro 2016 before that first game. I can point at the scenes on the pitch now and suggest that's a legacy image; it's a lovely scene. David Edwards' son comes on as well, again fully kitted in red and he has a decent right foot on him. He fires a shot into the net and the crowd roars. He likes it, so he gets the ball back and he does it again and gets the same reaction. It's a bit like a big, mad, noisy family get together, with twenty thousand aunties and uncles watching on proudly as the kids show off their skills. It genuinely does feel like 'family', the bond is that strong. These are our boys.

Eventually, we start to drift away. I feel a strong urge to celebrate. My phone's once more on the cusp of shutdown so I send out an SOS to Gary and Alun to ascertain their next movements. We keep it simple and agree to meet back where we were before the game. Megan's sent me a text to say she thinks Ashley Williams has broken his arm! This would be very bad news and I hope to heck she's wrong.

The bar's really close to the stadium and yet, when an opportunistic Eastern European guy appears on the pavement with a shopping trolley and a cool box full of chilled beers, I can't resist. I buy two, at €5 apiece! That is the sort of entrepreneurialism we'll miss post-Brexit. We came, we saw, we didn't lose to Northern Ireland! It's party time people!

The troops re-gather and reflect on a bad game but a brilliant result. The enormity of being in the last eight of the European Championships begins to sink in and it feels amazing. Wales is on the map now – sport does that – people who previously didn't know about our country now know about our country. The tournament has been everything anyone could have hoped for – and more – in terms of global exposure. The team embodies all the characteristics you'd want to showcase on such a public platform. It's only sport perhaps, but Wales now has the national identity it's been seeking for decades. It's Gareth Bale's 'top knot', his daughter playing on the pitch, Aaron Ramsey's bleached blonde hair and Joe Ledley's beard. It's a red shirt, a dragon, a stirring anthem, and a 1,000-year-old language that isn't English. Sheep-shagging bastards? You know who we are!

Then there's singing and beer and chatting and beer. It's a fabulous evening. Two sets of fans stand side by side and enjoy each other's company, and it's wonderful. I get the chance to talk to a group of Northern Irish fans, who are good people. Unusually, as they readily accept, they're a mixed group of Protestants and Catholics. They say the IFA is making good progress in opening things up to both sides of the community. Everyone in Northern Ireland loves football, they just struggle to love it together. But their supporters have been fantastic. There has been no sectarian chanting, it's very noticeable that most of the banners flown are in the green, blue and white of the kit, rather than the red, white and blue of the Union Jack. They've followed their team with great humour and good grace, they'll be a big loss to the competition.

In between conversations, I have to find more supplies and my search takes me up the road to a Chinese restaurant. They're happy to do 'off-sales' and I load a plastic bag with bottles of Tsing Tao in various sizes. Only when I get back to my crew for distribution do I realise I have no means of opening them. In desperation, I take a few steps out from under the bar's awning and try to knock the top off against a barrier on the subway parapet. It doesn't work. A voice calls to me, "Mister, I help?" I turn round and there's a homeless guy in a sleeping bag in the doorway. "I open?" he offers. "Sure, thanks!" I reply and pass him the bottle. He grips the top between his teeth and pops it off. "I drink?" he asks and I give him the thumbs up.

My big bag of bottles turns out to be a little over optimistic as Alun,

Kev, Euros and the chaps are off to get something to eat. I hang on with Rhys, Gwilym, Gary and the rest and we sing silly songs about getting to the last eight, but I'm aware that I need to get back to Gare Du Nord whilst the metro's still running, and I found the underground complicated enough when I was sober. I cannot afford to make any mistakes tomorrow morning in terms of getting home on time and in a fit state to continue the celebrations, so I need to make sure I'm back at the hotel at a reasonable hour tonight. I say goodbye to the guys then head off for the metro across the road.

This is the point where it's tough being a solo traveller. I need someone to help me make sense of this mad multicoloured spaghetti map that's supposed to tell me how to get from here to home. Eventually, I take the plunge and hop on a train. Then I hop off it because I need to change but also because I'm really desperate for a wee. I'm now on a long concourse with no sign of an exit at either end. As I consider my options my plight becomes worse and I have no choice but to tuck right in behind some sort of unmanned control hut in a quiet-ish corner on a concourse between platforms, aim at the wall and relieve myself. Never was a phrase more apt. At any moment, I'm expecting security staff to appear, CCTV cameras to spin round and point in my direction, alarms to go off and hordes of Japanese tourists to start filming with their camera phones, but nobody seems to notice me or the puddle forming around my feet.

I tiptoe away, trying not to leave a trail of footprints, and manage to find both a train back to Gare Du Nord and then from Gare Du Nord to Charles de Gaulle airport. The one thing I don't manage to find is my one day travel pass. Don't get me wrong, I've had my money's worth, I feel a bit like a mole I've spent that much of the day scurrying around underground, but another €10 to make the train journey's a blow. There's one more financial hit to come as well. Back at the airport, I head for the shuttle stop. I wait and wait but nothing comes, in the end I manage to hail a passing cab and he charges me €20 for the five minute drive back to the hotel.

I was up at 4am and it's now 1.30am the following day. It's been a cracker but I really need some sleep. Ridiculously, magnificently, I'm going to be back again – in four days time – to Lille, to face either Hungary or Belgium. Oh, and happy birthday Rachel!

6

Lille
Wales v Belgium

'The Belgium game was the best night of my career! It was tough for me at first because the Gaffer had pulled me over after the Northern Ireland game and said that I wouldn't be starting. When Belgium went one up, from that great strike, we still had confidence because we felt we knew them and we could still get something out of the game. Ash's goal was massive, it gave us a real answer that there was something in it for us at half-time.

After Hal's fantastic goal, when I got the call to go on, I was actually pretty nervous. I mean we were winning and I didn't want to be the one to mess up, there was a lot of pressure. I've watched the game many times since and I seemed to be mainly playing as a centre-half as we had our backs to the wall but then we got that free kick which gave me the chance to get up the pitch. Gunts put the perfect ball in and then – phew! – I had to get in front of my defender first, then direct it into that far corner. It did feel like the perfect header.

Our fans were so outnumbered so it was even better that it was at that end, our end, or our corner at least! My 'Old Man', my brother and some mates were in that corner, and I managed to spot them celebrating in the stand as we were celebrating on the pitch. It was brilliant. My dad was tearing down the aisle towards me and he tripped over the hoardings on his way! My mum and my missus were in the seats behind the dugout but my dad and my brother said they wanted to be with the fans.

At full-time, I was quite emotional. People have said I looked down, as if we'd lost, but it was just everything getting to me – not starting, coming on and scoring and the feeling of disbelief at what we'd just achieved.'
Sam Vokes

Sunday, 26th June

Technically not a new day, and it's only a few hours after hitting the hay that I'm back up and in a bit of a panic. My phone's bedside and for some reason the battery's still flat. I guess the socket doesn't work and I want to check-in before I get to the airport, so I stumble around the room looking for another one. It's found and I go back to bed to doze for a couple of hours. I'm back up and outside in good time to jump aboard the 8.30am shuttle bus, having finally worked out why my airline app on my, now recharged, phone won't let me check-in for this flight. I've read the small print and you can't check-in online for flights from Charles De Gaulle. I'm going to have to go to a desk to do it, 'old school'!

I'm holding it all together at the moment, just. The *moules et frites* was a long time ago and I haven't eaten since, but I have taken on quite a lot of liquid. I suffered a dodgy couple of minutes just before leaving the room so I'm still on the cusp of a hangover. The problem with that is, I can't afford to be anything other than on top form for my return home. I've been granted this dispensation to miss the actual, waking up next to my wife on her birthday bit, the first time that's happened since we've known each other. She's suffered my missing most of our wedding anniversary celebrations due to international clashes so the least I owe her is a bit of energy, full attention and big hugs, as well as a few presents of course. So, after a quick check-in, a long queue through boarding and a baggage check where the bloke tipped my bag over and emptied everything on the conveyor belt – I head for duty free and champagne! That's for Rachel of course, not to mark Wales' glorious march to the quarter-finals of the European Championships. I also need a bottle of water and a sandwich. That's for me, right here, right now. Medicinal.

I make the call home from the shuttle bus to the plane. A shuttle bus that is full of football fans, Northern Irish, Welsh and English. With that in mind, I offer a quiet rendition of *Happy Birthday* down the line as Rachel picks up. I'm hoping she's happy to hear that I'm all set for the big day, despite the fact that I'm still several hundred miles away. The flight's apparently on time so I'll be back before she's had brunch.

Then the phone pings as a text from Steve arrives, he's quite clearly more focused on the quarter-final game as he's already put together a plan. We fly to Paris from Doncaster again, pick up a hire car and drive to Lille. Then we find an apartment, as he's planning on bringing his wife and son for this one so, he wants to know if I can get three tickets? Wow, three!? For the biggest game in Welsh football history it's a tall order. I ask him to book the flights and I'll try my best with the tickets. Mine's already on order so, 'I'm alright Jacques'.

The flight's good and lands on time and, as we're waiting in the aisle to disembark, I get talking to one of the lads ahead of me. He's a Leeds fan and has been over for the last couple of weeks, following England. He's one of the many who expected England to win the group so pre-booked what looked like the ideal flight home, until they didn't win it. He's not impressed with Hodgson's selection for the Slovakia game, even though England have ended up with a game against Iceland. I ask him if he'll be back out for the quarter-finals but he says he's used up all his leave with work, so Doncaster looks like being the last stop on his tournament travels.

Not for me, of course, I'll be back in less than four days time. First though, home and fatigue takes its toll as I make a bit of a mess of what should be a straightforward 45 minute drive back up the A1. It ends up involving the M18 and the M62 and I arrive on the drive a little later than promised, but just before lunch, which is still pretty good going.

I do my best to be the life and soul but I'm very, very tired and I sneak off upstairs mid-afternoon, to 'get ready' which means to 'take a nap'. It's just a quick one, about twenty minutes, so I'm not really missed but it helps perk me up before we all go out to visit friends who've very kindly prepared a birthday tea. We transport the wine, I

176

bought on the ferry, into the house to help the party go with a swing and it's a lovely night, in great company, to round off a terrific weekend but there's no escaping Brexit talk. Gill and Jake were both Remain voters so everyone in the room's singing from the same hymn sheet, it doesn't make for much of a debate, more of a moan-in.

. Needless to say, there's always football when real life starts to get a bit tricky, so Jake and I steal occasional glances at Germany beating Slovakia, comfortably, then more lingering looks at Belgium v Hungary, by way of research on my part of course. The signs are not encouraging as the Belgians tear their opponents apart. The Hungarians actually make a lot of chances in an open game but where they miss, Belgium score – four times! It's the biggest win in the tournament to date. So we'll be renewing acquaintances with a side we've got to know very well over the last few years. Friday will be the fifth meeting in four years – our record reads won two, drawn two, lost one – but I must park those thoughts because now there's a discussion about Megan's forthcoming 'prom'. Another event that I'm set to miss due to 'bloody football'!

We have a taxi booked to take us home and bed, once again, feels good, very good. I make a resolution to stay 'dry' until Lille – a whole three days – and one last check on my phone shows I've missed another message from Steve. Evo may be after a ticket now as well! That's a challenge for another day, tomorrow.

Monday, 27th June

The day's first task, before I've even got out of bed, is to email Lucy and ask if there's any chance of getting four tickets. The UEFA hub opens for sales at 1pm, so that's the fall back strategy. Shoney's already booked his flights and Evo's now trying to work out whether he can get Thursday and Friday off work.

George Osborne was at work earlier than me, delivering a 7am statement designed to offer some reassurance to the financial institutions, seemingly rattled by the prospect of trying to work out what happens next. That seems a pretty big question all round today and nobody seems to have any answers. Iain Duncan Smith, a big Leave campaigner, doesn't help matters when he comes out with a classic explanation for some of the benefits promised post-

Brexit. It now appears that the Leave campaigners' "promises were possibilities". That's a line I must remember, could come in handy for the next time I fail to mow the lawn when I said I would.

There's chaos everywhere you look, Labour's shadow cabinet appear to be resigning *en masse*; they want Corbyn out. It all feels like the end of days. How did this happen? How did we hold a referendum on such a massive issue without apparently having the faintest clue of what was going to happen if people actually voted to Leave?

Whilst our political leaders fall out and apart we, the people, have to try and carry on doing what we do. That means Megan has to finish her final GCSE and I have to go and pick her up, amazed and a little emotional at the realisation that my firstborn has now finished the first part of her secondary education. It's a time to count your blessings, to focus on the good things and to try and shut out the bad. So, family, football, music and clothes it is then.

I get word from Evo that the UEFA hub's sold out but, as he's struggling to get time off anyway, he's not going to be able to make it. Then Shoney makes contact to say his wife can't go now either, so my request for four is down to a more manageable two. I pass that message on to the FAW as quickly as possible, before anything's processed. Lucy's team must be getting absolutely inundated with this sort of stuff, and they've already had months of it in the run-up to the tournament. The staff are all fans as well but I wouldn't mind betting they're ready for a rest. I need another power nap once everyone's back home, so I'm wide awake for the England v Iceland game in Nice.

Iceland's story is an incredible one, a population of just over 320,000 – smaller than Cardiff – and yet they've qualified for the Euros. Not only that but they've got through the group stage as well, finishing second with a win and two draws. Still, England must feel they've landed a plum draw compared to some of the teams they could have come up against, in what looks like the tougher half of the knockout format.

The Icelandic fans have already made their mark as well, for such a tiny country. In comparative terms they've brought the biggest support to France, approximately ten per cent of the population! Their haunting 'Viking' chant and synchronised clapping has become one of the images of the tournament. Like Wales, they're another great example of the significance of this experience to the teams who've never been here before: the small nations enjoying the big stage.

The game starts predictably enough with England getting a penalty and Rooney scoring. That should be it, but I promise myself I'll keep watching until they get a second. The second goal quickly follows, but it's not England who score. It's 1-1. A goal that comes from a long throw, a tactic they've already employed to good effect in the tournament. In commentary, Glenn Hoddle describes it as "80s football", which I think is meant to be a criticism, not of England but of Iceland. Maybe England need to go back to the future then, as another attack brings another goal for Iceland and a scoreline that's still hard to believe. It stays the same until half-time.

What's even harder to believe, after the players come back out for the second half, is the sheer awfulness of England's performance. I'm actually, genuinely, shocked at how bad they are. It isn't just that, 'didn't play well today' bad, it's full on 'my veterans team would give this lot a game' bad. It looks like the weight of expectation has just crushed these young players. They're almost gulping for air out there, like fish flipped out of the water and onto the land. It's clear they have no idea how to make this better. Not only is there no 'plan B', there's no 'plan anything'.

Wales suffered a horrendous 6-1 thrashing in Serbia some years ago, and they weren't as bad as this. Not only that, it was that calamitous result that led Chris Coleman to rethink the way he was working. From that point on, we've lost games, but it's always looked like they're playing to an agreed and understood plan. There's a plan for when we go in front, there's a plan for when we go behind and there's a plan for when we want to hold on for a draw. In this game, England have nothing. Suddenly, young talented players just look like young players. I have a sense that England need to go through a process that Wales have been through. Remove the expectation, take away the pressure to let the team grow together, lose together, and learn the international game together.

John Toshack was the man who oversaw what was a pretty painful experience, for them and us. But it's largely the same team now that was dubbed, by some observers, as being so bad it was suggested Wales should give up on the idea of having a national team altogether. I suspect it won't be Roy Hodgson who'll be tasked with initiating anything similar with Team England. Sure enough, within minutes of the final whistle, and with the Icelandic players pretty much still on the pitch celebrating, it's confirmed that he's gone. Even though I've supported Wales all my life, I was born in England and I take no pleasure from seeing England crash like this. The feel good factor, that can come from the international game, benefits everyone. International football is the one aspect of the game that still unites nations and brings in new fans in a way club football or the Premier League never can do. Wales will reap that reward in years to come, England have missed another opportunity.

Having said all that, the feeling of being the last side left from these shores is a good one. We've been written off by the English-based media as a one-man team, a team that only qualified because they enlarged the tournament. Here we are, still preparing for games when everyone else has gone home. Back in Wales, England's exit will be more wildly celebrated. It's one of football's oldest rivalries and England have enjoyed many more opportunities to gloat than Wales, most recently in Lens. Maybe that's why the Welsh players celebrated the final whistle in the Iceland game so enthusiastically. Incredibly, footage of their celebrations has already appeared on social media.

I see it and have to watch it again to confirm it's really the Welsh players. It is. I send a text to Ian Gwyn Hughes to warn him but I'm sure he already knows. My journalist antennae are twitching: this is going to become a story. Players aren't supposed to celebrate like this when fellow professionals lose. I don't actually have any problem with them celebrating as a group in the privacy of a hotel room, my issue would be with the fact that someone filmed it and then distributed it. Whoever did it is either very naïve to the consequences or actively trying antagonise England or undermine Wales, none of which is very good.

Tuesday, 28th June

A big day in the Shone household as the email comes through that confirms two extra tickets for the Wales v Belgium game on Friday. Steve's been busy on the accommodation front. Lille's proved something of a nightmare for finding anywhere to stay. As well as the game, it's coming up to the 100th anniversary of the start of the Battle of the Somme, and many people are using the city as a base for all the events that are taking place. The hotel rooms that are available, and there don't seem to be many, are exorbitantly expensive. It's another instance where you do wonder if UEFA might have looked at the wider 'events calendar' and decided that Lille wasn't the best choice of host stadium for this one? What do they think travelling fans do, sleep on benches or go straight home afterwards? That's actually a possibility for some of the Belgian fans but it isn't for the Welsh support, not when the game doesn't kick-off until 9pm.

In the absence of reasonably priced *en-suite* rooms, Steve has sought the assistance of Airbnb and has come up with a house on the outskirts of town, near a metro station. He has asked for the price for two nights – we're flying the day before the game just in case anyone decides to go on strike or flights get cancelled or delayed. It's far from cheap, in fact it's flipping expensive for a bed in someone's house, but we don't appear to have a lot of choice. Like UEFA, our French friends don't appear to be shy about squeezing every last Euro out of their visitors! He's booked the hire car as well, so now we have all we need. The trip is on!

In preparation, I'm giving my liver a rest, I'm still off the booze and I go out for my first run in a while, probably since Dinard! In the absence of regular exercise, my family are quick to point out that I've acquired a little beer belly courtesy of the Euros, something also mentioned by at least a couple of so-called pals out in France. I don't want to have to go up a size in SO58 T-shirts so I do need to get a few miles under my belt instead of a few pints.

As anticipated, England are getting pelters for their performance in news headlines, radio phone-ins, social media trolling, the works. This is the bit that Wales players didn't have to endure when they were struggling as novice internationals. The Welsh media remained largely supportive, whilst the English media lost interest as did the vast majority of fans, so they were allowed to take the set-backs yet learn in a relatively calm environment. That's a luxury that won't be afforded the England players. That one World Cup win 50 years ago has become such a burden!

I'm interested in the debate that rages around England's exit. Much of it centres on the role of the Premier League in failing to nurture young talent, with some saying the players leaving the top academies are mentally weak, that they can't think for themselves and problem solve when things don't go to plan. My take on this, having been there all the way as this Welsh squad's developed, is that England's most important requirement is to create the same sort of atmosphere in the group that now exists with Wales. To do that, they need to keep the players together, let them become friends, rather than occasional acquaintances, and let them gain confidence in each other.

As an example, it's been remarked upon that England players seemed reluctant to say anything of interest in their media conferences and interviews, probably because they've been warned – time after time – about not saying anything that might be 'twisted' or become a negative headline. The FA employ a team of people whose job it is to do just that. By contrast, the Wales players have been largely left alone over the years. They've been guided a little, but they're a bright bunch and they've worked it out for themselves. As a result, they perform confidently in front of the cameras, they anticipate the tricky questions and deal with them rather than avoiding them altogether.

My guess would be that this applies away from the glare of the media as well, that there is an environment in the Welsh camp that encourages discussion. The players are at ease in each other's company so don't feel daunted about doing or saying what they think is right. Many of them have been together for a decade or more, so they're a content and strong bunch of friends, but they also allow access and a voice to new members of the squad. Those new members are then confident that they won't get grief from 'the group' if they make a mistake. Furthermore, being part of 'the group' protects them from what people outside are saying.

This environment is surely what England need to build? It's what used to happen at successful football clubs – where a team spirit could be developed over years – but it doesn't anymore because of the high turnover of personnel. Wales have developed an 'old school' club mentality; like Revie's Leeds, Shankly's Liverpool, Ferguson's Manchester United or Graham's Arsenal. England have to try and do the same but it won't be easy for them. As we saw in Nice, where the England fans chanted 'You're not fit to wear the shirt' and, as we saw in Lens, where Harry Kane and Raheem Sterling were taken off at half-time, in full view of a TV audience of millions. There is huge pressure on every England performance. There's no hiding place. It wouldn't be surprising if some young players decided they didn't actually like playing for England after all. It doesn't look like much fun at the moment, and fun is a key and undervalued aspect of the international game. Very rich young men don't *need* to play for their country, they have to *want* to play for their country. If it's not for the money and it's not for the fun, why do it?

The Welsh players have been criticised for their celebrations at England's demise but, do you know what it signifies? It simply shows that they're a group of mates on holiday together, having fun.

Wednesday, 29th June

The clock's ticking down towards Lille and I'm keeping an ever more intense focus on team news. There's good news for Wales, Ashley Williams is okay, he's not broken his arm. I've watched the TV footage of him demanding to stay on the pitch in the final few minutes of the game in Paris. I can see the phrase, "I'm fine! I'm fine!" appearing on a Spirit of '58 T-shirt in the future.

Good news from the Belgian camp as well, as Hazard doesn't train and three key defenders are ruled out. Dembélé and Verthongen are injured, and Vermaelen is suspended. They're still red hot favourites to reach the semi-finals though, which is fine. Underdog status suits us best. We know what we are.

It's going to be harder to maintain that status in the wake of the latest FIFA rankings, with Wales now higher than England. It's a much derided system but, on the evidence of the Euros and despite the defeat in Lens, it would be hard to argue that they're wrong wouldn't it? I suppose this next game will give a greater idea of where Wales are really 'at', given that Belgium are now rated the second best team in the world, and the best in Europe.

I pack a bag, again, take Millie to Girl Guides and then pick her up before retreating to the guest room, again. The Shones are coming to collect me at 4.45am.

Thursday, 30th June

After a decent night's sleep, running and abstinence from the booze must have helped, I'm downstairs tucking into a bowl of porridge when there's a tap at the window. Two faces peer in. My lift's a little early, Steve and son having arrived in what must be Fergus' car. It's quite small and quite old and Steve's quite worried that we won't make it to the airport, but my car's stuck behind my wife's on the drive, and I'm anxious not to wake all the neighbours up shifting vehicles around at this ungodly hour so, the Fergus mobile it is.

There was no Fergus when I first got to know Steve through work and our Wednesday night football sessions. Now, he comes and plays with us whenever work or his studies allow. He's about to start another University course, he's travelled across South America with his mates, worked for various TV and film production companies and yet his dad still tut-tuts disapprovingly when he starts getting up to speed on the A1. I chuckle in the back seat, then remember that my eldest daughter will be eligible for driving lessons in a few weeks time. I may not be quite so relaxed when it's me in the passenger's seat!

As we arrive at the airport and follow diversion signs for the long stay car park – a similar process to the one I undertook just a few days ago – things get a little more complicated as Fergus drives right past the front of the terminal and through an automatic gate, then we find our path blocked by another automatic gate. This time, it appears, we have to insert money if we want to continue our search for the car park. This seems a little unfair, so Fergus pushes the button on the box and explains our predicament to the South Yorkshire voice that answers. The voice in the box is unsympathetic. "T'long stay's shut!" it crackles back. "But we followed your signs for it, they didn't say it was shut", Fergus responds, reasonably. The air of calm is then a tad undermined as Steve leans across and shouts, "Just open the gate!" I'm already pushing my hand into my pocket for small change at this point, concerned that we might still be stuck between these barriers as our plane departs for Paris. With audible grumbling being heard from the crackling voice in the box, the gate lifts and we're free to try and find somewhere else to park.

Walking into the terminal building is already acquiring a sense of familiarity. The staff are friendly, we're greeted at the check-in and, seeing our 'colours', the check-in woman starts bemoaning her country's woeful performance, "England shouldn't get paid!" she declares loudly, as Steve talks to her colleague.

We head on through to a very quiet departures lounge. I have a cup of tea and a catch-up with Fergus, then the flight's called – on time again – and with another handful of Wales fans, we board. The plane's pretty empty, this route doesn't appear to have been on the Welsh fans' travel radar. I tried to sell the seat that Steve had originally bought for his wife but there were no takers, despite it being considerably cheaper than many of the other flight options. It's at least a couple of hours from north Wales and one group of lads have made the trip over, it's already been a long day for them.

Lille's close enough to the channel ports to offer the option of going by car, and two of the Paris party I collected tickets for, Euros and Gruff are coming that way tomorrow. Again, I've been tasked as ticket-monitor for the boys, in case things get tight or the dockworkers call a lightning strike.

The flight to Charles de Gaulle is smooth, trouble-free and we arrive on time. Having been here before, I can then lead our small party confidently through the crowds, towards the rental car stands, on the same route that I took to the hotel shuttle just a few days ago. Getting out of the car park proves a little trickier but, with Steve at the wheel again, he successfully guides us out of our subterranean lair and we quickly pick up signs for Lille. It's about 150 miles, so we're expecting to be there in time for lunch. As we're in no hurry, Steve suggests a diversion, calling in at the Thiepval Memorial *en route*. It seems apt, given the Somme anniversary that falls in a few days time. Also, he wants Fergus to see it. Steve's been before, I haven't and I'd like to go. My *Taid* joined up in 1916, lying about his age. He served with the Royal Welsh Fusiliers and then the Royal Engineers and his two cap badges are amongst my most prized possessions. His older brother was killed in France in 1917.

I re-programme the satnav and, after finding ourselves on the same road we took from Lens back to Amiens a lifetime ago, we leave the *autoroute* and head off into the French countryside, passing through villages whose names are etched onto the consciousness of those of us who can still remember relatives recounting tales of their 'Great War'. This leads us to a diversion from the diversion, when we spot a sign for the RWF and Welsh Guards memorial at Mametz Wood. We head off onto the D64, drive through the village of Mametz and follow a narrow, windy lane, following another car with GB plates. To our left, we spot a raised and wooded patch of land and the memorial appears on our right, a small car park below it.

We park, then climb the steps up to the memorial, a Welsh dragon sculpture facing towards the wood. The attack at Mametz began on 7th July 1916, the 38th Welsh Division given the job of seizing it from its German defenders, the crack Prussian Guards. The Welsh soldiers were ordered to walk towards the wood, across open ground – the planned smokescreen having failed to materialise – young men from all parts of Wales, conscripts new to the war. Needless to say, they were mown down in their hundreds, by machine guns to their front, left and right. The wood was finally taken on 12th July, after fierce hand-to-hand combat in amongst the trees. As I stand and look across from the memorial towards the wood, I can't imagine how horrific the whole experience must have been for those who survived. It's impossible not to draw parallels with our own visit to this part of France. We've come for a sporting event and will go home afterwards. Despite everything, the world must be an eminently better place for the contrast. It's a shame we don't commemorate peace.

It's interesting to see how this region has embraced it's awful history, how the First World War memorials and battlefields are part of the tourist industry. After we leave Mametz, we see a coach coming on the other side of the road and, in the front seat next to the driver, a moustachioed middle-aged guide dressed like a British 'Tommy'. It's a battlefields tour bus. We pass another a bit further on: just like the *Résistance* memorial in Plouha, there are clearly lots of people keen to revisit these dark passages in our recent history.

This sense is reinforced as we approach Thiepval. There are TV broadcast vans parked in small villages, camera crews wandering about, reporters delivering 'pieces to camera' in front of gravestones or churches. Then the huge Thiepval memorial comes into sight, it's approach road blocked by security guards dressed in black. Steve's not daunted and ploughs on, but we're flagged down a couple of hundred meters short at least, of our intended destination. We're asked if we have accreditation. Steve ignores that question and asks if we can just walk up to the memorial but we're told that without accreditation it's not possible. All around us there are more TV people, clipboards, golf buggies carrying producers, and soldiers in full dress uniform smoking outside long marquees. It feels more like we're on the set of a Hollywood blockbuster movie. I feel quite angry that this place has been taken over by these people, preparing to cover the 100th anniversary of a battle fought by my forefathers, denying us the chance to visit the memorial to them.

With the rain falling, we turn the car round on a muddy car park and drive back to the road. Steve's next idea is to visit the Canadian memorial, a place where they have preserved some of the trenches. As we head away from Thiepval, the scene becomes even more bizarre. We see signs for the Ulster Regiment memorial, then be-suited, bowler-hatted members of the Orange Lodge, their sashes clearly visible under their suit jackets. Then we have to slow the car as, up ahead, there is a marching column of men, all dressed in First World War regalia of soft peaked caps, puttees, bandoliers and, at their head, a burly bloke with three stripes on his sleeve. It would feel like we'd stepped back in time if there wasn't a crowd of onlookers at the side of the road taking pictures of them on camera phones. It's hard not to get a sense that somehow we're celebrating something that was utterly horrific. This wasn't glorious, it was a pointless – months long – slaughter in the mud, across worthless fields.

The Canadian memorial offers no sanctuary. It's closed to the public as well and we're forced to perform another u-turn in another car park. The visit to Mametz Wood was the right thing to do, a chance to reflect, this is something very different. It's time to leave. As we drive back along more country lanes, through villages flying Union Jacks, we pass a roadside memorial with a familiar crest that catches my eye. Steve slows down. It's the PFA badge, and this is the plaque commemorating the VC won by Donny Bell, the only British professional footballer to receive the highest military honour during the First World War. He came from Harrogate, played for Bradford Park Avenue and was the first professional player to join up in 1914. In 1916, during the Battle of the Somme, and with his unit pinned down, he successfully attacked a machine gun post on his own, then led a counter attack. He was shot dead five days later. A lad from up the road from where I live, a keen footballer, a brave man, another life lost. After the bad taste left by the scenes around the major memorials, it's a suitably poignant way to end our short trip to the killing fields.

Back on the motorway, our arrival in Lille is further delayed by a big traffic hold up. Steve's already in contact with the owners of the house we're heading for. He's had to revise the time we'd be getting there a couple of times already, they seem relaxed enough and promise to visit when they finish work.

This is a real trip into the unknown. I've no previous experience with Airbnb but I've read that there are different types of place on offer, either rooms in an occupied house, or the house or apartment with the owners absent. I very much hope it will be the latter although Steve's not sure what the arrangements are. We approach our base through the run-down outskirts of Lille. The satnav struggles to identify the exact location as there's so much building work going on, it looks like this part of the city is undergoing major renovation.

Sure enough, we find the street, a striking vision of white concrete boxes to left and right. They are very much 'newbuild'. We locate the right number, collect the key as instructed from a box by the gate, behind which there's a small yard area just about big enough to park the car. As we unpack the car, a white cat watches us from the front doorstep.

We go in and quickly ascertain that someone lives in this house and they've been here pretty recently. There are dishes in the sink for a start, a pair of shoes at the bottom of the stairs and coats hanging up. As we explore further, it becomes apparent that there are only two bedrooms available, both with double beds in them. Just like Toulouse, this means that someone's got to find an alternative. Needless to say it's our intrepid backpacker Fergus, who gets 'volunteered'. There's a big leather sofa in the living area downstairs that faces a quite enormous TV, entirely out of scale with its surroundings. Fergus settles himself down for a play with the remote control.

The cat's banging it's paw against the back patio windows now. Fergus wants to let it in but I point out that it might not be the owner's, besides, I'm not fond of cats anyway – long story but it involves a furry bacon sandwich, a stolen chicken breast and a bedsit in Barrow. Steve heads off upstairs for a kip and I search for a kettle. A cup of tea would be good, it's been a long time since the last one in departures at Doncaster Airport. The French don't normally do kettles. They drink coffee so the kitchen has a *cafétière*. However, we're in luck. I find a kettle pushed away at the back of a cupboard. Then I look for milk in the fridge and it appears our hosts don't do that either, there's a strange milk-like substance in a bottle but it's not milk, it looks thick, more like sour milk. At this point, I concede that I'm going to have to take action. I'm also hungry, having not eaten since 4.30am.

I resolve to go out and scavenge for supplies. Outside the house, at the end of the road, there's a huge hole being dug. It's scale suggests it might be for a rail track but, in truth, the buildings beyond it, across a busy dual carriageway, do look pretty run-down. There is, however, an Aldi sign a couple of hundred metres away on the other side of the road. The road proves a challenge, it's like 'Frogger' trying get across it but I make it and set about gathering provisions. I'm more than happy to fall back on the baguette, cheese and ham combination that's served us so well so far. Add to that, crisps, beer (naturally), and milk and we're good to go.

I return to base, the hunter with his quarry. Tonight, the tribe will eat. Fergus tears up the French stick and I make the tea – we brought our own teabags. Still I'm thwarted. The kettle's clearly been out of action for while as large flakes of limescale rise to the top when I pour the water into the cup. I will not be defeated on this one. I swill water round the kettle, pour it out, clean the kettle, pour more water in, repeat the process and finally – finally – manage to produce a vaguely drinkable cup of tea. Fergus, the dutiful son, takes a cup and a bit of baguette up to his dad. I eat, drink and then decide I'd quite like a power nap as well so I head to my room. It's sparsely furnished, with a futon bed and some fitted wardrobes, already full of someone else's clothes.

There are no pictures on the wall. For what we're paying for this place, I would expect a little more. There isn't even a toilet upstairs. For some reason, it's downstairs. This is not a very well designed house. Still, I have a bed, a mattress and a duvet and that's really all I need at this moment in time. I wind the metal shutters down to block out the light and the sounds of the construction work taking place beyond the thin strip of uncut grass that constitutes the back garden. The cat's still meowing outside the backdoor. I sleep.

I awake to the sounds of voices downstairs, one of which at least, I don't recognise. This may answer the question as to whether we're paying for exclusive use of the house or not? I go downstairs to see Steve and a young guy chatting and I introduce myself. He is, indeed, our host. A very nice chap he is as well. His first language is Moroccan Arabic, and he clearly also speaks French but he speaks very good English. He came to France to work a few years ago, met his wife and they've recently bought this house together, in this new district of Lille. He works in IT and he travels quite a lot, although he can't travel to the UK because he's Moroccan and hasn't got French citizenship yet. As a non-EU citizen, he can't get in.

Needless to say, this leads to a Brexit chat and again, he seems bemused as to why we've opted out. He's delighted to be in, he's made a good life for himself here, has a French wife, and earns enough to be able to invest over €200,000 in this property. He goes back home occasionally, work took him back to Morocco recently, but he has no plans to return permanently. There's beer in the fridge, he's created a cinema room for himself as he loves films and he invites us to partake of both.

His wife then returns, a new black Mercedes now parked on the street. They're going out for a meal but they'll be coming back later and sleeping here before going to work early in the morning. That scuppers the idea of Fergus sleeping on the sofa. He'll be bunking up with his dad after all. If it was Evo, he'd already have his airbed out on the drive next to the car!

They leave and we bid them a fond farewell – nice people – it'll be a pleasure to share their house with them! Then we begin our own preparations for a night out. That means taking our host up on his offer, he's got a good selection of Leffe, a fine dark beer that also happens to be pretty strong. We fire one down each before we head off into another murky evening.

The metro station's about a ten-minute walk away. There's a busy road intersection outside it with cars queuing in rush hour traffic. As they pull up, a small dishevelled group approach them, knocking on windows. It appears to be a mother and her children. She's wearing a headscarf and a flower patterned dress down to the floor. The young ones are dirty-faced, their clothes scruffy and their hair matted. The woman holds a sign that says in English, in magic marker scrawl, 'We are Syrian, please help us'. Car drivers fix their stares straight ahead, the sad group moves between vehicles before the lights change and they have to skip out the way and back to the pavement. Whether they really are Syrian refugees fleeing the terrible civil war is impossible to say. They're a sad sight, wherever they're from.

Just like Toulouse, the metro's swift, smooth and driverless. How do we not have similar transport systems in the UK? As the next train glides in, I make a beeline for the front, where the driver should be. Steve and Fergus are less impressed by such wizardry and stand further down the carriage. I'm wearing another of Tim's SO58 T-shirts tonight, the one with a map of Wales in red, yellow and green, and the slogan 'Independent Football Nation'. A guy in a blue Ralph Lauren polo shirt, cargo shorts and Adidas trainers spots it and weaves over in my direction. I think he's here for the football and I think he may have had a drink. He points at me. "Hey, aren't you that #@*$ from Sky Sports?" he enquires in a south Walian accent. It's a little hard to know how to answer this – I do my best – "Yes, I am that #@*$ from Sky Sports." I reply. I think my honesty may have disarmed him a little as he puts his hand up and says, "Sorry about calling you a '#@*$', I've had a drink." Now, he needs my help. He wants to know how to get into town and tags along as we zip in towards the Gare Lille Flandres.

Half a dozen stops later, we've arrived. Me and my new pal get off. Seemingly stricken with remorse, the poor guy offers a final apology before we go our separate ways. "Don't worry," I laugh, "I grew up in Ruabon, I've heard worse!" Reunited with Steve and Fergus, we emerge from the station and into the centre of the city. There are a number of bars facing the grand colonnades in front of the building, which are pretty busy already so we head off to find somewhere we can sit down and eat. We head off the main drag and down a side street towards a church with an imposing steeple. Steve spots a Chinese restaurant. Clearly keen to recreate the pre-match routine of Bordeaux, he suggests we give it a go.

It's pretty quiet inside so staff move quickly to motion us in, sit us down and get menus in our hands. Drinks appear and food swiftly after. As we eat and chat, the ambience is somewhat destroyed as a group of half a dozen blokes tumble in from the street. It's about 5.30pm but they're already in that 'Get a Chinese' at the end of a long night out mindset. They're loud, quite aggressive with the staff and, obviously, Welsh. A couple of their party voice objections to the choice of venue and as quickly as they appear, they leave. Before peace returns however, there's more discord. A Welsh couple, I haven't noticed before, have an argument with the manageress about not being able to wrap up food to take away – I presume they've asked for a 'doggy-bag' or something similar. The man is tall, fairly elderly and pretty rude as he tosses insults in his wake on his way towards the door, his wife in tow. It's the very first time in this whole Euro experience that I've had cause to feel embarrassed at the behaviour of my fellow fans. Steve senses it as well and offers apologies to the lady on the receiving end. When all's said and done, it's just a few harsh words, we've done pretty well.

We leave the restaurant and head off in search of somewhere to pass the rest of the evening and to watch the Portugal v Poland game. Lille's got an 'old town', so we head in that direction, following street signs and the map on my phone. There are touts out, offering tickets and prices are high, the Belgian invasion's seen to that. We head across the vast Grand Place, it has bars and restaurants all around the edge. On the other side, there are narrow streets and we turn left then right until we emerge into another square, by an unusual concrete church. In front of it, there are seats and tables that belong to a couple of bars, one of which has a big screen TV. This is us.

Beers appear, the match kicks off and we're back in Euro heaven. Poland score early through Lewandoski and Portugal equalise before half-time, through their new wonder kid, Renato Sanches. I'll be honest, I wasn't really aware of him, but Fergus knows all about him and his growing reputation. I'm the football journalist but Fergus has grown up with the football PC and console games, creating teams from the vast and hugely accurate up-to-the-minute database these games utilise. He's been able to watch all sorts of European football – on the TV, on his laptop – and I'm often amazed at just how much football knowledge many young people have these days, it's encyclopaedic.

As the game unfolds, a dozen noisy Belgians find a table close by to create a bit of the big match atmosphere. They're singing, drunk and happy. There's a bit of banter with a passing band of Welsh fans, songs are traded, then everyone drifts off into the night. More touts arrive, looking and sounding like London 'geezers'. Expensively dressed, with lots of "Awright boys, anyone arfter any tickets?" They get into conversation with a table close by, no deal is done.

Still, our game goes on, into extra time and, by the time the penalty shoot out's starting, the bar owner's already stacking the chairs. He does at least leave the TV on as we sup up. A small crowd gathers around us, all watching to see who goes through. The Portuguese eventually triumph and go through to the semi-final. That means they will now play the winner of Belgium v Wales. There aren't many in Lille tonight who'd predict anything other than that being Belgium, but the mood in the Welsh ranks is clearly upbeat. As we get back to the metro station, there are lots of fans around, lots of singing and we're enjoying every minute. Don't take us home.

On the train, there's a group of German lads; Hamburg fans. I shout the name of Kevin Keegan, my first 'favourite footballer' from my earliest days in Liverpool. It was a genuine shock to the seven year old Bryn when he decided to leave to go and play in Germany. Why would he leave Liverpool, the best side in Europe? He made a big impression there though – he was nicknamed Mighty Mouse – and the Hamburg fans immediately launch into a Keegan chant when they hear mention of his name. They're a friendly bunch but I can't resist a quick shout of 'St Pauli!' – Hamburg's cross-city rivals – as we arrive at our stop. They laugh and offer *faux* outrage as we leap off the train and onto the platform.

It's all quiet 'back home'. We creep in, sneak a last beer from the fridge and then tiptoe upstairs. I get into my room to find I'm not alone. There's the cat looking at me from the bed as I switch the light on. It stares at me angrily as if to say, 'what the hell are you doing in my room?' I chase it out and pull the door to firmly behind me. I don't like bloody cats!

Friday, 1st July – Euro 2016 Match Day 5

White Rabbits, White Rabbits, White Rabbits! A new month dawns and we're still in the Euros! After a long day comes a deep sleep and it's well after 9am before I wake up. I go downstairs somewhat tentatively – clutching my breakfast Weetabix I've brought over with me – pushing my head round the door of the living room. There's no sign of anyone but Steve, already sipping tea on the sofa.

Fergus is still in bed. It would appear it's been a tricky night for him, sleeping on the floor at the foot of his dad's bed. Our hosts have departed, off to work, so we've got the house to ourselves for the rest of the day, under the watchful eye of the cat, of course.

It's another 9 o'clock kick-off tonight, so the day stretches ahead of us but I've got tickets to collect and Steve suggests we might as well drive in to get them, then come back, have some lunch and head back into the city centre later in the afternoon. It sounds like a plan. Upstairs, there's the sound of Fergus apparently having a shower, an impression reinforced when I head up the stairs only to be greeted with water rushing down towards me. The water's running out across the floor of the shower room, under the door and down the stairs. It's like an indoor water feature. Much like the camper van experience, I leap into action, grabbing towels to mop up as much as I can. You have to say, a shower room with the shower unit at floor level lends further evidence to the accusation that this house is not very well designed.

The flood stemmed, we jump into our little car and head for the hotel that'll be the ticket collection point. It's the Crowne Plaza, next to the Eurostar station, that we're after this time. As we get closer, the traffic gets heavier and we find ourselves in a slow moving queue that stretches off way beyond the station. It turns out we're stuck on the Boulevard de Leeds – how on earth did this road get its name? Was there a mayor in the 1970s who was a big admirer of the Revie boys? I leave Steve and Fergus to ponder on this whilst I jump out and head for the hotel. It's only when I get into reception and there's no sign of any of the FAW ticket team that I realise why – I'm too early – they aren't 'opening' until noon and it's only 11.45.

I take the opportunity to go for a very quick look around. It's clear from the traffic, the crowds of people around the station concourse and on the pavements that many fans are just arriving in the city, by road and rail. The fan zone is across the road so I go for a look, although there are gates and security checks so I don't bother joining the queue. I haven't actually been in one yet, walked round a few but never been in.

Back outside the Eurostar terminal, I hear my name called and there, walking towards me, is Kev, a Wrexham fan I seem to bump into on most trips with Wales. The last time I saw him was outside a bar in Brussels ahead of the qualifier there in 2014. I mentioned our chat in *Zombie Nation Awakes* so the first thing he says to me here in Lille is, "It was me you were talking about in the book wasn't it?" I assure him it was and ask who he wants to play him when they make the movie?

Further on, I'm stopped by two more Wales fans. They also have a question, "Have you got your ticket yet?" The reason they want to know is they've just bought tickets from someone outside the station and paid a lot for them. "Don't ask how much!" they say. Their one fear is that they've bought fakes so they want to compare them with one that's definitely genuine. I can't help yet but peruse them anyway. They've got a hologram on them, that's a good sign. Many years ago, when Liverpool played Wimbledon in the cup final, I was in college just down the road from Wembley. I fancied going to the game and bought a ticket from a bloke outside the stadium, a Scouser. It was the first year they'd introduced holograms, after loads of fakes had flooded the market in previous years. I asked my guy if the ticket I was buying had the new hologram. He pointed to a square of tinfoil on the ticket I'd just paid £15 for. I'd never actually seen a hologram but I knew they showed a 3D image. I couldn't see anything. "Ah, it's alright lah, dey put it under a special light and it shows up." He assured me before disappearing off into the crowds.

Ticket in hand, I joined a mass of people jammed around the turnstiles at the Wimbledon end and saw my first hologram over the shoulder of the guy in front of me. I could clearly see the Wembley logo on his silver square. I'd been had. I sold my 'ticket', tinfoil and all, to another desperate Scouser for a fiver and went back to college to watch it on the telly instead. Ten pounds poorer and a whole lot wiser.

I have one more objective before I go and get my own ticket, it's either the big match nerves or the Chinese last night, but I have something of a queasy sensation in my stomach. There's a big shopping centre opposite the station so I head there in search of a chemist. They're bag-checking at the entrance and, once inside, there's another fully armed patrol of soldiers walking amongst the shoppers. It's a reminder that a fixture like this must be causing the authorities great concern with huge numbers of people crossing the border from Belgium – but how can they check everyone and everything?

I find what I need, it turns out the French for diarrhoea appears to be diarrhoea, or maybe the assistant could diagnose my complaint by just the look on my face. I pop a pill and, it now being midday, I head back to the hotel. The station is now teeming with people and, out on the other side, there's a big crowd of Belgians – red, yellow and black from head to toe – marching behind a bloke with a big drum. They are chanting, waving flags and, even though it's only noon – nine hours before kick-off – there's a flare! The atmosphere is brilliant.

Over the road, in the hotel, it's pretty busy at the bar. Inevitably, there are quite a few people I know, including Kris O'Leary, the former Swansea player and coach. He lost his job when Garry Monk was sacked earlier in the season. He's desperate to get back to work but as he acknowledges, despite lots of clubs already starting their pre-season preparations, it has given him the chance to follow Wales around as a fan. After a lifetime in the game, it'll be doing him good to have a break, a chance to watch games without the worry of the personal consequences dependent on the result.

The ticket handover takes place, I exit the hotel and spot Steve and the car, now pulled over onto the pavement on the other side of the road. I get back in and we set off for our Airbnb home again, leaving the crowds and the traffic jams behind. There's a trip to Aldi to fit in. Today we will dine on ravioli and hot dogs. Steve loves his tinned ravioli, that much I have learnt about my travelling companion over the last few weeks. We also agree to stock up on beer now, with the intention of taking our own supplies into town later as we expect that it's going to be ruddy difficult to get served anywhere! There's quarter of a million Belgians coming over the border and those Belgian lads like a beer.

As we're leaving the shop with our food and booze, one of the staff calls over, "Wales? Gareth Bale?" We nod in acknowledgement but he's not done there. "Belgium win 2-0," he predicts. We laugh but don't disagree.

If there was any issue, the tablet's done it's work and I'm soon happily tucking into a hot dog and supping from the day's first bottle of beer. I have a decision to make about my attire for the afternoon. I've been wearing the long sleeved Wales away shirt that Barry Horne gave me. He found it in his attic recently. It was issued to him before a game in the very early 90s and he never used it, never even took it out of the bag. It's a lovely item but I have to bear in mind the weather. It's still dull and overcast but I have no choice to opt for the grey shorts, the Reebok Paris and the SO58 T-shirt combination that did the trick in Toulouse. All topped off with the bucket hat, naturally. I've brought both versions of the bucket hat with me and I offer the original, pre-Euro success one to Fergus. He accepts, gratefully. He's now officially one of 'us'.

We load our bags with beers. I've got my little packaway rucksack and it clinks away on my back as we set off for the metro station. We head up onto the platform, followed by a lads and dads group of Welsh fans. We get chatting as we wait for a train, one of them asks if it would be okay to have a picture with the lads, so we all pose and smile as a train arrives and then we have to break away and dive on before the doors slide shut. We all make it, bar one. Their pal's stuck on the other side of the glass as we pull away, much to the amusement of his two mates, "Shook him off at last!" they laugh. There are Belgian fans heading into town on our train as well, one wearing a very big, red hat and red jacket and trousers. Steve gets into conversation with him. He's a nice chap but he's very confident and can only see a Belgian victory. His English is extremely good, almost impeccable, but Steve tests it to the limit when, he remarks, "We have a saying, 'pride comes before a fall.'" This seems to confuse our Belgian friend. He gets off the train still trying to work out what it means, again prompting laughter from the Welsh lads, "You got him there!" they suggest. "Pride comes before a fall!"

We get out at the Gare de Lille Flandres again. The concourse is packed with fans moving in all directions so we head down for the main exit – the tall, Roman colonnades – and the steps down to the street level and a fountain in front of the station. An incredible sight greets us there. We hear the noise first. The singing, the cheering, the roars then we step outside to pandemonium. There's a huge crowd gathered on all sides of the station. In front of us, there's a hotel and in front of that, there's a vast crowd of Belgians, some of them with footballs, and they're launching them high into the air. Then there are roars as they come down only to be volleyed up into the air again. The hotel sign is being targeted as well. The HOTEL CONTINENTAL is now the H TEL CON INENTA . The first O hangs down precariously, only a bit of the last L survives and even as we're watching, another ball strikes a letter and there's another big roar. That's the scene in front of the station. To the side of it, the crowds stand in and around the bars, and I spot a big Newport County flag hanging across the awning below the Hotel de Londres. Welsh and French flags hang side by side from a balcony above a coffee shop. Loads of people are cradling plastic beer glasses but the atmosphere's great, and fans of the two teams stand together and talk.

We press on through the crowds in the direction of the main square. So far it's brilliant, but the sight that greets us in Le Place Charles de Gaulle, to give it it's full title, is just off the scale – one of the most amazing things I've ever experienced. It's packed with people. In front of us and to the right are crowds of Welsh fans with flags from every town and village, gathered outside of the bars and *cafés*. To our left, a huge crowd of Belgians and they're going mad. They're singing, jumping up and down and there are big scary bangs as flares go off, it's total craziness. Incredibly, the steps up to a balcony in front of the ornate theatre building are adorned with Wrexham flags, including Andy Yemm's famous Stoke Reds banner. The balcony offers a great overview of the madness below so we make our way to the top of the steps and look down on the sea of people; the red, yellow and black. Clouds of pink smoke drift across, another song starts, the Belgians bounce – crouching down *en masse* – then leap up together and continue their wonderfully joyous routine. Over and over it happens. Then they start singing *Don't Take Me Home* and up on our vantage point, we join in. Clearly, the feeling's mutual. It's the craziest party I've ever been to!

To get an even better view, I need to go higher and I pull myself up onto a narrow window ledge, maybe thirty feet or more above the crowds now. Standing here, on the window ledge, watching these people below being deliriously happy, I feel as happy as I've ever felt in my life. It often feels like a bad world we live in but here, in this Flemish city in northern France, for one afternoon at least, everybody's having the best time of their lives.

A guy in Belgian fan gear scrambles up to join me on my perch. I put out a hand to pull him up. Inevitably, he speaks good English. He asks me what I think about the game tonight? We begin a chat about our respective teams. He says he thinks Belgium will win but they are missing important players in defence. I remind him of our impressive record in recent games and the more confidently these guys talk about their team, the more confident I begin to feel about mine. He makes an interesting point about the scenes below. "They are so happy because they expect to win, they have had some beers and we are so close to Belgium. We must enjoy it because we will never see this again." It's a unique combination that's prompted such unbridled joy and it's great to be here in the midst of it but it does make me wonder if the Belgians aren't jumping the gun just a little. It's hours from kick-off still, how can they sustain this level of excitement through the rest of the afternoon and into the night? I think there's a chance these fans might have peaked a bit too early! As I consider this, a guy dressed as a chicken is being passed over everybody's heads in a rubber dinghy. He's kneeling in his craft, holding a paddle and, as he's doing a rowing action, he's being moved, quite quickly, above the crowd. This is completely bonkers.

Next, a middle aged woman, who looks very much like someone's mum, gets hoisted up above the heads of the crowd and she proceeds to lead the crowd in several more chants, arms waving above her head. There are police officers in the square but not many and they keep their distance. They know when they aren't needed.

I hop down from my ledge, say goodbye and good luck to my Belgian friend and go and join Steve and Fergus at the bottom of the steps. It's time to sample the scenes on the other side of the square, the away end! It's not quite so frenzied in the far corner, there's singing, large crowds but no dinghies. It's time to unpack the beers in the bags, fighting our way through to any bar seems too tough a challenge. So, we stand, we drink and we watch. It just feels like a time to soak it all up, to store away the images, the sights and the sounds for those dark days of winter, on a cold November night in Grimsby.

Groups of fans pass constantly, wearing fancy dress and silly hats. There's a father and daughter walking hand in hand, both of them wearing a silver foil reproduction of the Brussels Atomium on their heads. They make slow progress as they stop for every request for a picture. There are other nations represented here as well. Two guys in German shirts walk by, Steve calls to them and they come over for a chat. This is exactly what football should be, a big party, people brought together by a love of the game first, a love of their country second.

All of Wales is represented here, the flags give testament to that, including my village, Ruabon. My first Wales away trip was with the lads from my local pub, lads I grew up with, played football with and went clubbing with. They're here in Lille as well. I spot Spike and Aggie and we enjoy a reunion in the midst of this brilliant madness.

It's years since I last saw them but they're no different – the sparkle's still in their eyes – mind you, that might be something to do with the ale! Talking of which, our stocks are dwindling so I undertake a mission to acquire more. There's supposed to be some sort of ban on shops selling alcohol today, though there's little evidence of it based on the piles of empty bottles and cans around us. Sure enough, a couple of hundred metres off the square, there's a supermarket and the bag gets refilled.

I have one more task to perform and I'm not going to replicate the shameful scenes of the Paris metro if I can help it, so I end up climbing to the top floor of a swanky apartment store in search of a toilet. I must look a somewhat odd sight amongst the well heeled shoppers with my bucket hat, stubble and a small blue rucksack stuffed full of bottles and cans. I manage to make it up and down without attracting the attention of store detectives and return to my pals suitably refreshed and bearing gifts. There's another familiar face in the vicinity on my return, it's one of the police spotters who travels away with Wales. I've met him on a few previous trips and I catch his eye and wave a greeting. I try and keep it subtle as he's obviously working and I'm not sure whether anyone's meant to know he's a police spotter or not?

He's probably even more well known to the group of blokes he appears to be watching – lads in their 40s and older – they're all decked out in expensive coats, Adidas trainers, label polo shirts, no football shirts. If I had to guess, I'd say these were some of the Cardiff firm from back in the day, the infamous Soul Crew perhaps? They're doing what everyone else is doing, drinking, chatting and laughing. There's been trouble at Wales v Belgium games in the past but that was a long time ago and it mainly involved Wrexham and Cardiff fans fighting each other. Today, everybody stands side by side.

It's noticeable now that the crowds are thinning out a little and we agree it's time we started to make our way towards the stadium. The metro's going to get pretty busy with so many thousands of fans currently in the city centre. I still have the two tickets for Gruff and Euros and they still haven't made it to Lille. In fact, it's 5.30pm and they've only just arrived in France. They were meant to cross at 12.15 but severe delays on the Eurotunnel mean they're now touch and go to actually get here in time to collect those tickets. We're in touch by text and I promise to wait at the stadium as long as I can.

We head back up the steps and into the station. Predictably, it's packed. There are lots more Belgian fans than Welsh fans but everyone's getting on well. We have pictures taken with each other as we wait to squeeze through the barriers. Then we all squeeze onto the next train and it's yet another standing room only journey to a French football stadium. The Stade Pierre-Mauroy is served by the last stop on the line. Will it also be the last stop on the line for our great adventure? The Belgians around me clearly think so. They're unremittingly confident, I haven't met one yet who'd predict anything other than a win for Belgium. They clearly haven't suffered like we've suffered!

We all pour off the train and, whilst the majority head off up the road to the ground, we wait for the latecomers to arrive and collect their tickets. We're standing at a fork in the road and behind us there's a fence and then a field. The fence has now been drummed into service as a temporary urinal by fans who've probably just endured a fairly uncomfortable last few metro stops.

So much of the fun of this tournament has just been finding a good spot to stand and watch as the crowds go by, this is another such location – as long as you keep your eyes away from the fence. There's another silver foil hat heading our way, this time it's a Wales fan who's been busy making a full size replica of the European Championship trophy. It's an amazing construction, even more amazing that it somehow stays on his head. I'm hoping that I'm not in the row behind him in the stadium. Then, there's Dewi Prysor, a very well known figure in north Wales. He's another everyman, a poet, a writer, a composer, a language activist and a Wales away regular. I got to know him when he hosted a joint Spirit of '58/*Zombie Nation Awakes* event in Bala. He's a good guy and he comes over for a chat.

Then things become a little less conventional when a group of half a dozen young people of all sizes and ages come over. They're begging, I think. There's one older girl, maybe 14, then a younger lad and three or four little ones. A small hand is pushed out at me, palm upturned but I shake my head and look away in the manner of anyone who's ever turned down such a request, don't make eye contact! Steve and Fergus have adopted a different approach. Fergus is now carrying one of the little ones in his arms, Steve's laughing and joking with the older girl. Over the next few minutes I can only watch on in wonderment as the Shones and this merry band have a fine time together. I've had a few drinks so I have to double take as Steve now appears to be teaching them how to do Dai Hooligan's pincer movement. No, it's real, that's exactly what he's doing. They're all following Steve's lead, shuffling from side to side on the pavement, laughing their heads off.

In the midst of all this, the phone goes and it's Gruff. He's panting heavily but I make out that they've managed to get parked up and they're now running towards the stadium. I confirm our location and even as I do so, two pale faced middle-aged men round the corner at pace and seem set to weep with relief as they see me standing at the side of the road. The full horror of the journey is etched across their faces, the tension pours away as I take the tickets out of the envelope and pass them over. It's okay, they've made it, so let's go, let's get into the stadium for the biggest game of our lives!

Steve and Fergus say goodbye to their gang of young pals and we all set off towards the ground. As we walk-up Steve confides, "I'm feeling a bit drunk." The supermarket excursion has been a success! The security checks are the best organised of any we've encountered so far and we're up the steps and into our seats well before the anthems. It's quite a sight. We're in the corner again, Wales fans occupying an 'L' shape section at our end and the Belgians occupying just about every other section. It's a wall of red at both ends. The stadium's new, holds 50,000 and it's full and bouncing. Over our heads, the roof is open, despite the fact that rain falls heavily from a dark Lille sky.

The players emerge from the tunnel, far away on the opposite side of the stadium. They head to their line-up positions and the Belgian anthem's announced first. The majority of the crowd join in, of course, but they can't compete with what comes next. From our corner, from every Welsh voice dotted around the stadium, the sound of something incredible, an ancient language, a song of defiance, 'Gwlad! Gwlad!' Then the words rise to the crescendo, 'O bydded i'r hen iaith barhau!' 'Let the old language endure!' – and, in this moment, it does, on the lips of every man, woman and child supporting the little country to the west of England. And I'll guess that around the world, in a host of different languages, people are saying, "Wow! What a stirring anthem this place called Wales has!" It's almost too much to bear. It's one of those moments when I find myself overcome with the enormity of it all and I have to gulp down sobs as I stand, arms stretched wide. Alone again, in the middle of a crowd. Before the game kicks off, I reconnect, there are handshakes with Steve and Fergus, and then we're off, Belgium v Wales in the quarter-finals of the European Championships!

Our opponents begin the game like they want to get it wrapped up as quickly as possible. In their change shirts of light blue with red, yellow and black hoops around the middle, they look more *Tour de France* than Euro 2016 and they certainly set a blistering pace, whizzing down both wings and steering inside Welsh challenges through the middle. Hazard's everywhere and De Bruyne looks up for it. Defensively the team may look a little makeshift, but there's so much talent in front of the back four that attack must seem like the best form of defence.

Inside the first five minutes, crosses come in from both wings that cause problems, and the singing of *Men Of Harlech* seems so apt, given that it's wave after wave of attacks and our thin red line is continually being breached. It's unfair to compare sport and war because one is life or death and the other is essentially utterly trivial, but it's hard not to think of the young Welsh lads thrown into battle, a long way from home at Mametz Wood, 100 years ago. The phrase 'digging in' certainly comes to mind as Ben Davies blocks off De Bruyne as he sets off towards the Welsh penalty area again. It's a yellow card for Davies. I know what this means straight away. It's his second one of the tournament, so he'll misses the next game, although the next game seems an awfully long way off at this early stage. What a smack in the guts for poor Ben, saviour against Slovakia, but he's got to get on with it.

We're struggling to get hold of the ball, never mind getting it up to the other end. Belgium are throwing everyone forward, defenders included. That confidence we've seen and heard in their fans all day long, almost celebrating the win before the game, seems justified and the players appear to be of the same mindset. Wales should be swept aside on their way to a winnable semi-final.

The sense of destiny grows as De Bruyne launches forward and Romelu Lukaku sets up a shooting chance for Carrasco. It's on target and well struck but a big, yellow blur blocks it. The ball then bounces into the path of Meunier and he unleashes another shot, again heading for the goal, until a red blur leaps into the path of it and the ball spins away. There's no respite, however, as Hazard waits, then shoots and this time a clutch of red shirts throw themselves across it's trajectory and a deflection lifts it up and over the bar. It all takes no more than a few seconds but with each and every one of them, I'm expecting to see the ball hit the back of the net. Somehow, it doesn't. There are Welsh players picking themselves up off the turf as we celebrate their good work and our good fortune. Even then the corner causes more panic as Lukaku just misses out making contact at the far post. There aren't ten minutes on the clock yet and we're on the ropes!

The tide turns briefly as Hal heads into the hands of Courtois and then Gareth goes on a gallop that leaves defenders trailing, but his shot's not on target and flies into the side netting. He's not really hit the sweet spot with one of those yet this tournament, yet still, it's a reminder that we've got stars of our own. If truth be told, it's been an amazing first few minutes: breathless stuff. We're all transfixed, eyes following the action from one end to the other, each of us in our own world of worry or hope or excitement or maybe all three?

It's a rare moment of opportunity for Wales though as Belgium again move forward ominously, massed ranks moving up together to lay siege to the Welsh penalty area as we give the ball away. If I didn't know better I'd say it was Joe Allen. Nah, can't be?! I see the ball go out wide to Hazard, for the first time he's got space and time. The Welsh midfielders have dropped back to the edge of the area, the defenders are even deeper. The Belgians get to play in triangles, with little passes back and forth. Nainggolan is waiting just to Hazard's right – an easy and obvious ball – although a cross might be a better option as the guy with the blonde Mohican, the guy who's crazy header set up Gareth Bale's winning goal when the two teams last met, is a long way out. Hazard plays it to him anyway. With no red shirt close, the Belgian is able to let the ball roll past his left foot, onto his right and in one movement he sets himself perfectly to strike the ball with tremendous power and tremendous accuracy. I know where it's going as soon as he connects. The yellow blur that is Wayne Hennessey is leaping, stretching, bending desperately upwards but nobody's blocking this one. As the ball hits the net, it's hard not to applaud. Nainggolan has his revenge. What a goal!

Now, the stadium, or two thirds of it at least, erupts. We see footage on the big screen of the coach, Marc Wilmots, racing across the technical area to celebrate. After suffering at the hands of Wales before, this must be the start he dreamed of. The opposite end of the stadium is a seething mass of Red Devils. They've got their early goal, it's all going to plan. It's strange. I don't feel bad, I don't feel sad. I think I smile, reflecting on all the great things that have happened over the last few weeks. I'm okay with it. If they score again, that'll be that, but we've had a hell of a run. They're ranked the second best side in the world, they were meant to win. I'm in this state of detached contentment as the game goes on, the Belgian fans all flares and flags again. The intensity of those opening minutes dissolves a little as the party starts anew around the sides of the pitch. They start doing the dance with the crouching and the leaping up that we saw in the square, only this time it's tens of thousands joining in. It's quite a sight. The Belgian players are still pressing forward at every opportunity but they seem a little more relaxed now that they've scored. The onus is on Wales to find a way to break out.

Over the next few minutes, something incredible happens. The Welsh team, this band of brothers, begins to work it out, to come up with exactly that plan. There's no big huddle and the signs are intermittent at first but it's there. Players start to step forward again, defenders push up rather than nervously hugging the edge of the area. Midfielders begin to base themselves higher up the pitch and the two wing-backs start to venture up the touchlines again. Maybe the Belgians have put so much into that opening frenzy that, like their fans and their pre-match partying, they're happy to take a little rest now. The noise levels in the stadium drop, at one end at least. For the first time, the Welsh supporters raise their voices – every bit the rallying cry – although, to be honest I think we're responding to what we're seeing in the players. We're playing the game in the opposition half now and our midfield trio that was overrun for 15 minutes – Allen, Ledley and Ramsey – are working together, moving the ball between themselves and bringing the wing-backs into the game. When we lose possession, we fight to get it back quickly again.

Neil Taylor's showing his attacking worth once more, he's a good 'out' ball, and the game recalibrates. Ramsey has a shot blocked, Gunter gets booked for holding De Bruyne then Ashley Williams berates the ref for not showing a yellow card to Hazard for picking the ball up in anticipation of a free kick. They are little things but they irritate the Belgians, fans and players alike, it's all part of the fightback. Before the start of the last qualification campaign, Chris Coleman talked about wanting the players to be more 'streetwise' in international games, to learn the often cynical art of 'game management'. This is it. Break the game up in any way possible. Remind opponents that you're not about to give up the battle. A foul, a niggle, a shot, whatever it takes. All those years of watching Wales has prepared me for the worst at 1-0 down, now I'm watching this team turn the game round in front of my very eyes. It's uplifting, it's like it's our little secret about to be unleashed on the wider world. The mood around me matches what I'm seeing, *Hymns and Arias* gets an airing, the old Max Boyce rugby song, then *Calon Lân*. It's our own message of defiance.

Nainggolan whinges about a foul on the edge of the box as Wales get the ball back off him, Ramsey breaks down the right and whips in a cross from the byline. It arrives at the feet of Neil Taylor, unmarked on the penalty spot. It's one of those 'arms up in the air' moments as he connects well but it's a green blur that stops this goal, Courtois making a great save from such close range. Those arms drop and hands land on 15,000 Celtic heads. Neil Taylor? Never scored a goal for Wales until Toulouse, now he's nearly doubled his tally in Lille!

It lifts the volume at our end another notch. There's no doubt about it, our players have dragged themselves right back into this, they've steadied things, they're playing good football. The red shirts push forward for another attack and Robson-Kanu does his thing down the right, skipping past a challenge to cross, until De Bruyne blocks it and we get a corner. Ramsey's first effort is short, to Bale and another block so he gets another chance. The referee gets involved as the players are jostling for territory, ahead of the next corner. The Wales players are lined up as if shopping for baguettes, with Belgian defenders jostling to jump the queue as the next one comes over. Suddenly, Ashley Williams makes a break and seems to be running down an empty aisle as the ball sails towards him. From afar, we see him jump, stoop, connect and the ball hits the ground and bounces up and over the line, between defender and post. YEEEEEESSSSSSSSSS!!!!!!!!! Ashley spins away heading for the dugout, just like Gareth in Cyprus, and in the Welsh end, everyone around me, we all start leaping around and hugging everyone within reach. I'm locked in an embrace with Steve and Fergus and others I don't know. *'He's Ashley Williams! He's captain of Wales!'* YYYYEEEEAAAAHHHH!!!!

We've been box ticking in every game. Just let us see a goal – box ticked. Just let us win a game – box ticked. Just let us go through – box ticked. Win the group? Bonus box ticked. Scoring in the quarter-finals to equalise? Whatever happens, that's another box ticked! That's how it works for the older fans at this end of the ground. We don't ask for much from our team, it's the hope that kills you.

There are fans of all ages around me though and the younger ones must presumably now think that Wales can go on and win the game. I've a had a lifetime of believing that this is a brief moment of euphoria before reality intrudes, like Lens. But this team is making it different. They don't have all the old baggage, the old anxieties, they don't remember Bodin's penalty or Jordan's handball or the faulty floodlights at Swansea. We were behind for the first time in the tournament, now we're level. Now, we need to push on, and that's just what the players do.

A hero up front a few minutes ago, Ashley Williams now earns another huge roar with a fantastically robust but clean challenge on De Bruyne on the edge of our area. De Bruyne looks like a sulky school-kid with his bottom lip curled, Williams runs right through him – men against boys. They're not out of it, Carrasco whips a ball in that Hennessey stretches to tip away, but we're the only ones making any noise now, *"You're not singing anymore!"* booms out – a retro number from the depths of the archives – picked out and dusted down. The perfect riposte after a day spent watching and listening to nice but noisy Belgians.

Gareth sets off again, fires off another shot – right foot this time – that Courtois saves and now nobody can deny that Wales, little Wales, the one-man team, are on top, in control and taking the game to the second best team in the world. Belgium can't get out of their own half as red shirts swarm all over them. The movement's brilliant, the Welsh players constantly offering options to the man in possession, making runs, overlapping, it's breathtaking stuff. It's football on another planet to anything I've witnessed from a Welsh team before. Given the quality of the opposition and the magnitude of the occasion, it's beyond Russia in Toulouse. We win corners, Chester and Williams get on the end of crosses, Ramsey shoots, Hal has a header and the soundtrack to it all is the anthem, chorus after chorus, *'Gwlad!'* after *'Gwlad!'* Now, I feel different. I feel like the young fans around me. We can win this game!

The half-time whistle comes as an unwelcome interruption. We roar our approval as the players disappear down the tunnel but the break gives Belgium the chance to regroup, it's not that they were bad, it's just that we were better.

The fifteen minutes at least gives everyone the chance to take stock and let the heart rate drop. It's Fergus's first experience of a live Wales game, I can tell he's loving it. If every game was like this, every ground would be full, always. He's grown up mainly watching the game on TV and on computers, there's nothing to compare with this, this is why UEFA feel they can get away with charging such exorbitant prices, because we have to go, have to be 'there' in the knowledge that it might be like this, but no guarantees and certainly no refund.

There are signs of activity on the far touchline now, I can see the hugely distinct figure of Marouane Fellaini, or rather I can see his hair. The afro's now streaked blonde, hopefully making him even easier for Joe Allen to spot if he throws another elbow like he did in the qualifier in Brussels. I'm heartened by his appearance actually. Wilmots has done something similar in previous meetings. When things aren't going well, he likes to chuck on the big lads and a skilful player like Hazard becomes less important as they start to hoof the ball into the area more often.

We've got three central defenders who all leap well, and that change of tactics has suited us well in those previous games. Carrasco's been sacrificed, which is also a surprise, as he often seemed to be a good option for them down the right in the first half. It would appear that 'get it in the mixer!' was the half-time message, as Belgium race out the blocks again. It's appropriate that *Men Of Harlech* is the new backing track. We have something of the look of the South Wales Borderers staunchly defending Rorke's Drift as the Belgians bang their shields and launch a fresh wave of attacks. There's a big miss as Romelu Lukaku, his brother now playing too, gets up above our defenders and a cross drops on his forehead. It's one of those moments when you feel most helpless as a fan, with a half-second to contemplate what happens next. It should be crushing disappointment at another Belgian goal, instead it's a surge of relief as he fails to do what Ashley did from a similar position in the first half. It's a chance a centre-forward of his size and stature should take with glee – it goes wide.

We're penned back now though, as the game's clearly swung back in their favour once more. De Bruyne's involved again, having faded after the skipper's big hit before half-time, and he has a shot that goes over. Then Hazard suddenly comes to life. He really doesn't seem to get much luck against Wales: nice in the approach but as we've seen in those previous games, not the accuracy or penetration at the business end of the move. So, he sets off on a weaving run from the left, gets into a good position for a shot but puts it just a little too wide of the far post.

The Belgian fans are reinvigorated by the players revival and they find their voices again as the team seeks to live up to those sky-high expectations. There's the biggest ovation since the goal when they force a corner kick. Even from where we're standing, a long way away, it has the feel of a period of play that's building towards a goal. The captain uses his head to good effect to keep another cross away from Lukaku, Ben Davies hacks the corner away and then Joe Ledley has a little row with the ref about a throw-in on the halfway line, so there's a pause in play: slow it down, break it up, get the shape back.

Gareth Bale picks up a pass on the right and Aaron's made a good forward run so Gareth goes long to drop the ball into his path. It's just about the first time we've seen red shirts up our end this half and there's a collective lean forward as the ball's moved quickly through Aaron and into Hal Robson-Kanu in the area. He's got his back to goal and Neil Taylor's bombed up from the back to support him. There are three light blue shirts around him in the area so he seems to need that assistance. Except that one second he's facing our goal and the next he's facing the Belgian goal. It doesn't compute, neither does the fact that those three Belgian defenders all seem to have disappeared, all of a sudden it's just Hal and Thibault – Hal wins! Kanu beats Courtois, the net bulges. BOOM! The Welsh end explodes! EXPLODES! I'm literally screaming, we're all screaming, but I'm also leaping up and down, I'm screaming and leaping and so is everybody else. Then I'm, we're, looking round for someone to hug, to hug and scream and jump up and down, then someone else, then repeat. Ian

Gwyn Hughes' son, Daniel, is two seats down from me, our eyes meet and then we're jumping up and down in each other's arms. Steve and Fergus have both been off hugging strangers but we return to find each other. More jumping, more hugging, still screaming. Belgium could have kicked-off and equalised by the time some semblance of order returns to our 'end'. On the big screen above our heads, they're still re-running the goal and we can see how the magic happened, for magic it truly was! It was a turn, a Cruyff turn! I've never seen a player do one 'live' in a game before, no wonder I didn't know what had happened! This is Hal, rejected by Arsenal as a lad, unattached after leaving Reading at the end of the season, spent most of his career at Championship level – often as a sub – and yet he's just produced one of the most exquisite moments of pure skill you'll ever see. This is Hal, born in London, earned caps for England at U-19 and U-20 level, switched to Wales when Brian Flynn found out he had a grandmother from Caerphilly. This is Hal. He's done it in a finely poised quarter-final tie of the European Championships, in front of 50,000 people in the stadium and millions, tens of millions more watching around the world. For Wales. Who now lead Belgium by two goals to one. This is 'Hal, Robson, Hal Robson-Kanu'.

Did I say I've never been happier than Toulouse? It doesn't do to make bold statements like that with this team. Transporting Wales supporters to new levels of euphoria, that's this team's mission. I was tense when we took a narrow lead in the qualifier against Belgium in Cardiff. I'm not like that now. Qualifying, that was the big one, the really big one. This, this is pure easy street after the decades-long purgatory of seeing them try but fail, time after time. This is easy, another box ticked. Take the lead v Belgium – ticked. Do it with a goal of breathtaking beauty – bonus box. Enjoy it while it lasts – I'll be ticking that one too.

I climb up on my seat for a while. An urge takes me. I want to look around, to survey the scenes. The game's going on but Wales are keeping the ball so that's fine. I need to soak this scene up, now, at its height, for this might be the happiest moment any of us ever experience as Wales fans. This may yet prove to be our last game in this tournament, so remember this bit, when we were in front. I don't feel an urge to sing, I'm happy to watch as a huge chorus of *Don't Take Me Home* rises from all around. It's one of those choruses that everyone joins in with, even the ones who've stood with their arms folded. But I want to watch this time, I do the actions, arms spread wide, up on my seat, and as we're singing, Wales win a corner and Courtois flaps and Wales nearly score again. Ashley Williams denied. *'He's the captain of Wales'.*

Then, there's another song from the back catalogue, *'Are you watching Ingerland?'* Back in the day, we used to sing this one whenever we were in front against good teams but I was never sure why. It just seemed to highlight an unhealthy obsession with what happened to the team across the border. As if us being better than England for one afternoon or night was a substitute for us actually being successful in our own right, regardless of how England are doing. The real nature of the rivalry with England's just been exposed by the referendum, Wales voted with England when nobody else in the UK did. For the majority, it's just a Saturday afternoon rivalry. So, I don't join in. I know plenty of people in England who will be watching. Some will have been riled by the footage of the Welsh players celebrating the Iceland result but most will be supporting Wales, including my own family – I hope so, *'Are you watching Rachel, Megan and Millie?'*

The sense of soaking it all up now heightens a little as Belgium line-up a free kick just outside the penalty area. I retreat to my usual mental refuge, 'Ah rats! They're bound to score, it was good while it lasted.' But that's not really working for me anymore. Something has happened, I've been rewired; maybe it's the screaming? I don't think Kevin De Bruyne will score. He doesn't, it's a poor shot straight at Hennessey. Do you know what? I'm enjoying this! I'm not racked with tension, feeling a little bit sick, like usual. I'm genuinely enjoying this. Why wouldn't I? We're not fluking this like we have in the past, it's not 'get ahead then cling on', we are well organised, intelligent, committed, talented and confident. The players are doing okay as well, boom boom!

We get two more corners and from the second Joe Allen sees his goal-bound shot deflected, the ball comes back to Captain Fantastic and he almost produces an acrobatic volley to score a second. It's that sort of evening. We're playing like Brazil!

The pattern follows that night in Cardiff, the period when the crowd sang the anthem and the Belgian players seemed to stop playing, alarmed at the intensity of it all. They're going through the motions,

Wales can keep possession, move the ball around, run the clock down. It's like that for a few glorious minutes. After all the frenzy, it's an emotional oasis and more chance just to suck it all in, cram it all into memory banks for cold winter's evenings and grandchildren on knees.

With fifteen minutes to go, and a humiliating exit beginning to look more of a reality, the Belgians rouse themselves a little. It's pretty basic stuff, bomb some balls into the box for the big lads, but it almost works. Aldeweireld's the unlikely source of a cross into the box that's just too high for James Chester but perfect for the distinctive golden afro. Fellaini's been largely anonymous so far, apart from the usual untidy scraps with opponents but this is his moment. This is what he's here for. He meets the ball just to the left of centre, we wait for the net bulge, the telltale ripple. Instead, his hands go to his head, as do the hands of the massed ranks behind that goal. The ball goes wide.

Just as it feels like we're invincible, unstoppable, Aaron Ramsey attempts to block a through ball, moves his body towards it and it hits him, it hits his hand. The referee, an impeccable performance up to this point, reaches for his pocket. I know, Aaron knows. His reaction to the yellow card conveys his devastation. He's out of the semi-final. Like Ben before him though, he's got to put it out of his mind. Those of us of a certain age remember the Gazza moment in Italia '90, the tears as he got yellow carded, ruled out of the final, and Gary Lineker's 'finger to the temple' gesture to the bench, as if to say, 'Careful, he's lost it.'

We've got to get there first, he can help us. He'll be okay, he's a strong character. There's work still to be done for sure as Belgium throw another ball into the box and Fellaini climbs to head it goalwards. It goes wide again but only a foot or two in front of Witsel's outstretched leg. It's not desperate defending yet, but we're getting to that time where anywhere will do. During the qualifiers, I'd be anxiously checking the stadium clock every couple of minutes, I haven't been doing it tonight. In fact, rather than wanting the game to be over, there's a part of me that wants it to go on forever. If there's an event in time you could choose to be trapped in, this would be it. The game goes on forever, we're always winning and we're always playing this well. Eternal bliss!

Still, if you're going to play until eternity, you need to make changes, freshen it up a bit and the board goes up to call Joe Ledley back to the dugout for a rest. If truth be told, he looks spent. He's been quietly going about an immense amount of work in that midfield, harrying, chasing, offering support. As he walks slowly over to the touchline, the inevitable '*Ain't nobody like Joe Ledley*' chorus follows him over to the high-five with Andy King. This team's blessed, not only with great players, but also with great characters and professional sportsmen who aren't afraid to display a personality. Joe is the beard, the dance moves, the cool clothes.

It's a mark of the strength of this squad that we bring on a player who won the Premier League title with Leicester. In years gone by, Andy King would have been a regular starter, a possible captain, but he's been a loyal servant at a time when the national team's been blessed with a glut of talented midfielders. He's utterly reliable and just the man you want to bring on for the last ten minutes or so of a game of this magnitude.

Other changes are afoot, Sam Vokes appears on the touchline, ready to come on. The board goes up again and it's another hero who departs, Hal Robson-Kanu. You know the phrase 'legend' that's used in relation to sport stars? Well, Hal has just achieved that status. He could retire tomorrow and everyone in this stadium and everyone back home will remember that moment, forever. His name echoes around the ground, over and over, I wonder if he'll manage to get himself a club for next season now? Real Madrid perhaps? Sam jogs on, ten minutes left to make an impression.

Inevitably, the emphasis is on defence now, and the referee redeems himself to an extent when a clutch of attacking players buzz around in our box and Naingollan goes down as Ashley Williams goes in to challenge him. It's almost identical to an incident at a similiar stage in the game in Cardiff, when Hazard went down. The outcome's the same as well. Get up you big Jessie! Play on!

The truth is, apart from a clumsy challenge like that, the only tactic Belgium seem to have is a ball into the box for someone to head. It won't be Romelu Lukaku though, he's had his chance and failed. He follows his brother in being taken off, neither have had a night to look back on fondly around the family table. For all his imposing physique, for all his classic target-man looks, the big guy up front, having seen him quite a few times, he doesn't seem to be much of a header of a ball. Wales have cause to be thankful for that.

The changes have helped waste time and taken a bit of the heat out of things but they're coming at us again, an attack down the right side, this time. Yet every time, there's a red shirt, two red shirts, a challenge, a block, a header. The concentration levels are incredible, these lads just haven't switched off and as another corner comes in, another head arrives to meet it and direct it away from the area. Aaron Ramsey completes the job with a proper hack up into the Belgian half. When the ball comes back, he wins it again and he's fouled. More seconds elapse.

All around me, the mood's almost indescribable. Our focus levels match those of the players on the pitch. All eyes follow every ball, no one talks. Every noise is directed at the pitch, to raise the players or question the ref. I don't know what this is. I've been going to football matches since I was about six years old, when my dad took me to a youth cup match at Anfield – an entry level fixture before I quickly graduated to the big stuff. My first proper games were at Goodison and Anfield before I became a regular at Wrexham. My first Wales game was a big one, against Russia at The Racecourse in 1981 – a thirty thousand crowd – we drew when we needed to win. The big games only really involve your own team, that's when it matters. I've seen a few of those down the years but this is the one, this is above everything else I've witnessed in over 40 years of being a fan.

Then, James Chester plays a ball out of defence, parallel with the touchline in front of us and Chris Gunter races after it, now almost in line with our position so he can take it to the corner flag perhaps and more precious seconds will elapse. No. Instead, he swivels and whips the ball beyond the covering defender and it sails over another defender on the edge of the six-yard-box and behind him there are two more players, one in red and one in pastel blue. Both leap at the same time but it's the man in red who gets there first, turning his head from right to left as the ball connects with his forehead, the movement alters the course of the flight and sends the ball arcing up and over the long, outstretched arm of a man in green.

I know where it's going, Fergus knows where it's going, Steve knows where it's going, Daniel knows where it's going and Sam Vokes knows where it's going. Super, super, super Sam Vokes knows where it's going. The ball sails on its way, it would fly forever if it wasn't for the net, the net that stops it, that breaks it's flight. The ball hits the net and drops down to the grass and as it stops and rests there, on the grass, inside the goal, life changes.

Everything that's happened up to this point on this fantastic journey, the ecstasy, the euphoria, the joy, the celebrations, the madness, the screaming, the jumping, the hugging, it's all nothing in comparison to this. This. This is the highest high, off the scale, lunar, oh my God! It's not words, it's just an internal explosion of happiness, but it's a tidal wave and I'm engulfed in utterly perfect happiness. I've never taken any drugs, nothing, so I've no knowledge of an 'instant hit', but it can't be any better than this. And all around me, there are people experiencing exactly the same sensation of pure and utter happiness, thousands of people. And down in front of me, right down in line with where I'm standing, my arms in the air – perfect happiness pumping through my body – there's Sam Vokes. My mate, Sam Vokes. One of the friendliest, most down to earth footballers I've ever met. A lad who's career I've followed with interest ever since I first saw him play for Brian Flynn's fabulous Under-21 team nearly a decade ago. He's had to scrap hard since he started at Bournemouth – a move to Wolves didn't really work out – he then went off to half a dozen clubs on loan before arriving at Burnley. There, it all took off. He's a Premier League striker now but he's exactly the same bloke I first interviewed all those years ago. Sam Vokes has just scored the best headed goal I've ever seen. And he's down on the pitch-side, pushed into the barriers, punching the air, surrounded by his teammates, his mates, the same guys who came through that Under-21 side with him. Chris Gunter, the man who put the cross in, Gareth Bale, Aaron Ramsey, Andy King, Neil Taylor, they're all there with him. We're all there with him and they are here with us. We're all mates, we're all together. We love them and they love us, and now we're all going to the semi-finals of the European Championships!

As the players drift back towards the centre circle, five minutes plus a couple to play out, the last drops of tension have poured out of the Welsh support. Now is the time for a party. As I contemplate the enormity of the achievement, the gloriousness of the football we've played, the fact that it's us, my team, Wales and the world is watching on, it's all too much. I can only stand on my seat again, arms out wide, the biggest, widest smile stretched across my face, tears rolling down my cheeks. I'm sobbing with joy.

Don't Take Me Home is being sung now, louder than ever, longer than ever. It's from the heart because who could ever want this to end? Nobody's really watching the game anymore, somewhere away down the other end, the players are doing what they've been doing all night – all tournament – working hard, defending with discipline; corners are conceded and cleared. It's irrelevant. The Belgian fans know it, many are heading for the exits. Somewhere in their midst, there's a chap with a big red hat, who's just worked out what the phrase, 'pride comes before a fall' means.

The stadium clock hits the 90-minute mark and *Hen Wlad Fy Nhadau* rises up from our ranks. The Belgians must be sick of the sound of these impromptu renditions of the anthem, sick of the sight of Bale and the boys, no wins in the last four meetings, beaten in the last two. The second best team in the world? No, some great players maybe, but still not a team.

We have a team, a fantastic team, the best team our country's ever produced. As a man, they raise their arms in the air when the referee brings the whistle to his lips and the three blasts signal the end of the game. We're all a bit stunned I think as it's a reality now – Wales in the semi-finals – down to the last four. One game, just one game away from the final! Portugal or Wales to decide which one will be playing in Paris in nine days time. How can that make any sense? How has this happened? The players start making their way over to our corner, to our end. In the middle of the group, Gareth Bale, motions them all to line up, we know what's coming next. Like Bosnia, they join hands and race in towards the fans before leaping and sliding across the turf, slick from all the evening's rain. In Zenica, I was already interviewing Chris Coleman as they slid past me – working and elated – but trying to be professional as they celebrated qualification. The travelling fans were on the other side of the fence that night. Tonight, I'm so proud, so, so happy to be back amongst the fans, delighted that I can do what they did there; sing, dance, cry, shout. I'm just a fan. It's why I came into the job in the first place. Watching football for a living is great but nothing beats this.

Our celebrations go on and on, nobody's wants to go home, nobody wants to even leave the stadium because when we head out, it's over, and we're onto the next one. The players stay out with us, they join in with our chants, they sing *Don't Take Me Home*, then stand and bring their hands together above their heads as the Icelandic fans' Viking chant gets nicked. It's not just the players out there now either, all the staff have joined in. I've seen them in action, their roles unheralded but every one of them completely committed to the cause. It's more than the players, this is the team, the video analysts, masseurs, physios, fitness coaches, kitmen, the lot. The stadium's empty now, save for our section and, after some more moves from ol' snake hips himself, Joe Ledley, the players begin to drift back towards the tunnel and the dressing room and, I would imagine and hope, a few beers.

So our little team turns and, somewhat reluctantly, heads for the exits. Fergus has picked a pretty decent game to make his international debut. He'll never forget his first cap! It's dark, chilly and damp outside, as we head back to the metro station, knowing what awaits. Sure enough, huge queues, thousands of people all waiting for trains back into the city centre. It's pretty quiet out here, now is the time everyone begins to realise just how knackered they are. As the queue snakes slowly, very slowly, round towards the station entrance, patience begins to wear a little thin. Like Bordeaux, the idea of having a new stadium linked to the city centre by a single tramline must have seemed a good idea at the time, not so good when pretty much everybody's hoping to use that one route after the game. Wembley has many faults but I've always found the tube service, with different stations and different lines all serving it, works efficiently in getting everyone quickly away afterwards.

As we wait, some ahead of me start to discuss their plans for the next game, Lyon in five days time. They're talking about getting the train, they've already booked tickets and mention the name of a website when I join in the discussion. As I stand and wait, I check prices. The addition of a return ticket to Leeds makes it very expensive, so someone suggests a flight to Paris, then the train. The TGV goes from the airport direct to Lyon. This sounds a good alternative so I go back to the Flybe website and book yet another return flight from Doncaster. The price is reasonable, obviously still not a route that's caught the eye of too many in Wales. I book a flight out on Tuesday rather than the early flight on Wednesday. I'll stay at the airport again, then get the train down in the morning. That removes the risk of any major flight delays on the day of the game, then I'll fly back the day after, an evening flight meaning there will be plenty of time to get back to Charles de Gaulle from Lyon. I'll leave the train booking until tomorrow, a quick glance suggests it takes a couple of hours and there's a regular service. I've lost Steve and Fergus by now, our queues have split and we've been parted, so I can't check what they might plan to do.

There's one more major task to undertake still, the big one, tickets! I ticked the boxes on my FAW order form all the way to the quarter-finals but the leap in cost from the last eight to the last four was massive, a 300% increase, unjustifiable. That's how it seemed at the time anyway. Now, in the queue, I'm beginning to wonder? One thing's for certain, I have to go. I can't not be there, it's become an addiction. I have to see this thing through to the end, no matter what it takes. I need to make contact with Lucy! As I'm still shuffling towards the platform, I send an email asking about availability. I factor in the possibility that there may be more interest from the Leeds Dragons, poor Lucy and her team are about to be deluged with this sort of stuff for the third time in a little over a week. We're all now experiencing the logistical craziness of these tournaments, having to make complicated travel plans for the next game whilst still waiting for a train to take us away from the scene of the last one!

There may also need to be some negotiation with the powers that be back at HQ, home that is. My wife's just sent me pictures of Megan's Prom, she looks amazing in her dress, like I've never seen her look before. She's normally a big fan of trainers, jeans and hoodies. The fact that I've missed it, like I miss all Megan's birthdays because of Wales internationals, won't have propelled me to the top of the popularity stakes. The fact that Wales have won again won't necessarily have been a cause for celebration for my wife. For other fans, there will be similar concerns: the family, the finances, even just the act of getting more time off work. Nobody really thought we'd still be playing games of football in France four days from the end of the entire tournament. "It's only two weeks love, then I'll be home...".

Eventually, maybe 40 minutes after leaving the stadium, I manage to get onto a train. It's quite late now, approaching midnight, and we're up early in the morning to drive back to the airport for a flight home at 10am. That means we've no plans to extend the party. Instead

I opt for civilised reflection on the events of the evening in the company of a Belgian fan who sits down next to me as we head back towards the Gare de Lille Flandres. He's a lovely guy, obviously gutted about his team's failure but magnanimous in defeat and fulsome in his praise of Wales, the team and the fans. He bemoans the fact that his team may have lots of star names but doesn't have anything like the same sort of 'side before self' attitude displayed throughout by my team. He concedes the fans were overconfident, that they hadn't ever regarded the possibility of anything other than a place in the final, given the seemingly favourable draw. He says the manager will pay the price now. As he arrives at his stop, we say our goodbyes and share a little embrace before he heads off into the night, the perfect way to end the most amazing, life-affirming day. The Belgian fans' contribution to this whole experience has been immense. They're fabulous people.

Steve and Fergus are waiting at the station and we walk back to the house together, creeping in once we get there because all the lights are off, our hosts must be in bed. There's enough baguette left for yet another ham and cheese sandwich, the first food we've had since we left the house, and there are a couple more beers in the fridge, so we enjoy one final toast, '*Iechyd da*! Here's to Lyon'.

7

Lyon
Portugal v Wales

*'It was like when you look forward to something, something you've
always dreamed about and you've thought about just how good it might
be and then, when you're actually experiencing it, it's a hundred times
better! I've never been to war, I hope I never have to, but when I saw
30,000 of our fans in someone else's country, it felt like we were all
going to do battle together. That's why we're so desperate to do it again,
to have that feeling again.'*
Chris Coleman

Saturday, 2nd July

Four hours after heading off to bed, I'm creeping back downstairs
to dine on Weetabix and tea ahead of our departure. Apart from a
lengthy delay at the *peage*, we make the airport in good time. As we
drop the car off at the rental office, the guy checking it over says,
"You're Vayles? I want Vayles to win!" It happens again as we go
through the security check, when the guy looking at my bag notices
my shirt – Barry's gift – and says "Vayles? Well done!" I thought we'd
be *Pays de Galles* to everyone but it seems 'Vayles' is the popular choice.
I don't think they have many/any French words that start with a 'w'
so maybe they pronounce it like the German 'w'.

Once we're through, with a little time to spare, my priority is to find
a copy of this morning's *L'Équipe*. I race around duty free shops trying

to find one, but it's early and copies don't appear to have arrived yet. Eventually, I have to give up my search as the flight's called and we move to the gate. As it turns out, there's a little shop adjacent to it and I'm able to purchase a couple of copies. The front page is brilliant, the headline reads, '*Quelle Folie!*' which I translate as 'What Madness!' and there's a picture of the Wales players celebrating at the end of the game.

As I'm sitting trying to translate the match report, a Wrexham fan I know comes over. Richard was one of the Supporters Trust board members who helped oversee the takeover of the club. Like many amongst our club's fan base, he combines watching club and country whenever possible. He bemoans the cost, particularly as he's now trying to weigh up how he's going to get out again in a couple of days time. He's put the lot on the credit card so far, with little idea as to how he's actually going to repay it and advances an interesting observation, suggesting he might have to retire from watching football after this – that we're at the pinnacle now. "It'll never be like this again!" It's true that Wrexham v North Ferriby is going to be a tough ask after Lille last night.

On the shuttle bus to the plane, there are more tales of terrible trips. Some of the lads flew out from Doncaster on the later flight on the day before the game. As the plane approached Paris, already descending towards Charles de Gaulle, something went wrong with one of the engines and they had to turn back, despite being only ten minutes from touching down. They landed back at Doncaster, then sat on the plane for two hours before taking off again. Having finally arrived in Paris, hours later than scheduled, they turned up at their hotel only to be told it had been overbooked and they'd all have head off to another hotel. At this point, it seems, some gave up and just found a bar for the rest of the night. They do all look very tired.

Despite all that, they too are contemplating the implications of another trip, particularly on maxed-out credit cards. One of them has some cracking advice when it comes to the prices of things when you're sorting out the flights, tickets, hotels etc. for Lyon, "Don't look, just book!" We board the plane before being told the flight's delayed. It gives me the chance to check train times and I think I'll opt for a 9am train, figuring that most people will fly out on the day which means they won't be in Paris in time to catch this one. You have to book a seat on the TGV so, once they're full that's it. I discuss these travel plans with Steve. He now wants to come but wants to travel on the day of the game. It doesn't look like Fergus will be coming but, as we're sitting on the tarmac, Evo sends a text to confirm that he's managed to get Wednesday and Thursday off so he's definitely in. He can't get any time off on Tuesday so he proposes doing the flight from Doncaster then the train but, as he checks the SNCF website, it seems my theory was correct as the trains after 9am are all booked up now. All over Wales and beyond, people are already tapping away at computers or tablets or staring at their mobile phones trying to work out the best, cheapest way to get to Lyon. Prices will be rising accordingly.

Evo comes back with another suggestion – a hire car from Charles de Gaulle. It's a five or six hour drive down to Lyon. It wouldn't be worth even contemplating that trip on the British motorway network but France offers greater hope. Shoney's keen on that idea. The flight gets in at 9am, meaning they should be in Lyon for mid-afternoon. Evo's right on the case now, and comes back again with details of an Airbnb in Lyon, an apartment in the city for just €24. He's been in touch with the owner and it's available so he gets the thumbs up to book it from us at the 'Paris office'. €24, between us, it's got to be good for that hasn't it?

I make contact with Megan, she's been camping out after the Prom. It seems she's just got back home after having not had any sleep. There's going to be a lot of tired people in the Law household later on.

We finally take off an hour late and I treat myself to a little bottle of Prosecco. This is in *lieu* of the celebrations we had to forego after the game last night. Back at Doncaster, there's more interest from the security staff – the guy at passport control watched the game – and we're offered his congratulations. I suspect our paths may well cross again in the not too distant future. I'll soon be on first name terms with the staff at the airport at this rate. The lads who endured the bad trip out, head off to the car park and a long drive back over to north Wales. "See you in Lyon", we say, as we go our separate ways. Don't look, just book.

An hour later, I'm back home and there's the Welsh bunting up across the front of the house for my arrival. The dog runs out to see me and my wife's on the doorstep to greet me, so far so good. Things get a bit trickier once the negotiations begin. Now Megan's finished school, she's been invited to go and stay with my mum and dad. They both help out with the staging of the International Eisteddfod in Llangollen and they've enlisted my daughter for a support role this year. Megan's really looking forward to it – she's even taking a pal with her – the only issue is, they need a lift over and that's clearly going to be me. I suggest going over on Monday, when I'm not booked on a flight to Paris, whilst Megan insists she wants to go on Tuesday, when I am. Lack of sleep and what might be her first mild hangover have hardened Megan's resolve – she's not for compromising. As I'm swiftly reminded by her mother, I've missed numerous events in her life due to international commitments, including last night's Prom. "Deal with it!" is the terse instruction from my other half. I deal with it, changing my original flight to a later one, at a price needless to say.

It's probably a good job that everyone clears off for the afternoon. I'm still 'coming down' from last night, genuinely struggling and down in the dumps as serotonin levels readjust. I need a hit, so I sit down to watch a rerun of the game. I get through the entire thing before they come home and I quickly turn the TV off and dry my tears, scared of getting caught. I have work to do anyway. I still haven't got a ticket for the semi, so I put an appeal out on social media and send requests to various well-connected people I know. My efforts bring varying results, Lucy replies to say sorry, she can't help, but that's offset by positive responses from two different sources on Facebook. It already looks like I'm going to be able to get what I need. I have the offer of two category three tickets and one category four. The first two belong to a Swiss guy who's willing to sell at face value plus booking fee, the extra one belongs to another Bryn – Pritchard – Gary's brother. He has a ticket but can't get more time off work, and again at face value. I have a real feeling there will be a lot of tickets on sale on the day, particularly those ridiculously expensive ones but I don't want to take the gamble. The Swiss fan connection had come via an intermediary so he passes my message on and I await further developments.

I'm banished to the 'other telly' for the evening as I want to watch Italy v Germany, research for who we might play in the final. It's a poor game and an even worse penalty shootout but the Germans, as ever, prevail.

Sunday, 3rd July

I awake and progress arrangements on the ticket front. I have contact details for my man in Switzerland, Bryn Pritchard's happy to pass his ticket on and Evo's now booked everything including the car and the apartment. Shoney's now staying in his new caravan in Whitby and he claims an intermittent phone signal is hampering his internet access, so he asks me to book his flight for him. I also need to get a hotel for Tuesday night, which I quickly sort on my booking app. The Swiss guy gives the all clear, we swap phone numbers and agree to arrange a meet up on the day in Lyon. All this done from my bed, before breakfast! I should set up a travel agency, I'd never have to get up.

Finally, I need to ensure I can get Megan over to north Wales and still catch a flight from Doncaster on the same day, so I organise a pick up *en route* with my mum. My dad will be dispatched to meet us just the other side of Chester at noon, giving me plenty of time to get back over to Yorkshire. All sorted!

The pressure's off now, everybody's a bit happier and calm settles on the Law household once more. I go for a run and on my way back bump into Tony, my next door neighbour. He's a rugby league fan, if he likes any sport, and rugby league fans in Leeds are often pretty hostile towards football. Tony knows what I do for a living but he's never once mentioned football in conversation with me before. Today, he's all about Wales! He's watched the games, thinks we've got a good chance in the semi-final etc. This is further proof of the extent to which we've grabbed the imagination of more than one nation.

Mind you, that comes at a price. The London-based media outlets are all turning their attention on Wales now and I get reports from the camp of the impact that's having on the questions being asked of the manager and players. There are lots of England-related questions thrown at Chris Coleman at the day's press conference and when Osian Roberts, his assistant, answers questions in Welsh for the Welsh language media, it's hard to hear him as some of the other reporters start to chat to each other as he's talking, which seems a bit disrespectful.

Back home, it's all a lot more straightforward. We don't care where the players hail from, they give their all for the shirt and they're the greatest ambassadors Wales has ever had. The nation is responding. Huge fan zones are springing up to show the games across the country. Wrexham, shamefully, the home of Welsh football and the birthplace of the FAW, refuses to join in. The Council says it's too hard-up to organise an event that might attract thousands of people. I'm told there's hardly any reflection of this being a glorious time to be a Welsh town, with no flags up or anything. It's puzzling in the extreme, how short-sighted is that? Wrexham should be crowing from the roof tops about the fact that football's been played in the town since 1864, that the Wynnstay Hotel was where the FAW was formed on 2 February, 1876, but instead, nothing. The townspeople give their own verdict and I watch footage on YouTube of thousands celebrating in front of that same Wynnstay Hotel after the Belgium game. Perhaps Llewelyn Kenrick will have been looking down happily: the founder of the FAW, the father of Welsh football, the man who started it all.

I treat the family to a meal out, to assuage my guilt prior to yet another departure and the fact that I'm missing Millie's school awards night. This European Championships is having a detrimental effect on my relationship with my children! There'll be no 'Dad of the Year' award for me in 2016.

There's more research to conduct tonight with the last quarter-final match. I've heard people suggesting they want a Wales v Iceland final, although I'm sure that prospect would be enough to make a UEFA marketing official faint. France quickly and emphatically ensure that won't happen. They're four up by half-time! The Iceland fans do their big 'OOO' chant a few times but it has to be said, they've got nothing like our repertoire. Still, those fans have been a big part of the best bits of this tournament. Another fairy story comes to 'The End'. Only one left unfinished!

Monday, 4th July

The calm before the storm. A day for dog-walking, lawn-mowing and food shopping. Over in France, Alex has just set off on a 600-

mile drive from the team base in Brittany to Lyon. Eight hours at least in one go. UEFA claimed this was going to a be a 'green' tournament, but it's difficult to see how that can be true when we've all spent weeks driving up and down or flying-in and out of the country? The tournament must have a carbon footprint like a sasquatch!?

Tuesday, 5th July

There's a lot of travelling to be done today as I criss-cross England then fly back to France and there's an awful lot that could yet scupper my carefully prepared itinerary. For a start, the French are striking again and some flights are being cancelled. My flight operator recommends I keep checking on their website to ensure all is as it should be.

The roads are the next challenge. We pick up Megan's pal and then head over the Pennines and into the midst of the world's longest, slowest set of motorway repairs on the M60 around the top of Manchester. It's the usual crawl through that but we make the meeting place, the Cheshire Oaks retail park, with time to spare so Megan and her pal go for a little light shopping whilst I remain at the rendezvous point waiting for my dad. Once he's turned up, he takes the girls off for a coffee and some lunch and I say my goodbyes, promising to return to collect Megan on Friday. What I don't say is that if Wales actually go on to the final, I'm not sure I'm even going to be back in the country on Friday, but let's leave that thought for now.

The drive back over to the east takes me on a different trans-Pennine route, fewer lanes but far more scenic as I climb up beyond Manchester then drop down on the other side in Sheffield. There's one moment of panic when the hands-free rings in the car and Evo's name comes up on the dashboard screen. I immediately panic, is this about strikes and delays? "Yes? What's up?" I greet him nervously. "Just ringing to say everything's okay with your flight, it's still showing as being on time." I laugh with relief.

After a couple of hours more on the road, I'm back on familiar ground, the Robin Hood airport short stay car park. Then, it's all old friends as I go through the security checks. The guy with the trays greets me with, "Now then, are you going to beat Portugal?" and the bloke on the scanner is the same one I had a chat with the other day. I must be their most frequent flyer?

With no more driving to do today, I can finally afford to indulge in a pint at the Wetherspoon's and then settle down to wait, checking my emails. There are various ticket messages still coming in. Alex has been chasing one himself, despite the fact that he's working for Sky. As a non-rights holding broadcaster, there are no media passes available and he's trying to source one, the same as everybody else. He's finally bought one from the UEFA website, category 2 for €295! I get the offer of one in another email, the price is £375. This merely underlines my sense that there are going to be a lot of tickets available tomorrow. The fact that the organisers are already charging astronomical prices means the touts will be expected to stick even more on top. On that basis, people simply won't bother going.

There are a few more Wales fans around the lounge than has been the case before, perhaps because it's a later flight, and one guy from Mold comes over for a chat. He's unimpressed with the event organisation and makes the observation about simple issues like the lack of signage or people to help with information, something I'd agree with. There's another guy from Wrexham as well, a massively loyal fan who travels everywhere with Wales. He's known for wearing a kilt, or *cilt* as they're called in Welsh, on these trips. Today though, disappointingly, he's more conventionally attired in cargo shorts. I point at them and he shrugs – the explanation follows. He's had to leave the kilt, the lucky kilt, at home because they haven't been able to find anywhere to stay in Lyon, so a night on a bench beckons. However, some standards have to be maintained and with kilts having no pockets, spare underpants, a toothbrush and toothpaste are all shoved down into the cargo shorts. We both know what this means – the seriousness of the situation – the absence of the lucky kilt could be significant. I have packed the same combination as the Lille and Toulouse games in my hand luggage so if Wales fail, it won't be my fault.

Before the flight's called, I have an interview to do with an American soccer podcast, the story of Wales success is travelling around the world. I head off to find a quiet corner of the departures hall – not a big problem at Doncaster – and for the next 20 minutes I join in a conversation with the three hosts about Welsh football and the glorious Euro adventure, our chat only curtailed, appropriately enough, as the Paris flight is announced as boarding.

We leave on time, and I'm regaled on board with more tales of terrible trips, this one involving an attempt to claim a couple of quiet days in Bilbao between matches that turned into a nightmare of cancelled and redirected flights, taking in Brussels and Barcelona, and nearly 48 hours spent either in the air or in terminal buildings. When the lads finally got to the digs they'd originally booked, completely knackered after their odyssey and desperate to get to bed, the owner greeted them with the good news that they'd arrived at Fiesta time and tonight everybody would be out on the streets partying!

It's pretty incredible really that I've managed to avoid any such disasters, driving for the first part of the tournament probably helped, at least you're largely a master of your own destiny when you're going by road. Neglecting to book the internal flight from Bordeaux to Lille for the England game seemed like a bad miss at the time, until I spoke to the lads like Gary and Gwilym who did use that route. Their homeward flight after the game was cancelled, they spent the night in a hotel, then faced the prospect of more time waiting in Lille with no sign of a replacement plane, so insisted the airline drove them to Paris to catch a flight from there instead. A bus was booked for their early morning departure but it took the wrong turn at Charles de Gaulle and got wedged inside a tunnel. With the next flight about to depart, our intrepid travellers pushed open the first door they could find, then raced up several flights of stairs, trying to open every door *en route* to see if it led to departures. Eventually they emerged in the security staff canteen, probably not the best place to barge in through the door in a big group, but, rather than shoot them, someone led them to where they were meant to be. They caught their flight, just. By contrast, I'm in on time again and there's even a hotel bus waiting to take me on to my resting place for the night. I've booked with a chain called Nomad for the night, there are two hotels of that name and I head into reception of the wrong one, the posh one but luckily, the budget one's next door.

It's pretty good as it turns out. Instead of having a TV, there's a projector that uses the opposite wall as a big screen. Everything in the room, the curtains, lights – including the mood lighting in the shower unit – heat, is controlled from a tablet. I fiddle around with it and find a French football show, with a panel and a studio audience. Tonight's topic for discussion is Bale v Ronaldo! Downstairs, there's a clever buffet arrangement and a little bar, so I eat and drink before going back up to change the shower lighting from light blue to green.

Barry sends me a message, he's booked a flight from Doncaster on Saturday, ready for the final. A phrase from *Zombie Nation Awakes* comes immediately to mind, 'Too soon Barry, too soon.'

Wednesday, 6th July – Euro 2016 Match Day 6

As if I needed any more stress in my life today, as I go down for breakfast there's a woman screaming at the guy behind the reception desk! She's demanding someone drive her somewhere, the French staff look at each other and roll eyes and shrug a lot.

My departure is more straightforward, after coffee and pastries I'm on the bus back to the airport to catch my train south. Like many other aspects of this whole travel saga, the French display a surprisingly laid back approach to organising passengers. There are very few members of staff around for a start, the TGV platform's approached not through a ticket barrier but via a normal door. The only ticket check is by a person in uniform at the head of what might loosely be called a queue but is really more of a free-for-all. Once on the platform, a train pulls in and I'm amongst a group of passengers attempting to board it, only to be told that there are actually two parts to this platform and our train will be on the other one.

The European Championships must have added to the amount of passenger footfall through this station and I'd have expected an army of people on hand to help you out. No such thing. Still, I'm getting better at this independent traveller lark, I've had plenty of practice over the last few weeks and I find my designated seat in the final carriage of the Lyon train. I note with some satisfaction that it's the quiet carriage, which means it's got double doors separating it from the rest of the train. There's only me and a French couple in it as well. The rest of the train appears to be packed.

As we slide out from the station, I get quite excited. I've always fancied a ride on the TGV system; this is my first time. It's about 350 miles to Lyon and it's going to take two hours, with just one stop. We're well underway when the sliding doors open and a group of Wales fans stumble in, checking their tickets. There are two families here, mum, dad and teenage kids. They split-up and find themselves seats. Now our little haven is as packed as the rest of the train. After they get settled in, we start to chat. They're from Cardiff – that's obvious from the accents actually. The two men are regulars at Cardiff City and often go and watch Wales whilst the ladies and the kids have all wanted to join in with this adventure as well. This has been a very inclusive experience. It's been great to see so many people travelling as families and it bodes really well for the long term future of the game in Wales. Like pretty much everyone else I've met, the little – "No Surrender" – bloke on the metro in Paris apart, these are good people. We discuss the whole 'box ticking' exercise the older regulars have all been undertaking and the logistical challenge tournament football presents. Their biggest upheaval came when the guy I'm talking to confesses he booked flights from the wrong Paris airport earlier in the tournament, getting his Orly mixed up with his Charles de Gaulle, a mistake nobody noticed until they arrived at check-in, at the wrong airport!

It's a pleasant trip down in their company, the TGV proving to be a civilised and punctual service. They have, apparently, bumped the prices up in line with everyone else intent on exploiting football fans in France but it's still cost me less than Leeds to London return, which is a much shorter journey. We get into Lyon bang on time.

I have a mission to undertake as the advanced guard. I have to go and find the apartment and collect the key from a man called Pierre. Evo's sent me all the details, including his mobile number. A text also tells me that they've arrived in France and they're on the road south now, expecting to arrive at about 3pm. I get my bearings on the platform before heading down the steps and into the station below. It's a busy place, crowds of football fans move about amongst the locals and no sooner have I set foot inside than I spot Jonny Owen, the first time we've had chance to chat since the day of the game in Bordeaux. There's an awful lot to catch up on. As we get stuck into it, Gwilym Boore arrives, with his son in tow. So, now we're all chatting away, recounting tales of our Euro experiences in the middle of Lyon station, like it was the most natural thing in the world. We're all Wales away veterans, battle-hardened, ultra-realists, but even so, there's some crazy talk about Paris and how we'll get there and where we'll stay? I have to put a stop to it, it's not the way we do it. As we stand and chat, guys walk past holding up bunches of tickets. I don't think they're going to find many takers, not unless they're going to start at face value and work down.

I've got an appointment with Pierre now, so I have to say *au revoir* to the lads – I've a metro system to tackle. The instructions seem quite straightforward. We're near a stop that's served by one of the lines from the station. I find it, get a ticket and speed off to my next destination. On arrival there, I have to walk up the road, look out for a big mosaic on the other side of the roundabout and the apartment is in the adjacent building. I spot the mosaic and send Pierre a message to say I'm close by. He responds by saying he's been delayed a little, so I make a detour to get some provisions in. That primarily involves milk, a ready-made chicken sandwich and some beer. I walk up to the building and sit on the step, waiting. After a couple of minutes, a dishevelled looking bloke weaves his way up the pavement in my direction. I have a bad vibe about this already. I hope to God this isn't Pierre. It appears not as he doesn't greet me. He just sits down on the step and starts talking away in what might be French, I'm not really sure. As he talks I focus hard and begin to understand what he's saying. He says he's had a bad time – I think he says he has no work – he's from Poland but can't afford to get home. In between the faltering French, there are bits of Polish so having a conversation is all but impossible. There's a distant look in his eyes, this chap's way out there. I have a sense where this is leading but before I can produce any cash, he peers into my bag, spots the cans of beer and lifts one out. He gestures, I think, if I'm ok for us to share it. I decline the offer and, as he's opened the can already and taken a swig, I suggest he might like to keep the beer as "*un cadeau*" – 'a gift'. He still doesn't move so I take the initiative and wander off, leaving him to enjoy his drink alone.

From the other side of the street, I keep an eye on him until he leaves and I head back hoping desperately that Pierre isn't going to keep me waiting much longer – I don't fancy losing my last can to another passing '*clochard*'. I resume my place on the step and clutch my plastic bag tightly until my man arrives and offers his hand. He speaks reasonable English but trying to convey, 'a tramp stole my beer' proves beyond me in either English or French.

He leads me up to the top floor and opens the door to our living space for the next few hours. He's come from work, he explains, and this is where he lives. That much is obvious from the clothes horse just inside the doorway, which has his shirts and pants draped over it. This Airbnb thing is a bit of a puzzle to me. I know it was a relatively short notice booking but I can only imagine the scenes in our house if we were renting out rooms and someone was coming to stay. My wife would instigate a frenzied tidy up and we'd all be shoving stuff into cupboards and wiping down surfaces. Pierre, like our friends in Lille, seems a lot more laid back about the whole 'tidy up' thing. It's a bachelor pad, with all that implies.

He gives me the tour, which doesn't take long. We're standing in the dining/living room/kitchen, then there's his bedroom and one more room, our room. It's quite narrow, a sofa up against the wall with pillows and a mattress propped on top of it. "How many of you are there?" he enquires. "Three" I reply. "Ah, okay, two of you can have the sofa bed, the other one can use the mattress." The room is about six feet wide and maybe eight feet feet long? Pierre's plan is for me and Steve – chunky lads – to sleep with Evo – a giant – in this tiny room. As I'm assessing the implications of this suggestion (well, what do you expect for €24 you might ask?), I think he is too. "Maybe I will stay with my girlfriend tonight?" he suggests. This seems like a terrific idea.

Tour over, he gets out a big map of the city and places our current location on it, then offers various suggestions as to places we might want to head for a drink or for food later. He's actually a thoroughly nice chap and after a quick chat, he has to go back to the office. He wishes us well, says he doesn't like Portugal, for reasons unexplained, so he hopes we'll win. He leaves me on my own, amidst the washing, and I re-examine the contents of my plastic bag.

I pull out the last remaining can and go and sit on the balcony to drink it. It's a pretty nondescript view but it does offer the chance to check out the parking situation: Evo and Steve are going to need somewhere to leave the car. Text contact says they're making good progress but they're still a couple of hours away. I fire off a message to my Swiss ticket contact, just to reassure him that I'm still coming to collect them. He suggests a meeting place, the McDonald's near the fan zone in the centre of town. I check it out on Pierre's big map.

It's time to venture out again. I go back downstairs and walk back towards the metro station. There's a bar close by, the sun's shining, I need to make the most of these quiet moments, so I pull up a chair, order a beer and sit back to watch the world go by. It's time for some quiet contemplation of what lies ahead. If Aaron was playing, I'd be very confident. He's been at his very best in two of our last three games – arguably more important to the team than Gareth – and his assist rate for our recent goals has been crucial. How do you replace that? Andy King's a great player, if he's the option, but he's a different sort of player. In my mind, I wonder if the one person who could add that attacking assistance is Emyr Huws? He's not here though, pretty unlucky not to make the final squad. Ben's a big miss as well. He's been brilliant. The clearance off the line in the first few minutes of the first match is arguably the defining moment of the tournament so far. His presence gives us great mobility and a bit more pace in that that defensive three.

My pre-match musings are interrupted by a couple of Barnsley fans who are sitting a couple of tables away and come over for a chat. They have been following England and arranged their travel on the basis that Lyon would be the semi-final venue. They've come to take in the atmosphere anyway, at least their club's had a great season, even if their country didn't do so well.

I head back to the flat to guide the chaps in. There's no parking on the street down below, it's for residents only until the evening, so Evo's got directions from Pierre as to where they might be able to leave the car. That means they're approaching on foot, so I head up to the balcony, and we employ a combination of mobile phones and me waving to guide them in. I meet them on the ground floor, take them up and show them the full horror of the sleeping arrangements. Shoney's got a solution. If Pierre's not coming back tonight, he's going to use his bed. Evo's also got his eyes on the big leather sofa that dominates the middle of the living area, so, as long as Pierre's staying away, it looks like it'll only be me on the mattress after all. He hasn't left any duvets or anything, so I have a root around in a cupboard and find a sheet.

Now that they're settling in, I have to get straight out again, as I don't want to be late for the Swiss bloke who's got the tickets, for me and Evo at least. Evo's brought cash, as requested and I shove it all

– mine and his – into an envelope, pushing the envelope right down in my pocket. I need that security guard again!

I arrange a meeting place with the chaps later, I'm meant to be doing a radio interview at a pub called The Elephant & Castle later, so that's where we agree to rendezvous. I also have to arrange the collection of Steve's ticket – Gary has it at the moment and he's out and about in the city centre as well. I'd be lying if I said I wasn't just a tiny bit stressed, having taken on the responsibility of sorting out everyone's tickets. They've travelled out here on the basis that they're going to watch the game and it's down to me to make sure that happens. So, the first stop is the metro for a train to Bellecour, then out of the station and find the McD's. I've sent my contact a photo of myself, taken in Paris after Northern Ireland, so I'm wearing exactly the same gear now. Mind you, a bright red, yellow and green bucket hat isn't exactly the beacon it should be, given that pretty much everyone's wearing one in the area around the restaurant when I find it. Still, a sixth sense and the sight of a young chap in a Swiss cap encourages me to go over and ask, "Are you Dane?" I suppose he should check left and right and then reply, "Who wants to know?" But he doesn't, he says, "Yeah, hi, do you want the tickets?" Instead, I look left and right, then surreptitiously slide the envelope out of my pocket and pass it to him in what I hope is a discrete movement. "It's all there." I whisper, then check left and right again as he hands me an envelope in return. I don't look in mine, he doesn't look in his. We are both very trusting. At this point, I guess we should go our separate ways and slip off into the crowds but we don't, we have a quick chat about the match. He was hoping he'd be here supporting his country today but that wasn't to be the case. We talk about Aaron's absence, a bit about Bale and then shake hands before saying goodbye.

Actually, my attempt at being anonymous is largely undermined by the fact I'm outside a place surrounded by Wales fans, a couple of whom shout 'Alright Bryn?' as I head off to my next rendezvous.

The pub's located on the other side of the river and doesn't appear to be too far away, so I walk. There are some great looking backstreets, full of interesting shops, little eateries and bars and hidden squares. Every now and again, I hear a snippet of song, get a glimpse of another group of red shirts, Wales' red that it, rather than Portuguese red, or is that maroon? Anyway, whatever colour it is I haven't spotted any of it yet. I suspect there are going to be lots more Welsh fans at the stadium tonight.

That suspicion's enhanced as I round the corner then cross the bridge over the river to the pub. There are big crowds outside, all Wales fans it appears. It's interesting: earlier in the day, in the station, as I chatted with Jonny Owen, he raised a point about a key difference between England and Wales supporters. A friend of his spotted it, over here. When England fans descend on a bar or pub, they stand outside, facing out. Like its their territory and they're waiting for you to try and take it off them. As I look at this pub, surrounded by Wales supporters, all I can see are backs. People are facing in, talking to mates, singing amongst themselves, basically unconcerned by what anyone else might be doing. Perhaps England's reputation is now such that, like 'Wild Bill' Hickok, they have to effectively sit with their back to the wall – always wary of an attack – or maybe some still seek that confrontation.

It's not going to happen here. Happy, noisy vibes prevail and people are dancing round to The Barry Horns who are sounding better and better with all the gigs they've been playing on their first ever tour of France. Radio Wales are broadcasting from a small table outside and the queue at the bar's three or four deep.

I wait in line, the prize at the end of it is a decent pint of real ale, I think this place is part of the same chain that owns the Charles Dickens pub we frequented in Bordeaux. I head back outside, where fans are now spread across the pavements and over the road to the bridge on the other side. Now, there's work to be done. First of all, I have to track down Gary. A flurry of text messages are exchanged then a phone call, can I see a red bridge downriver? Yes, I can. He'll be under the cantilever structure. I'll direct Steve and Evo straight to him.

The information's then related to Steve and Evo and I sip my pint whilst surveying the wild scenes on the other side of the road. The Barry Horns are playing, fans are singing, the sun's shining, it's yet another picture of Welsh football paradise, except, I'm not quite feeling it. I don't know why, maybe because I haven't got my mates here with me, or maybe we're all getting a bit too used to having great fun in France. Perhaps complacency is setting in, or maybe I'm just stressed about ticket handovers. Gary hasn't seen them yet so I ring

Evo, to reiterate that he's still waiting on the red bridge over the river. "Which river?" Evo asks. "There are two." This is a bombshell! Two rivers through the city?! I've only seen one, the one I'm on now. I have to describe what I can see from where I am before we can ascertain that I must be by the Saône and they've been looking on the Rhône. Finally, we've worked out where we all are in relation to each other and they head to the red bridge, I contact Gary to assure him that they are most definitely on their way. The jigsaw's almost complete. It's time for another pint, I think. It's time to settle my nerves.

As I work my way through the masses again, I see the person's who's going to be doing the radio interview, Elis James. He's a well-known comedian, actor and broadcaster, he's also a big football fan and is recording a series of programmes on the Euro experience. He's already done one great one for Radio Four which laid bare the myth that rugby is Wales' national game, so, although we've never met before, he's alright by me. I introduce myself and interrupt his lunch.

He's been and bought himself one of those small bowls of pasta and is now standing and eating it outside the pub. It seems a little incongruous in these surroundings, a little too civilised perhaps? A small bowl of pasta and chips I could just about accept. He's got a producer with him who has all the gear required but he's still working on a live broadcast from the table by the door of the pub.

Then, finally, Evo and Steve arrive. The ticket has been collected. I have Evo's ticket. We all have tickets. Soon we will all have beer, then we'll be ready. Elis is ready now as well so we follow him round to a quieter corner and there, across the road from the Elephant and Castle is a smaller bar, with tables outside on the decking. I've overlooked it because it's called Ninkasi, which sounds like it might be something to do with sushi, but it's not. It's a little French craft beer and burgers place which is exactly what is required. Evo's very much into craft beers – he brews his own – I'm a fan as well and we're starving so this is the perfect place!

Elis finds a table and I follow him with a beer to do the interview, which is good fun, particularly as we're talking over the sound of singing and chanting from around the corner, to give a real flavour of the tournament. Once we're done, the food's ordered, more beers arrive and we sit down to what might well be our last supper. Good food, good ale, good company and enough of that pre-match beer-induced buzz that's the real difference between working and not working.

We have to keep some of our wits about us still because the next bit promises to be tricky. The stadium isn't in the city. It's in a suburb called Décines-Charpieu. I've seen differing estimates on the distance from the city centre, from as much as 20 kilometres to just under 10, but even if it's the latter, that's a fair hike from where we are now. It seems we have to get a metro then a tram. The trams run from the train station and, given previous experiences of French match day transport, we're ready to set off before 7pm, anticipating an hour's journey. It's a brand new stadium and I'm sure it'll look great and the sight lines will be fabulous and all that but why can't they build a new ground in walking distance of the city centre for once? The Millennium Stadium has its faults but it's glory is the fact that you leave the pub and five minutes later you're queuing up to get in. Five minutes after the game's over, you're back at the bar.

Needless to say, there's a general exodus taking place as Welsh fans head off towards Décines-Charpieu and a date with destiny. There's been an awful lot of singing all afternoon but I've not seen the level of lunacy the Belgians attained in Lille. I genuinely think some of the 'Euro Veterans' are beginning to flag now. It's been a bewildering few weeks of, planes, trains and automobiles, with games every few days, tickets to chase, strange beds in strange places. We've stumbled from one city to another and now they're making us work hard again just to get to the ground. We follow the crowds from the metro station to the tram stop. Then, another Euro tradition, as we're all jammed on board like a rush hour tube on the Central line. I share my small square of space with some young Costa Rican guys, all decked out in their national team shirts. They're big football fans and have made a trip over to France to watch Euro 2016 matches. Inevitably we talk Bale but I have the chance to educate them a little more about Wales. They didn't know there was a Welsh language and are curious to learn more, so we do a little session – some of the basics – then we all fall back on joining in with another chorus of *Don't Take Me Home*. This is the bit that makes me realise just how massive this whole event has been for the country, for Wales. All over the world, lots of people now know a bit more about Wales. It might only be the fact that Gareth Bale comes from Wales. It might only be the fact that our flag is a dragon, it might only be the fact that we sing an anthem in a language that isn't English. Whatever it is, they know a little bit more about Wales and that fact makes me feel immensely happy.

As I stand in this crowded carriage, I can reflect on the way the team travelled back from Bosnia having finally qualified. On the plane home the players were expecting fireworks and crowds lining the streets. I was on the flight with them and they called me over to discuss the feasibility of open top buses and the like. In the event, on arrival in Cardiff, there was nothing. Nobody came to greet them. Even before we arrived in France, I had a real sense of just how massive this could be for the country. I work on Premier League games that are broadcast to every corner of the world on a Saturday afternoon. Football is the global game. It's the one unifying force from Timbuktu to Tehran and, as sad as it seems, if you watch footage from virtually any warzone in the world, I'll guarantee you'll see football shirts – primarily English Premier League shirts – being worn by the protagonists. If Arsenal called for a ceasefire in Syria, they'd have more chance of success than the UN. I'm here with guys from Costa Rica, Steve's met blokes who have travelled from Tanzania and all they want to see is Bale play for Wales. There have been many famous and talented Welsh people – poets, politicians, even pirates – but who has done most to make the world aware of our existence? Gareth Bale, of course.

Once upon a time, as an idealistic teenager, I was a member of Plaid Cymru – the Welsh Nationalist party. I wanted an independent Wales, I learnt Welsh at school and I went around my village pushing leaflets through doors before the General Election in 1987, but then I went to University in England and I've lived in England ever since. I married an English woman and my children are English, hold on, even I'm English-born! So, I've become more relaxed about the concept of 'independence'.

Since those days, the advent of the Assembly government seemed to have given Wales a degree of autonomy and helped underline a growing sense of identity, even if only because people now put flags out and served Welsh cakes on St David's day. I still had a sense that one day, Wales might achieve a greater degree of devolution under the umbrella of the European Union, a small nation within a bigger, supportive federation, a bit like the Republic of Ireland. The Brexit vote seems to have brought an end to those ambitions.

I do think Wales is different from England. The language is just one factor, a big one admittedly, but I think the people are different as well. It might be something to do with the fact that Wales seems a more egalitarian place than England. There's a middle class and a working class in Wales but there's almost no upper class. I grew up in a largely working class village. I was middle class, but my parents were both teachers so I went to the local comprehensive and, before I left for university, I drank in the local pubs, played Sunday league football, played the trombone, went with my mates to the match, wrote poetry, acted in plays, went nightclubbing, had fights, got good 'A' level grades etc. I wasn't unique, I've met so many Welsh football fans who can point to a similar upbringing.

In England, I've found the dividing lines are just a little more clearly defined. Even at primary school in Liverpool, I was taunted with the bizarre nickname of 'Poshnob no.1'! I suspect education's key to all this. In Wales, many parents either don't or won't take the option to send their children to an independent school, in England, aspirational parents often seem to follow that route regardless of the local options available in the state school sector. On top of that, England has its establishment schools – Eton, Harrow, Winchester etc. – where it's future leaders tend to be educated. Wales' establishment is something different, it's more likely to involve a family link to the Labour Party or having parents in the media.

The Welsh 'establishment' tends to be south Wales based and the perception would be that it regards rugby as the country's sport, hence the empty arrivals hall when the team first returned to Cardiff after qualifying. Tonight, you can bet, every politician and media darling who's ever been to Barmouth on holiday will be flooding social media with messages of support. The Welsh football team has done the greatest job ever of selling the country to the world. Nothing in Wales' history, except the awful tragedy of Aberfan perhaps, will ever have drawn the focus of the world's media to the country like this game this evening.

We all spill out of the tram on the long walkway up to the stadium. There's a broad avenue, filled with fans, Welsh mainly but Portuguese as well, and Germans, amongst others. A group of German lads stop to talk and to entertain us with their newly composed song – which apparently they've been working on since they drove down –

especially for this game. To the tune of 'We are sailing', they serenade us with, "We hate dolphins, we hate dolphins, we hate dolphins, save the Wales." They have another one about Ronaldo as well which is a little less PC – there does seem to be an element of the world united in their dislike of Portugal's star player. We link arms with them and join in with the dolphin song before pictures are taken, hands shaken and we agree to meet again at the final on Sunday. There are more bizarre scenes as Steve spots a group of fans all dressed in Mexican wrestling outfits and they stop for more photos as we edge our way closer to the stadium.

All the time, there are people wandering around holding up tickets. We stop a couple to ask about prices. They momentarily perk up before realising it's just an exercise in acquiring information. As predicted, face value appears to be the best they're going to get. One guy who says he's a fan rather than a tout has a handful, bought in advance, before mates let him down. He can't get rid of them at face value and he's just trying to recoup some of his outlay. The problem for him is, there have been plenty of tickets around all day, and anyone who travelled without one has surely picked one up by now? The closer we get to the stadium, the bigger the price drop. It's pretty obvious that if we'd held on, we'd have paid a lot less for higher category tickets than the ones we've ended up with. UEFA's overpriced them so there'll be empty seats, at a European Championship semi-final, where's the sense in that?

It's about time to go our separate ways as well, with Steve in one section of the stadium and me and Evo elsewhere. We've seen neutrals, we've seen hordes of Wales fans, where are the Portuguese? They've not had a great tournament, despite reaching the last four. The shootout we watched in Lille apart, they've only actually won one game so far and they managed to scrape through the group stage despite drawing all three games. I'm guessing the lack of backing, relatively close to home, must be something to do with a lack of confidence in the team.

We climb the steps to enter the stadium, stopping to buy a plastic beaker of something called Tourtel Twist, it's an alcohol free beer with a flavour of lemon. The 'Twist' is that it tastes horrible. The sole reason for making the purchase is that it's served in a plastic cup with the game details printed on it. Well, it was in Lille. Not in Lyon as it turns out, which makes this €4 purchase very much a wasted one. We take our drinks over to the wall around the edge of the stadium. Evo and I lean on it and look down. It offers a view up the long esplanade with the sun setting behind it. The crowds are thinner now with just a few people making their way towards the ground. It's all quite chilled out really, not what I was expecting this close to such a big game. It's been a long day, it's been a long tournament. We've all got to lift ourselves for one more push.

So, we head to our seats. I love that moment when you first emerge into a stadium you've never been to before. It doesn't really matter what its size is, it's the sight that satisfies, the neatness of the four sides or the perfect bowl or the strange portacabin construction behind one goal. Lyon's new ground looks impressive. We're high up, second tier, and we have to look across the stadium to the far end, behind the other goal to see the block of red that marks out the territory held by majority of the Welsh supporters. We're not amongst them, that's the price to be paid for buying tickets from someone from Switzerland rather than the FA of Wales. As we take our seats, we excuse our way along a row of the kind of people I'd take for neutrals. There are no 'colours' up here, and there's one major difference between this and all the other games so far, everyone's sitting down.

Actually, there are two major differences, as we're minutes away from kick-off and there are lots of empty seats around us. In fact, there are lots of empty seats around the ground. Only the Welsh section seems to be completely filled. The Portuguese fans are down below, a smattering of three or four thousand maybe, behind the goal. If they couldn't fill the category three seats that we occupy, I can only imagine how hard the touts must have had to work with those cat one and two tickets outside. They're probably giving them away right now.

The impact on the experience of not being with Wales fans becomes immediately obvious as the teams walk out, then line up for the anthems. There's singing down at the far end, but we're detached from it and as the anthem starts, it's even worse. For the first time in six matches, I can hear myself sing. Me and Evo stand side-by-side, belting it out, but it's hard not to feel a little self-conscious. There are no tears tonight. When the anthems are over, we do something that feels all wrong, we sit down again.

The team lines up with James Collins and Andy King in for the two suspended players. They're excellent, experienced replacements to be able to call upon and I'm really chuffed for James, or 'Big Ginge' as he's always known. He's the last survivor of the team that was playing when I first started covering the games for Sky, 13 years ago. He had a full head of hair in those days, hence the nickname, although the legend lives on in the form his lustrous beard. He's the last of a different breed, a proper centre half who likes to head it, kick it and enjoys the odd beer after a game. He fell out with the manager and dropped out for a bit. Then they made up, he came back and now here he is, 32 years old, earning his 49th cap in what might be the biggest game of his career?

All eleven are wearing the strange charcoal grey and lime change strip that was selected for this tournament. I'm not a fan. Wales' away kits should be always be yellow or white. We've only worn this kit once before, when we had to change against England, even though there was no colour clash. We lost that game of course, if you're looking for omens. Don't forget the kilt as well. For some unknown reason, Portugal are also wearing their change strip, which is even more unpleasant than ours. It's a sort of toothpaste green. Sartorially, this semi-final is a bit of a disaster.

The game gets underway and Wales get straight up the other end of the pitch – a statement of intent perhaps – but Portugal cause the first flurry of excitement as Ronaldo gets tackled by Ashley Williams on the edge of the area and rolls round in characteristic style before turning round to the referee, arms stretched wide, asking for the free kick. He gets nothing but a chorus of boos from all sides of the stadium. He really isn't very popular, is he!?

The ref does give one Portugal's way soon afterwards – Joe Allen receiving a yellow card – and then Portugal get their first decent ball into the box. Down below us, James Collins wrestles with Cristiano Ronaldo, manhandling him out of the way of the cross like a bouncer ejecting a drunk from a bar and then nods the ball away himself. Ronaldo's down again with the same plaintive look towards someone, anyone – 'Look! I've been fouled!' No one's interested and play continues. Advantage 'Big Ginge'! The ball comes back in again and CR17's back on his feet, ready to attempt a spectacular overhead kick, but James Chester gets his head to it first this time. Portugal come again as the sound of *Calon Lân* drifts across from the other end and Mario drags a shot wide. It's not exactly relentless pressure but we're not creating anything. The two teams seem intent on keeping possession, men behind the ball, waiting for the chance to counterattack. They look well-matched to me, a star man each, some experienced internationals and one or two lesser-known names.

In the Bale v Ronaldo sideshow, our man gets the chance to strike first, from Wales' first corner. Joe Ledley takes it, as Aaron's watches from the stand. Instead of curling it in, he side-foots the ball towards the edge of the area, a big empty space as it happens. In a flash, Gareth runs out of the crowd, towards his own half and in one move spins 180 degrees and wraps his left foot round the ball. He can't quite keep it down and it flies over. We're up on our feet for the first time, it's a shot, some encouragement, and we aren't the only ones to react.

There are other pockets of Wales fans dotted around this upper tier. It's a lot better from our side now. Bale makes a run down the right, his cross to the near post's cleared just before Andy King can meet it, then Gareth wins the ball back in our half, shrugs off one pursuer and heads, at pace, towards the penalty area. This is classic Bale, space to run into, a sight of goal, the crowd around us rises expectantly as he unleashes a shot from his left foot. There's power but not the accuracy, it flies straight and into the arms of Rui Patrício. He's one of the Portuguese players who's impressed me in the games, or bits of games, that I've seen. This save's an easy one. We haven't seen Gareth make one of those attacking surges count yet, can tonight be the night, please?

Both sides have enjoyed periods of being on top so far but things even up over the next few minutes and the pattern reverts to keeping possession, probing, but not getting drawn out. The stadium noise levels drop accordingly, the Welsh fans quiet for the first time in nearly a month. Andy King goes close, connecting with a cross from the right, but the defender gets across just in time to deflect it behind. At the moment, Andy looks like our best chance with these late runs from midfield but what he can't provide quite as well as Aaron is that killer ball to Bale. Those two have a telepathy, always sensing each other on the pitch. That might be the difference tonight.

As it is, it's difficult to see either side scoring. 'Big Ginge' heads away another cross, leaving Ronaldo standing in his shadow, and half-time's almost upon us before we're reminded what we're up against. A cross from the left goes all the way to the back post, where Ronaldo waits. Chester stretches but can't get a touch and right in front of the Portugal fans, their hero puts his header wide. It's a warning though, something to dwell on during the break, as the referee blows his whistle at bang on 45 minutes.

It's time to breathe again. It's so strange watching the match amongst people who don't really care, when we both care more than we've ever cared about a game before. To my right and left, during the first half, people have been chatting away to each other, checking their phones, looking around them. I've been sitting, arms either folded or elbows propped on knees, chin resting on my thumbs, utterly focused on what's going on below.

As the teams reappear, we both sink back into our seats. I've a feeling this one could go all the way. Portugal's only win came in extra time so they've not actually managed a victory within 90 minutes yet and we're at the penultimate round of the competition! The second half begins as the first half finished, with the same pattern: win possession, advance as a group, lose it and drop back into the defensive formation. Joe Allen's finding the going tougher tonight. The opposition have done well in keeping the ball away from him. The midfield trio's not been as effective in getting it and keeping it. Getting it has been tough enough and Joe concedes a free kick just inside our half. It's swung in long towards the box and then knocked behind for a corner.

There's the usual jostling in the box but the corner's a surprise. It's taken short and rolled to the bald bloke, Guerreiro, standing a couple of yards up the line from the corner flag. It's one of those balls that you follow in, fearing the worst. It's got that 'whip' on it as they say, so it curves away from goal but it's high – heading towards the back post – and then you see it, the flash of green, the rocket launched, rising straight up out of the crowd. The head makes perfect contact and the ball flies straight into the back of the net. The number on the back of the shirt reads '7' and the letters spell RONALDO. Cristiano may be unpopular with the rest of the world but he's very popular with the whole of Portugal. His teammates, subs, coaches all run to the corner to dive on top of him. Our best hope now might be that he gets suffocated – okay winded – underneath them all. As they prise themselves off, he springs up and, for the avoidance of any doubt, plants himself in front of the steadicam operator, the guy who has to run up and down the touchline following and filming the action. Ronaldo knows all about the steadicam man, he knows the shot will get used a thousand times. He stands, legs spread, back to the lens and, with his head turned to the side – via the stadium screen – we all get a long look at the name and the number on the mint green shirt. That's probably why he's so unpopular. He is one hell of a player though!

It's a blow, a massive blow but I have faith in this team. They won't throw in the towel, they'll redouble their efforts and sure enough, within seconds, Gareth's carrying the ball forward. He's fouled so we get a free kick and the chance to respond quickly. It really is too far out this time so Gareth curls the ball into the area instead, the goalkeeper comes off his line and instead of catching it, panics and punches it away. It's a good response. We're up and shouting again, me and Evo, it's time to take the initiative. We're still in this.

Portugal attack again, they shift the ball from left to right. Ronaldo takes aim from outside the box but he's scuffed it and it's rolling wide before a mint leg stretches and pokes the ball into the net. Even from the far end, my immediate instinct says 'offside!' How can there be two Portuguese players in our six yard box and only one defender and it not be offside? 'Big Ginge' is that one Wales player and he's got his arm up, appealing, looking to the assistant but the scorer, Nani, is already on his way to celebrate with his teammates. The referee's heading back to the halfway line. It's a goal, another goal, right off the back of the first one. If it's a goal, then it's poor defending. I wonder straight away if Ben Davies would have been the other side of Nani, or a bit closer to make the block. The truth is, it doesn't matter. It's a bad goal to concede certainly and the reality is, that's it. Job done.

Reality's a place we've not really visited these last few weeks or months. Reality has been turned on its head. Over the course of the qualification campaign and now this tournament, the reality has pretty much become Wales winning, or certainly not losing. Even when we lost in Bosnia, we qualified, so it felt like winning, and, despite everything, I still hang on to a sense that one goal to get back in it and we've got a real chance. This is a team that won't give in, although now, for the first time in France, we look tired. The fans see it and give it one big go, the anthem's roused the team to new heights in the past, so *Hen Wlad Fy Nhadau* it is. The Portuguese have finally found their voices on the tier below but they can't compete with the emotion of this one. Sam Vokes comes on to replace Joe Ledley, then Hal departs for Simon Church and Jonny Williams comes on for James Collins. The formation changes, we go to a flat back four and begin to enjoy limited success in terms of pushing the opposition back but, they're happy to defend, wait and then launch a counter attack. They still carry the greater threat. It's clear that Gareth's getting frustrated, he goes deep to collect the ball but if he's back in our half, who's going to trouble this well-drilled backline at the other end? It'll need to be something special, like the 30-yard volley he lets fly that dips and moves but still ends up in the hands of the keeper.

The clock ticks down way too fast now. It's almost time to accept the inevitable. Portugal almost wrap it as Gareth loses the ball on the edge of our box and the big midfielder Danilo runs through the gap where James Collins once stood. He's through and shoots. Hennessey saves but the ball squirms under him and it's going in but he dives on it again, just before Nani arrives to tap it home. There's still life, still a little hope. Bale again, even further out, 40-yards perhaps, strikes one with his left foot, that moves in the air – we can see the line from where we are. Rui Patrício drops left to follow its original trajectory, then has to readjust swiftly to push it around the right hand post. It's our best moment of the second half. The first half we maybe edged, this half has been decisively in favour of the other team. Their experience of regularly playing in tournaments has shone through. They've battled their way to this position whilst we've swept all before us but as we've stumbled in sight of the line, they've just picked up the pace when the bell for the last lap rang.

I know it's over when we actually get our first free kick in Bale range, his shot hits the wall and he's clattered before he can pick up the rebound. Gareth's free kicks never hit the wall, they always go up and over. I think it's a sign that he's spent. They all are. As I consider that though, for the first time this evening, I get emotional. This group has given everything and then some and it feels like they've done it for us, they've done it to make us happy, to make us proud. And I am, I'm happy and proud. As the clock hits the 90-minute mark, it's the Welsh anthem that rings out around the stadium, the volume high, intense and more soulful than usual – more like a lament. It's the last time the world will hear this magnificent noise, for a couple of years at least. Tonight, we are all, in the words of the song, *'enwogion o fri'* – 'famous, esteemed people' – tomorrow, back to life, back to reality. Once the anthem's blown away on the cool, evening breeze, *Men Of Harlech* begins and it keeps going and keeps going, way beyond the final whistle, beyond the players handshakes with their opponents and beyond the Welsh lads walking up towards the Red Wall, to raise their arms in salute. It goes on and on until the players just stand and watch. Far away, at the other end of the stadium, on the second tier, two lads from Leeds join in. The seats around us are largely empty, a few people check under seats for bags, take a last selfie, head off for the exits, but me and Evo stand defiantly, arms outstretched, Dur-de-dur-de-duh-duh, clap, clap. We're desperate for the players to turn around to us, well I am – I'm sure Evo is – but they're transfixed by the fans at the far end. Even the Portuguese are nearly done celebrating now and still the singing goes on and on. The whole FAW party gathers in front of the fans. There's a big huddle, all the staff members included and Captain Ashley in the middle, "It's fine! It's fine!" They put on T-shirts, red T-shirts, over those awful, unlucky charcoal and lime shirts. It's too far for us to be able to read the print on the front but on the big screen, we see the words, *Diolch* and *Merci*. It's the last word. Reluctantly, we take our leave and head for the exit.

It's pretty quiet outside. There's a small group of Portuguese fans celebrating with a drum, all around them the silhouettes of Welsh fans drift past, heading for the queues and the trams and the city centre. We find Steve. He was in the Welsh section, singing, I envy him that. The last chance to let loose, to be uninhibited, has now passed us by. We're back to being middle-aged men, with mortgages to pay and children to try and get through school and university.

I ask Evo to take a last pic as we walk away, one with the stadium in the background. This was the last stop on our epic journey. Ah well, I've already been to Paris. Eiffel Tower? Done that! The next bit's predictable, huge queues for the tram. It snakes round the barriers for 100 yards or more. It's going to be another long journey back. Even if we were celebrating, this would be a struggle but at least I've had a decent night's sleep. Steve and Evo left home at 4am. Nearly 20 hours later, they're still travelling. The ordeal doesn't end with the tram, after the tram there's another queue for the metro. On the metro, there's another small group of Portuguese with a drum. One of them bashes it whilst the others dance and sing. I should enjoy this, maybe the last of the football festival moments, but it's hard. I guess the boot's been on the other foot for the rest of the tournament, Lens apart, and rival fans have taken our celebrations in good part. It's up to us to do the same. Of all the groups of fans we've encountered though, the Portuguese I think, have been the most reticent. We didn't see many pre-match, but it wasn't like the it was with the Slovakians, the Irish or the Belgians. We leave them to their little party. I'd imagine there's a very big party going on back home. A team that barely qualified for the second stage is now going to be playing in the final.

Steve and Evo need feeding, fuel in the tank and all that, so there's a quick stop at a kebab shop. They're already showing a rerun of the game in the restaurant next door. As I'm waiting for the lads, from a side street appears a familiar face. It's the pirate from Ynys Môn, the guy we first met in Toulouse – on the campsite – seemingly years ago. He comes over for a chat and to recount yet more tales of another terrible trip, involving multiple flight cancellations, missed connections, numerous airports and a zig-zag journey across several countries before they finally arrived in Lyon. He deserved a win after something like that but he'll have to settle for a kebab.

The chaps eat and walk as we agree to go in search of a nightcap. They're driving up in the morning and I've got a return train but not until 4pm. I've been offered a place in the car but a bit of sightseeing, some shopping and a last French lunch appeals by way of an afterword to this thriller. So, no need for an early start in the morning. If we'd won, I could have stayed out all night!

We head first for the the Elephant & Castle which is fairly busy, then decide to try next door again but Ninkasi's shut. We wander down the alley and come out into a small square with a wine bar and a pub to the right. The pub's called The Smoking Dog. We should be put off by the pub sign – a bulldog, smoking a cigar in front of a Union Jack – but there's music playing inside and they serve real ale, so we wander through the bar and find a table.

There are quite a few Wales fans coming in now, so the staff switch to the playlist they must belt out over the PA when they're showing Wales games on the big screen during the Six Nations. It's all Tom

Jones, the Stereophonics and other sing-along classics. It's all pretty corny but we need lifting and it's hard not to join in when *It's Not Unusual* comes on.

Then, a larger group of Welsh fans come in and claim the back room for themselves. I know one of them at least, it's Iolo Cheung, a young writer who interviewed me for a magazine piece when *Zombie Nation Awakes* came out. He's a first language Welsh speaker, an Everton fan and, yes, as the name suggests, he's got a Chinese father. He's in a mixed group, male and female, – all in their twenties I'd guess – all wearing Wales shirts and a few in SO58 bucket hats. They order a round of shots to go with their beers, then another, and as they down them, they sing. It's not another chorus of *Don't Take Me Home* that I'm beckoned over to join in with, it's a new song, one they've developed amongst themselves and it's about Chris Gunter. Chris Gunter, who hasn't got a song, but now he has, if this one catches on. Chris Gunter deserves a song. I find myself, in the early hours of the morning, singing the new Chris Gunter song in the company of this happy band. They crouch down together – the song's got movements – then it goes quieter, then they leap up and it goes LOUDER! We're smiling, laughing, still having a good time, the party goes on.

It's a great way to finish the journey. The young people in this back room are the future. They are the future of Welsh football and they are the future of Wales. Bright, optimistic, energetic and naturally interchanging the Welsh and English languages without discrimination. If Wales can harness this, Wales will be okay. Three last pints arrive. Evo, Shoney and I, raise a glass to Wales, the Euros, France and each other. The lads have been up nearly 24 hours now, top effort!

A taxi home and Pierre's done the right thing and stayed out. Steve nicks his bed, Evo claims the sofa, I crash out on my mattress. It's been the greatest month of my life. Now, please, take me home. *Diolch. Merci.* Thanks.

Epilogue

Even as I was enjoying my TGV trip home the following day, social media was awash with speculation about Chris Coleman's future. The FAW had announced a 9.30am media conference for the following morning. As we whizzed through the French countryside, I checked with Ian Gwyn Hughes. Nothing to worry about, just routine, he told me.

Even still, I was back home – up and out of bed – in time to watch the live coverage on Sky Sports News the next day. As promised, it was a routine event, designed to give a summation of the tournament experience. Chris Coleman made it clear he didn't want it to be regarded as a 'one off', that he wanted the prize money, running into several million Euros, to be invested in the grassroots game, better facilities and better coaches. He also joked that it was pity he signed his new contract just before the tournament, given the amount the FAW had just earned from it's time in France.

This light-hearted line took on a little more seriousness when, a few weeks later, managerless Hull City courted Coleman in the run-up to the start of the new season. Hull's approaches were rebuffed by the FAW but rumours about the national team manager's willingness to at least listen to what they had to offer persisted until the season started.

The Welsh players and staff returned to Wales later on that day, Friday 8 July. Unlike after the qualification-clincher against Bosnia, there were fire engines spraying arcs of water over the plane as it taxied to a halt at Cardiff airport, then crowds waiting to greet the players as they boarded the bus for the city centre.

What followed next were scenes unlike anything witnessed in Wales before. Around a quarter of a million people came out on the streets of the capital as the players and staff travelled in open top buses from the airport to an official reception at the Cardiff City Stadium.

For those of us who'd spent most of the last few weeks in France, it was a clear indication of just how much the team's achievements had gripped the imagination of the nation. Two thirds of the population, a record audience, had watched the semi-final on TV and in the run-up to the semi-final, major multinational brands like CocaCola and Budweiser were using Welsh in their social media advertising campaigns.

Despite doing more to promote the language on a global stage than anybody has ever achieved previously – or could have ever imagined – the FAW, the players and management staff, were all passed over for nomination to the *Gorsedd* in 2016. The *Gorsedd* is the body that is meant to recognise contributions to Welsh culture, specifically through the medium of Welsh, inviting those who've been instrumental in promoting the language to join it.

The Archdruid Geraint Lloyd Owen rejected criticism of the omission by saying that 'If they can't speak Welsh, I don't see how we can welcome them.' The omission caused much controversy in Wales and the decision was later justified on the grounds that the nominations for inclusion had to be made by February, before the tournament began.

When Wales qualified in October 2015 the players wore T-shirts bearing the word *Diolch*, the Welsh for 'Thanks'. The FAW had promoted the Welsh version of the #TogetherStronger hashtag – #*GydanGilyddYnGryfach* – throughout the qualifiers, and the Welsh speaking players like Joe Allen, and Ben Davies, as well as the coach Osian Roberts, had all done numerous interviews in their native language. Aaron Ramsey had also tweeted in Welsh to his over one million followers. At the time of writing, it remains to be seen whether anyone from the FAW will be nominated for next year's list.

As for me, well, I don't know what demons I exorcised or which doors in my mind I opened but I've felt like a different man since the summer. The shouting, the singing, the euphoria, the release of so much stuff, that's what the Euros did for me. Only now can I see how much mental baggage I must have been carrying around as a result of watching Wales continually fail. I knew it was having a negative impact on my life in general and, for the time being at least, I've let it go. If Sarah Powell asks me for a score prediction ahead of another international, I might even say I think Wales will win! Okay then, draw. Let's take this optimism thing one step at a time.

For Steve, it was more than a football tournament as well as it turned out. We'd talked for hours on end whilst we were driving up and down France but only after we'd got back – several weeks after actually – did he feel able to share the real reason as to why he was so keen to accompany me on the journey.

Steve's younger brother, Andrew, stuck with Wrexham when Steve switched allegiance to Crewe but the lads, like their dad, both supported Wales and all three would go to watch the national team play together. Shortly after Steve had moved to Leeds, at the age of 17, Andrew was diagnosed with leukaemia. Steve was the donor for a transplant but there were complications and Andrew became confined to a wheelchair. Despite that he'd still go and watch Wrexham games with his dad and Wales games with Steve, and the pair of them travelled down to Cardiff to see the second leg of the Euro2002 play off with Russia. On the way down, they discussed organising a trip over to Portugal to follow Wales in the tournament the following summer.

Sadly, Wales lost 1-0 and on the long drive back north, both fed up after seeing the national team fail again, the two brothers quarrelled over something trivial. Their parting at the end of the journey wasn't on the best of terms.

That was the last contact Steve had with Andrew before being told three days later that his brother had contracted pneumonia and been taken into intensive care. Steve didn't get chance to talk to his brother again. Andrew passed away at the age of 37.

So, Andrew was with us all the way in France, in spirit. I'm sure there were many others out there who'd lost relatives and friends before they got to fulfil the dream of going together to finally see Wales play in a summer tournament. They were all there with us.

The Shone family come from a village in north Wales called Hawarden, the same village where Gary Speed grew up. I'm pretty sure Andrew and Gary will have watched the games together.

*'We didn't so much feel under pressure to win,
we felt under pressure to make people proud.'*
Chris Coleman

St David's Press

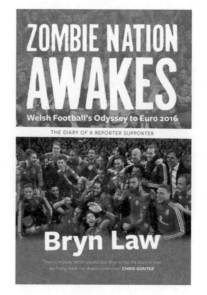

'When Chris, the players, and our amazing fans were celebrating in Bosnia, I just know that Gary was there, chuffed to see the country he loved finally achieve its dream, and knowing that he'd played his part. It's a great story and Bryn is the right man to tell it.'
Roger Speed, from his Foreword

'This diary tells the greatest story the nation's enjoyed since our one and only previous involvement in a summer tournament way back in 1958. A story told by someone who once travelled away to support Wales as a supporter and now travels with the side as a reporter.'
Chris Coleman, from his Preface

'Bryn's a fan and he's been as desperate as we have to see Wales qualifying... there's nobody better placed than Bryn to tell the story of how we finally made the dream come true!'
Chris Gunter

This is the book that many Welsh football fans thought they'd never get to read; a tale of outstanding performances at home and away, qualification success and a FIFA Top Ten ranking, and the best thing is...it's all true!

Packed with passion, tinged with sadness, and written with great humour, Bryn Law's diary of the campaign perfectly describes the emotions of following the Welsh national football team; when years of despair vanished in a wave of glorious euphoria to the sounds of Zombie Nation. It will bring a tear to your eye and put a massive grin on your face.

978 1 902719 467 - £13.99 - 320pp - 76 illustrations/photographs

St David's Press

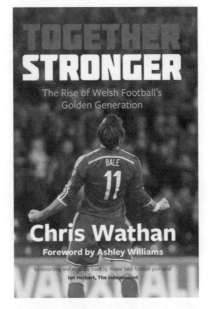

'There are no writers who have been as close to Welsh football as Chris over the last ten years. It is a story that's worth telling, worth reading and definitely worth enjoying!
Ashley Williams, Wales captain, from his Foreword

'A must-read for anyone with an interest in Welsh football, how a country that has always produced great players, finally produced a team with the quality and the unity to reach a first major tournament since 1958.'
Sam Wallace, Chief Football Writer, The Telegraph

'An absorbing and essential book by Wales' best football journalist.'
Ian Herbert, Chief Sportswriter, The Independent

'Well-informed insight into Wales' rollercoaster ride to the Euros. Chris Wathan writes with authority and sensitivity. The devastating chapter on Gary Speed's death is deeply moving.'
Henry Winter, Chief Football Writer, The Times

'Wonderful, I loved it. Only someone with Wathan's access to the team and unrivalled football knowledge could have written a book like this. It will be cherished by Welsh football fans for many years to come. You've done Welsh football proud. A superb achievement.'
Elis James, Comedian, Actor and Welsh football obsessive

978 1 902719 481 - £13.99 - 312pp - 68 illustrations/photographs

ST DAVID'S PRESS

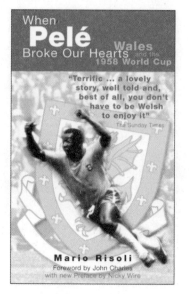

'A beautifully written and expertly researched book, which gives an insight into Wales' greatest football triumph'
Nicky Wire - Manic Street Preachers

"...a brilliant book...a thoroughly good read...I warmly recommend it"
Adrian Chiles Radio 5 Live

'If you were to write a surreal football comedy script tinged with pathos, personal tragedy, heroism, politics, adventure and endeavour, you couldn't begin to emulate the story of Wales in 1958 ... well-crafted ... meticulously researched'
Total Football

'a great tale, diligently researched and well told'
GQ Magazine

'excellent ... an intriguing story, compellingly told'
Four Four Two

'terrific ... a lovely story, well told and, best of all, you don't have to be Welsh to enjoy it'
The Sunday Times

When Pelé Broke Our Hearts is the definitive story of the Welsh team's remarkable 1958 World Cup campaign in Sweden, the first and only time Wales have played in football's premier tournament.

978 1 902719 023 - £9.99 - 180pp - 44 illustrations/photographs

ST DAVID'S PRESS

It is said that the human mind responds far better to an image than a word
and the saying, 'a picture paints a thousand words', was never truer than
during the fabulous French summer of 2016 when that now famous 'Red
Wall', our quite fantastic supporters, rose to the challenge. This is a collection
of their photographs, their experiences and memories captured on the front
line, a true record of the fervour, happiness and friendship that marked their
personal experiences at Euro 2016.
Nic Parry, from his Foreword

Roedd rhaid bod yn Ffrainc i sylweddoli maint y parch a'r edmygedd fu tuag
at angerdd, cyfeillgarwch a chwrteisi y cefnogwyr rheiny - fe syrthiodd Ewrob
mewn cariad â chefnogwyr tîm Cymru. Ond, fel dengys y gyfrol hon, nid dyna
oedd eu hunig gymwynas â ni. Aethant ati i gofnodi eu profiadau , a hynny
mewn llun. Eu lluniau hwy sydd yma, eu cofnod real hwy o eiliadau personol,
cofnod o iwfforia, o anghrediniaeth, o gyfeillgarwch ac angerdd - y cyfan yn
y foment, heb ei gynllunio.
Nic Parry, o'i Ragair

Allez Cymru is a full-colour and bilingual illustrated celebration of that amazing
and never-to-be-forgotten summer of football and fun in France when tens
of thousands of Welsh fans followed their team to the finals of Euro 2016.
Packed with photos and memories of the tournament, Allez Cymru will appeal
to all Welsh football fans from 5 to 105.
   Llyfr llawn-lliw dwyieithog i ddathlu'r mis o bêl-droed anhygoel a'r hwyl
aruthrol gafodd cefnogwyr Cymru yn Ffrainc, yn ystod Euro 2016 yw Allez
Cymru a llyfr i'w drysori i gefnogwyr o 5 i 105 mlwydd oed. O Bordeaux
i Toulouse ac o Lille i Lyon mae Allez Cymru yn llawn-dop gyda lluniau'r
cefnogwyr sy'n clyfleu'r balchder, emosiwn a chyfeillgarwch o fod yn aelod
ffyddlon o'r 'Wal Goch'.

978 1 902719 023 - £9.99 - 80pp - Fully illustrated in colour